The English Association:
One Hundred Years On

The English Association:
One Hundred Years On

by

William Baker

and

Elaine Treharne

with

Helen Lucas

The English Association
1906–2006

The English Association
University of Leicester, University Road, Leicester LE1 7RH

©The English Association and individual authors 2006

All rights reserved. No part of this publication may be reproduced, stored in a retrieval system, or transmitted, in any form or by any means, without the prior permission in writing of the English Association, or as expressly permitted by law, or under terms agreed with the appropriate reprographics organizations. Enquiries concerning reproduction outside the scope of the above should be sent to the Rights Department, The English Association, at the address above.

ISBN 0-900232-25-0

Produced by Jeremy Mills Publishing Ltd.
www.jeremymillspublishing.co.uk

Contents

I	The English Association: Beginnings	1
	The Context	1
	The Foundation	2
II	The First Decade	9
	Establishing a Reputation	9
	Early Executive Committee Meetings	9
	Recruitment	11
	Determining Strategy, 1908–18	12
III	From World War I to World War II	18
	The Newbolt Report	18
	Meetings, Business, Banquets	22
	Officers of the EA, 1918–1939	23
IV	World War II and Its Aftermath	25
	1940–1967	25
	Meetings, Business, Conferences	34
	Presidents	37
V	The 1960s and Beyond	40
	Meetings and Business	40
	Conferences	47
	The Presidents	48
VI	Publications: Annuals	52
	Essays and Studies	52
	1940–1956	59
	1967 to the Present	66
	The Year's Work in English Studies	68
	1921–1940	68
	YWES 1940–1965	73
	1967–2005	79
	The Year's Work in Critical and Cultural Theory [YWCCT]	85

VII	Publications: Journals	87
	From *Bulletin* to *English*	87
	The Bulletin	87
	English	88
	Occasional Publications of the EA	97
	The Best Seller: *Poems of To-day*	97
	Short Stories, Prose and Miscellaneous Publications	101
	Other Journals and Publications	104
	The Use of English	105
	English 4–11	106
	EA *Newsletter*	107
	Pamphlets	108
VIII	Provincial Branches	112
	The Early Years	112
	The Scottish Branch	113
	The Growth of the Branches	114
	Overseas Branches	120
	Overseas Branches 1940–67	125
	The 1960s to the present day	128
Bibliography		131
Index		133

Acknowledgments

This history could not have been undertaken without the generous assistance of many individuals. First of all, thanks must go to Helen Lucas, a most gracious and helpful host, copy editor, and Indexer, and Gordon Campbell and Elaine Treharne of the English Association, who suggested that I write it in the first place and who generously gave me access to the EA archives. My close friend, Emeritus Professor Donald Hawes, was most encouraging and read the manuscript in its various incarnations making his usual astute observations.

Others most generously supplied information often in the form of extensive emails include: James Alison, Joyce Bazire, June Baxter, Bernard Beatty, Martin Blocksidge, Nichole Bradbury, Peter Bury, Richard Cullen, Martin Dodsworth, Brian Gibbons, Trevor Griffith, Philippa Haywood, Andrew Hook, Margaret and Robert Jackson, Lionel Kelly, Peter Kitson, Roger Knight, Owen Knowles, Ann Merchant, David Mills, Michael O'Neil, Stephen Regan, Catherine Rees, Norman Reid, Margaret Reynolds, David Seed, Hilda Spear, Andrew Stables, Michael Stansfield, Gordon Valentine, Jocelyn Wogan-Browne, Helen Wilcox, and Wim van der Wurff.

Geoffrey Bellamy's University of Leicester MA Dissertation 'The Genesis of the Newbolt Report on the Teaching of English in England: A Study of the Early Years of the English Association' was extremely informative. Jayne Crosby is to be thanked for the difficult task of making sense of my handwriting. The debts owed are so many that if any person has been inadvertently omitted, then please accept apologies.

William Baker
July 2006

Additional thanks go to Professor Greg Walker of the University of Leicester and Professor Richard Madelaine, University of New South Wales.

Elaine Treharne and Helen Lucas

I
The English Association: Beginnings

The Context

The English Association was formally established on 7 July 1906 'to help to maintain the correct use of English, spoken and written'; 'to promote the due recognition of English as an essential element in the national education'; and also 'to discuss methods of English teaching' at both university and school level. Brian Doyle places the EA's creation in the term of a general historical and social movement.[1] By the opening decade of the twentieth century, 'English was coming to be called upon to sustain a "national ideal", which was traced back to Matthew Arnold. Its role was to assist in the educational work of transcending "individual self-interest" by subordinating the "individual self" to "common aims"' to use the words of the Vice-Chancellor of the University of Leeds. This, Doyle argues, is the context for the foundation of the EA, which was sympathetic to the 'view of English as the most natural candidate to lead a mission of cultural renewal'.[2] Doyle views the EA 'not so much as a pressure-group founded to further the professional interests of teachers of English, but rather as a class-based mobilisation which drew in not only most professors of English Language and Literature but also like-minded politicians, administrators and "men-of-letters"'.[3] Krishan Kumar places the foundation of the EA in a wider context of the creation of a concept of 'Englishness' and a 'new historical consciousness' of national identity.[4] This movement developed over the nineteenth century. At the start of the new century, it was part of the struggle of English language and literature 'to find their place in the national education system'. Further, 'the climactic moment … in this movement to establish English at the centre of the national curriculum came with the Newbolt Report of 1921'. Behind this report was the EA, founded in 1906 'to promote the due recognition of English as an essential element in the national education'.[5]

Ian Reid's *Wordsworth and the Formation of English Studies* sees the EA as essentially the inheritor of the formerly influential Wordsworth Society. The aims were the same: 'to forge a normative curriculum and pedagogy for English'.[6] Reid sees the EA as London-based, a metropolitan rather than Oxford or Cambridge centred organization which 'became for many years a powerful shaping force at all levels of education'.[7] He explains its power, which lasted for at least a quarter of a century, as

---

[1] Brian Doyle, 'The Invention of English' in Robert Colls and Philip Dodd, eds., *Englishness: Politics and Culture, 1880–1920*, 1986, p. 97.
[2] Doyle, pp. 98–102.
[3] Doyle, p. 103.
[4] Krishan Kumar, *The Making of English National Identity*, 2003, p. 222.
[5] Doyle, p. 222.
[6] Ian Reid, *Wordsworth and the Formation of English Studies*, 2004, p. x.
[7] Reid, p. 72.

emanating 'from the fact that its members overlapped with those of various groups active in shaping initiatives in education policy during the early years' of the twentieth century.[8] The EA's 'membership included a Who's Who of political and cultural luminaries as well as academics and educational bureaucrats'.[9]

The foundation of the EA was part, too, of a larger movement witnessing the establishment of formal professional groups, such as The Library Association, founded in 1877; the Modern Languages Association (1892); the Geographical Association (1893); the Classical Association (1903); and the Historical Association (1906). The last years of the nineteenth century witnessed tremendous changes in schools and education. Royal Commissions into university affairs in the period of the 1850s and 1870s proposed transformations in curricula. Subjects such as English and Geography had to justify themselves and to demonstrate their seriousness. Problems of what should be taught and examined, indeed of what constituted subjects, preoccupied university based academics and those teaching in the schools. The foundations of the English Association then have much in common with these other associations, which were partially a response to changes in education and to changing attitudes towards subject-based studies. In the case of a subject such as English, as with others, specialist practitioners felt the need to explain and justify the discipline, to clarify its boundaries and parameters at the school and university levels. These factors, combined with a movement for ensuring 'the transmission of a cultural heritage'[10] and a preoccupation with 'Englishness' that created the intellectual climate culminating in the formation of the EA.

The Foundation

In his July 1928 Presidential address, Sir Henry Newbolt recalled that 'the original suggestion' for the creation of the EA 'had come from several members of the teaching profession who desired to establish some kind of fellowship among themselves and at the same time to get into touch with the world of English letters'. There was never an 'attempt to assume the form of an Institution'. The impetus came from 'an instinctive common feeling' and common perspectives. These were: (1) 'to promote English scholarship'; (2) 'to raise the standard of education and especially of self-education'; (3) 'to increase…membership to the utmost, and to recruit it from the whole British Commonwealth'; and (4) the 'desire for fellowship and for a wider and more immediate touch with contemporary English writers and critics'.[11]

In his 'A Half-Century of the English Association' appearing in the 1956 'Jubilee' volume of *Essays & Studies*, Arundell Esdaile observed 'It is no unique paradox that the English Association …traces its first conception to a Scotchman'.[12] Easton Smith Valentine, M. A. (1868–1940) was head of English at Dundee High School and

---
[8] Reid, p. 86.
[9] Reid, p. 72.
[10] Doyle, p. 5.
[11] Henry Newbolt, *The Idea of an English Association*, Presidential Address 1928, pp. [3]–4
[12] *Essays & Studies*, 1956, p. 1. First footnote here.

author of *An Atlas of English Grammar, to be Used Along with all Grammars* (1890) and *Wordsworth's Country as Interpreted by His Poetry* (1900). On 15 January 1906, he sent a letter to four influential figures—Professor John W. Hales, Professor A. C. Bradley, the Reverend Stopford A. Brooke and Canon H. C. Beeching of Westminster Abbey, in which he wrote:

> Dear Sir,
>
> In looking through the Directory of Educational Associations, I have been struck with the want of a Society to foster the study of English and the teaching of that subject in our schools. Other departments of educational work are adequately represented; they are the Classical Association, the Mathematical Association, the Modern Language Association, the Historical Society, the Geographical Association, the Association of Science Masters in Public Schools, the Society of Art Masters, the Gymnastic Teachers' Institute, The Union of Directors of Music in Secondary Schools and many more. Indeed the only subject of primary importance in schoolwork that is altogether omitted seems to be what is vaguely termed 'English'.
>
> There are at least two good reasons why there should be an Association of Teachers of English. The term is somewhat vague; its connotation should be defined. Subjects like geography and handwriting, long associated with it, should be relegated to their proper departments; its various branches, given their due relative importance. Moreover all teachers, and especially the younger ones, need from time to time to have professional ideals, standards, and methods placed before them. Magazine articles may do good but in too consultory a manner. What is wanted is the constant force of a strong association—a union whose chief raison d'être would be the dissemination of right ideas on the teaching of English. It should, be a society with many branches in close affiliation with a central body, and one able to keep its members in touch with what is freshest and best in this special department of educational work.
>
> Again, the Association I have in view should be one of defence, if not even of aggression. We live in an age of competition, and not even school subjects are exempt from the struggle for existence. 'English' has in these days to prove itself worthy of a place in the curriculum. No doubt in so far as the term means 'reading' its position as one of 'the Three R's' is secure; but there are certain branches of the subject on which managers and even inspectors look askance, and the whole subject is sometimes starved for want of time. A strong association might do much to secure for the study of our language and literature a place in even the highest forms of all school curricula.
>
> I beg to submit the foregoing remarks for your consideration and criticism. If you approve of the object, perhaps you will be so good as to suggest the steps to be taken for founding the association and the names of prominent educationists whose sympathy might be enlisted in the movement.
>
> I am,
> Faithfully yours,
> Easton S. Valentine

The society that Valentine envisaged had three objectives: to make English a major subject in the school curriculum; to make teachers conscious of the purpose and importance of literary study; and to disseminate what Valentine regarded as the 'right ideas on the teaching of English'.

Valentine received remarkably similar replies from all four: all thought the idea of a society splendid, all regretted that other commitments precluded their taking an active part themselves. Beeching's, Brooke's and Hales' replies were brief. Beeching (1859–1919), a respected clergyman and man of letters, replied on 20 January 1906:

> My dear Sir,
> I thank you for your letter. I fear, however, I could be of no use to your society. I have never taught English Literature, and I have now ceased even to examine in it; so that I should not be in touch with practical questions. And besides that my duties here, of a domestic nature, in the Abbey, take up so much time, that I have to abstain from all committees that are not absolutely unavoidable.

Brooke (1832–1916), whose publications included *On Ten Plays of Shakespeare* (1905) and a *Primer of English Literature* (1876), replied on 21 January 1906:

> Dear Mr. Valentine,
> I think some such association as you outline would be of great use, but it would have to be linked up with the Schools of the country, and that would need long business. For my part I am too old now to give the attention and labour which such a work would demand. The Organisation would need younger men than I.

John Wesley Hales (1836–1914), Professor of English Language and Literature at King's College, responded on 31 January 1906, but his letter is only partially cited in the EA archives. The response reveals a genuine professional concern for the stature of English and a realization of the significance of what is being proposed. Hales writes that Valentine's 'idea strikes [him] as excellent, if only it can be properly and worthily carried out—carried out on the lines of the Classical Association, for instance'. Hales continues: 'To begin with, can you form a really <u>influential</u> and <u>commanding</u> committee with an effective list of Vice-Presidents, headed by a President who is a conspicuous scholar—such as Prof. Skeat?'[13] While Hales' health precluded him from undertaking 'any active part in the Association', he wrote again to Valentine on 6 February 1906. He agreed 'that the literary, as opposed to the philological side of English should be insisted on' and suggested that the politician and grandee Rosebery should be the first President. Hales, together with Skeat, Stopford A. Brooke, and Edward Dowden, the critic, all became Vice-Presidents.

The fullest and most significant reply to Valentine was that from A. C. Bradley (1851–1935). A noted scholar, in 1882 he was appointed to the first Chair of Literature and History at the University of Liverpool, subsequently taking up a Chair at Glasgow, and then the Professorship of Poetry at Oxford in 1901–06. His authorship of the highly influential *Shakespearean Tragedy* (1904), made him 'one of the greatest of the English critics of Shakespeare'.[14] Bradley's reply to Valentine doubts the efficacy of an English Association for school-teachers, but goes on:

> I do not know if I am right in thinking (but I believe I am) that in the English schools there are rarely teachers of English in the sense of teachers whose sole or main business it is to

---

[13] Indeed, Skeat, the first Elrington and Bosworth Professor of Anglo-Saxon at Cambridge, became a founding member of the EA.
[14] *Dictionary of National Biography*, M. R. Ridley (*DNB*, 1931–1940, p. 99).

teach English. In the secondary schools 'English', I believe, is taught by the form master, and I rather think it is so also in most primary schools. If this is so, it would perhaps be a difficulty. I mean that these masters would perhaps not care to form a separate society in addition to those to which they already belong.

However, as I say, I am ignorant, and it might well be that the University teachers would care to form a society, and that others would join in it. Perhaps your best plan would be to consult some of the leading Professors of English in the Universities…But, to speak frankly, I have no idea myself whether it is worth doing. I suppose it is possible again that the easiest way would be to form a separate section of the Modern Language Association.

… Of course, if an association were formed I should be happy to belong, though I should be able to do little.

In fact, Bradley became a life member of the EA, being co-opted as a Member of the Convening Committee at the preliminary committee meeting of Friday 18 May 1906. He was a very active member of the executive and was 'responsible for collecting and editing, in 1910, the first of its annual volumes *Essays and Studies*, also another volume in 1920'. He also produced various EA 'lectures, addresses and pamphlets',[15] and in 1911 he served as the Association's fifth President.

Bradley suggested that amongst others Valentine contact Oliver Elton (1860–1945), King Alfred Professor of English Literature at Liverpool from 1901. Elton was an enthusiastic respondent to the ideal of an English Association, writing to Valentine:

I agree there would be room and much use for such a body if it were well organised. I myself would join it, like Bradley, but my time is mortgaged to other work than that of organisation now. It is a spirited proposal.

Elton showed Valentine's proposal to his friend G. E. S. Coxhead, English Master at Liverpool College School and President of the Assistant Masters' Association of England and Wales. Coxhead consulted his colleagues, contacted Valentine and organised a meeting in Liverpool. Prior to this meeting Coxhead wrote to Valentine in February 1906 to reveal that teachers he had consulted seemed in 'general agreement' that 'A Society for promoting the study of English is desirable'; that it should 'be either (a) independent or (b) affiliated with a section of an existing society'; and that 'there should be held a prelim[inary] meeting of all university and school teachers interested in the subject'.

As Valentine notes in Correspondence now in the Archive of the EA: 'After further correspondence, I went to Liverpool on 16 March and at a preliminary meeting it was decided to proceed with the scheme. Voluminous correspondence between that date and the constitutive meeting in London University in April'. No written record seems to have survived of the 16 March 1906 preliminary meeting with Elton, Coxhead, Valentine and others. A letter signed by 56 conveners invited interested parties to attend a meeting public meeting at the University of London on 28 April 1906. The meeting was organised by Philip Hartog (1864–1947), Registrar of

---

[15] J. W. Mackail, 'A. C. Bradley', *Proceedings of the British Academy, 1935*, p. 390.

London University and author of *The Writing of English* (1907). Some of the flavour of the meeting is conveyed in a detailed report found in *The Scotsman* for 30 April 1906:

> A meeting was held on Saturday at the University of London, South Kensington, for the purpose of forming an Association 'to foster and develop the study of English as an essential element in our national education by (1) determining the relative importance of its various branches; (2) encouraging a high standard of scholarship in the teaching of our literature and language; (3) discussing methods and the interrelation of school and university work; and (4) affording opportunities for friendly intercourse and co-operation amongst all lovers of English language and literature'. Sir Arthur Rücker presided, and amongst those present were Professor Bradley, Mr E. S. Valentine, Dundee; Mr J. I. Low, Stirling; Canon Bell, Westminster; Dr. Furnivall, Dr Heath, Board of Education; Dr Scott, Board of Education; Professor Israel Gollancz, Mr P. J. Hartog, Registrar, London University; Mr Sidney Lee, Miss Clara Thomson, Cambridge; Miss Kennedy, Cambridge; Miss Bevan, Liverpool; Miss Laidler, and Miss Faithfull...
>
> ...Mr Hartog moved—'That there be formed an Association of persons interested in the teaching of English, to be called the English Literature and Language Association'. He said the situation was more eloquent than any words of his. In the majority of the greatest boys' schools of this country no English was taught. Corresponding to that they had on the part of the boys who left those schools an almost complete inability to write their own mother tongue, and a complete ignorance of the great masterpieces of English literature. There was a great national work for the Association to accomplish. They would have, if they were to judge from the reports of the Classical Association, very strong opposition. It was therefore of the utmost importance that they should be united both in their aim and their methods.
>
> Miss Clara Thomson, Cambridge, said that very often in her experience as an inspector she had found, while classics and mathematics were in the hands of specialists, the teaching of English was generally entrusted to the least qualified member of the staff. If the Association were formed it would raise the qualifications of the English teacher. The amount of time given to the study of English was insignificant. No literature was taught; the entire time was taken up with analysis and parsing. Encouragement was needed for research work in English. At present we had to go to German, French, or American scholars.
>
> As to the founding of a new association for the study of English, however, [Dr Heath] reminded them that there was already an association which had that end in view in the Modern Languages Association, and that there were there were two publications which were designed to further the study of modern languages. He thought they might join with that Association, and work towards the formation of a tradition of modern scholarship. In classics there was a tradition, and therein lay their strength. He moved an amendment that a committee be formed to inquire into the best means of compassing the aim of the Association, and that it report at a later meeting after conference with the Modern Languages Association.
>
> ...Dr Furnivall said William Morris once said to him, 'I say, Furnivall, damn the classics. What do you say?' (Laughter.) An enormous amount of time was wasted on the study of the classics, and English ought to be substituted.
>
> Professor Israel Gollancz said that before they could amalgamate with any body they must found an association. English was a modern language, but it was something more. The time would come when at that University there would be a special board which would watch most vigilantly, and with the utmost care, to see that the great literature and language of this country received first and foremost attention. (Applause.)

> …Mr Hartog, in replying to the discussion, said that he sympathised with much of what Dr Heath had said. To have a new publication would be an unmitigated evil, but to have the new Association would be a great benefit. As far as English in the schools was concerned, the Modern Languages Association might have been friendly, but its friendliness had done nothing.
> A vote was then taken, when the amendment was defeated by 29 to 25.
> …The business terminated with the appointment of a committee, with power to add to the number, to consider the position and arrange a meeting at a subsequent date.

As may be seen, a proposal to create an English section within the Modern Language Association was defeated by a narrow vote and the Association became established as an independent professional society. From its earliest days, membership was broad. At this first meeting, there were at least five women present, and a glance at the EA 1907–1908 membership listing reveals that out of an Executive Committee of 22 members, six were women. In addition to Miss C. Linklater Thomson, these include a number of headmistresses: A. E. Clay, Queen's School, Chester; G. Clement, Godolphin and Latymer Girls' School; and M. A. Gilliland, Aske's School, Acton.

The Chair at the 28 April 1906 meeting, Sir Arthur William Rücker (1848–1915), differed from the great majority of the other attendees. He was not professionally engaged with English Studies but was a member of the Royal Society and a distinguished physicist. In 1901 he became the first principal of London University, a position he held until his retirement in 1908; his election to the Chair of the initial meeting illustrates not only his standing, but also the close interconnection between the EA and the University of London.

The Interim Committee appointed at the meeting, and chaired by Rücker, included Frederick Samuel Boas (1862–1957). His election to the Interim Committee began a life-long participation in Association affairs that ranged from his becoming the first General Secretary, to his editorship of the EA's major bibliographical publication, *YWES* (*The Year's Work in English Studies*), from 1926 to 1955. He was a founding member of the EA in 1906 and became its president in 1917.

The Interim Committee held its preliminary meeting on 18 May 1906 with eight members in attendance: Israel Gollancz, F.S Boas, Miss Faithfull, Hartog, Dr. Heath, Miss Laidler, Professor W. Rippman[16] and Miss C. Linklater Thomson. Gollancz was elected Chair, and A. C. Bradley and A. McCormick, Secretary of the powerful Carnegie Trust based in Edinburgh, were co-opted from the General Committee. At a subsequent meeting on 23 June the committee prepared the papers for the general meeting to be held on 7 July, at London University, South Kensington. At the July general meeting Furnivall was appointed to the Chair and the Interim Committee's proposals, put forward by Gollancz and seconded by Bradley, were carried unanimously:

---

[16] Who seems to be the connection between the MLA and the EA in these early months, and who was a member of the EA only for the first year.

1) That an English Literature and Language Association to be called the English Association be and is hereby formed and that the Conveners of this Meeting together with other persons present and willing to join be the first Members thereof.
2) That the objects of the Association be (a) to afford opportunities for intercourse and co-operation amongst all those interested in the English Language and Literature; (b) to help to maintain the correct use of English, spoken and written; (c) to promote the due recognition of English as an essential element in the national education; (d) to discuss methods of teaching English and the co-relation of School and University work; to encourage and facilitate advanced study in English Language and Literature.
3) That the formation of local branches, or the recognition of local societies as branches be one of the chief methods by which the Association shall seek to carry out these objects'
4) That the policy of the Association be to encourage local branches to organise their own affairs, provided they accept as one of their main tasks the advocacy of the objects of the Association, and contribute to a central fund an amount to be fixed hereafter; and that local branches be represented on the Central Committee.
5) That a general meeting of the whole Association be held once a year, the first general meeting to be held in London.
6) That a provisional Committee consisting of 35 members, with the power to add to their number up to a maximum of 40, be formed for the purpose of administering the affairs of the Association until its first general meeting, and of drawing up a list of Officers and a Constitution to be submitted to that Meeting for consideration; and that the quorum of the Committee be five.[17]
7) That this Association is in favour of establishing relations with kindred bodies with a view to co-operation.

---

[17] The Committee Members are named as: Miss Bevan (Liverpool); ~~Professor Boas~~ (London); ~~Professor~~ A. C. Bradley (London); Mr. L. Cope Cornford (London); Mr. G. E. S. Coxhead (14, Normanby Street, Liverpool), to act as Secretary; Professor Dowden (Dublin); Professor O. Elton (Liverpool); ~~Rev. J. R. Wynne Edwards (Leeds)~~; Miss Faithfull (London); Mr. J. H. Fowler (Clifton); Mr. N. L. Frazer (London); Dr. Furnivall (London); Professor I. Gollancz (London); Mr. Hawkesworth (Rugby); Dr. F. heath (London); Professor C. H. Herford (Manchester); Mr. Edgar Jones (Wales); Miss Julia E. Kennedy (Cambridge); Professor W. P. Ker (London); Miss Laidler (Goldsmith's College, New Cross, London, S. E.) to act as Secretary; Professor Lawson (St. Andrews); Mr. Sidney Lee (London); Professor Littledale (Cardiff); Mr. J. Low (Stirling); Miss Macirone (London); Miss Powell (Cambridge); Professor W. Raleigh (Oxford); Professor Saintsbury (Edinburgh); R. P. Scott (London); Professor W. W. Skeat (Cambridge); Mr. C. G. Steel (Rugby); Mr. F. Storr (London); Miss C. L. Thomson (London); Mr. E. S. Valentine.

In the Minutes, Boas' name is written through, as is the name of the Rev. J. R. Wynne Edwards (Leeds). 'Professor' has been deleted from Bradley's name since he retired from his formal academic positions in 1906.

II
The First Decade

Establishing a Reputation

Within six months of Valentine's initial letters to Hales, Bradley, Stopford Brooke and Beeching sent out in January 1906, a national English Association was created, and by the end of its first year the EA had a remarkable 1000 members. A Scottish branch was formed in Edinburgh on 22 September 1906, and on 12 January 1907 the first annual meeting of the Association was held at University College, London.

In 1910, J.C. Smith noted that 'the last four years have witnessed a marked improvement in the English work done in English schools'. He adds that 'this improvement coincides with the rise of the English Association, and is undoubtedly connected with it at once as cause and as effect'.[18] Smith notes, too, the importance of the EA's three types of publication, which even within this short period of time had become established academic and pedagogic tools. These comprised an annual bulletin 'under the editorship of that excellent scholar and experienced teacher…Percy Simpson' detailing the EA's work and international output; leaflets 'issued to full members at irregular intervals—sometimes as many as half-a-dozen in a year'; and an Annual, edited at this time by A. C. Bradley with other eminent contributors.

Early Executive Committee Meetings

Organizational structure dominated the early meetings of the EA. The Committee met first on Saturday, 13 October 1906 in the University of London with Furnivall in the Chair. In a discussion about the potential co-option of Committee members, Gollancz proposed that co-option of only two members be deferred to a subsequent meeting. H. F. Heath supported this proposal,[19] contingent however, upon the inclusion of 'a large representation' from 'the public schools'.[20] The motion was carried, and subsequently 'Many names of public schoolmasters were submitted to the meeting, and after a vote, it was decided to co-opt Canon Bell', the former Headmaster of Marlborough College, who thereafter became one of the first Vice-Presidents of the EA.

This first Executive Committee meeting was much concerned with an organization structure and frameworks.[21] The general rubric of 'Questions of General Constitution' in the Minutes is sub-divided into the central concerns of 'Officers',

---
[18] J.C. Smith, 'English Association', *The Educational News*, 21 October 1910, p. 1097.
[19] Heath was a distinguished civil servant, an English lecturer, and a Librarian of London University.
[20] This debate reveals a friction in the EA between its membership and work in schools and with schoolteachers and its academic membership and activities, which was to continue for some years.
[21] In general, EA Minutes do not record the content of detailed discussions but merely convey decisions.

which was left blank; 'Committee'; 'Vice Presidents'; 'Subscription'; 'Accounts'; 'Life Membership'; and 'Subcommittees'. It was agreed that 'A central committee shall be elected annually. An executive committee of not less than 12 shall be appointed by the general committee from among its own members, with a quorum of 5'. It was then moved by Sidney Lee and carried 'that there be Vice-Presidents'. During the meeting, in addition to adopting the Constitution, E. S. Valentine was confirmed as Honorary Treasurer, F. S. Boas, Honorary General Secretary, and J. Inch Low, 'Hon. Secretary for Business connected with Local Branches in Scotland'. G. E. S. Coxhead became 'Hon. Secretary for Business connected with Local Branches in England and Wales'. The meeting then turned to the matter of subscriptions, where an intense debate—perhaps about the amount to be paid by local branches to the central EA—resulted in a proposal that 'The subscription if paid to the Central Association, shall be 5/–; local associations shall fix their own subscription, but of this subscription at least 1/– a head shall be paid to the Central Association, and members of such local associations shall be considered full members'.[22]

Following the debate over subscriptions, the meeting adopted a 'A proposition from Mr. Sidney Lee that a subscription of £3.3.0 [should] entitle life membership'. The success of this measure may be gauged from the 1907–1908 Membership Lists where life members numbered 16 of the total of 332 members. This group of sixteen is generally representative of EA membership more broadly at this time:[23] in gender terms, almost a third (5) were women; seven members lived outside London; six were active in Higher Education; four were active in public school education; and one, E. K. Chambers, was a Civil Servant active in educational philosophy.

The 1906 meeting then turned to the formation of three major sub-committees. The first, consisting of Heath, Bradley and Lee, would suggest officers for 1907. The second, constituted 'to draw up rules relating to the affiliation of local societies and the constitut[ion] of local com[mittees]', was formed by G. Coxhead,[24] E. S. Valentine, the instigator of the EA, and Miss C. Linklater Thomson.[25] The third sub-committee was charged 'to consider what arrangements can be made with existing journals for the temporary publication of the proceedings of the associat[ion]'. This area of the EA, its publication activities and future programmes became a crucial element of its subsequent activities. The three members were F. S. Boas, Francis Storr,[26] and Leslie Cope Cornford.[27]

---

[22] Subscription charges, given an initial membership of more than three hundred, were not considered excessive by the standards of the day.
[23] Rev. E. A. Abbott of Hampstead; A. C. Bradley; E. K. Chambers; Dr. T. Gregory Foster, University College, London; E. Margery Fox, Clapham High School; Mrs. Ernest von Glehn of Kensington; C. B. Heberden, Brasenose College, Oxford; J. E. Hodgson, Anerley, South East London; Adolphus A. Jack of 35 Kensington Square, Central London; Miss M. E. Jones of the Ladies' College, Harrogate; W. P. Ker; Sir Oliver Lodge, Birmingham, F. R. S.; Rev. Harry W. McKenzie, The School House, Uppingham; Dr. W. H. D. Rouse of the Perse Grammar School, Cambridge; Mrs. Henry Sidgwick, Newnham College, Cambridge; and Mrs. Tyndall, Hind Head House, Haslemere.
[24] Headmaster of Hinckley Grammar School and subsequently the 'Hon. Secretary for business connected with Local Branches in England and Wales'.
[25] Thomson was granted power to co-opt other members, lived in Ealing and represented the metropolis and the interests of the 'Central Body' in London.
[26] A former public school master, author and Vice-President of the Modern Language Association.
[27] A London-based journalist and naval correspondent.

Recruitment

The fruits of these early deliberations by EA committees can be seen from the 1907–1908 Officer and Membership lists. The sub-committee which met to suggest officers for 1907 set in motion an interesting choice for the first President of the EA. Henry Montagu Butler (1833–1918), the Master of Trinity College, Cambridge, was not elected until he was proposed at the first General Meeting held in January 1907 with Sidney Lee in the Chair. Butler was the son of a clergyman, a common pattern amongst EA high officials in the early years. Also initiating another familiar pattern, he had been Headmaster of a distinguished public school—in this case, Harrow. Unlike many other pre-Second World War EA Presidents, he was not a Balliol College, Oxford product, but rather a Cambridge graduate: elected President of the EA at the age of seventy-four, in many ways Butler represented another age.

The advice of Professor Hales about prospective Vice-Presidents gave rise to the appointment of leading literary authors and university scholars; among them, Thomas Hardy, J. M. Barrie, Henry Bradley, H. Montagu Butler, Edward Dowden, Frederick Furnivall, George Saintsbury, Walter Skeat and A. W. Ward. These were augmented by distinguished Headmasters and former Headmasters, including the Rev. H. M. Burge of Winchester, Canon Lyttleton of Eton College and Canon George Charles Bell, Headmaster of Marlborough College and then Principal of Queen's College, London.

The 1907–1908 membership listings reveal a large General Committee of thirty-five with a smaller Executive Committee of twenty-three members. These consisted of representatives of public school masters and mistresses including Miss Dingwall (Clapham High School for Girls), J. H. Fowler (Clifton), N. L. Frazer (Whitgift School, Croydon), Rev. E. C. Everard Owen (Harrow), and C. G. Steel (Rugby). Elementary and secondary school teachers were Miss Clara E. Grant (London County Council, Devons Road School), J. Kelly (Council School, Dudding Hill, Willesden), and J. A. White (L. C. C. Acland School). Head teachers were represented from both the private and public sectors including W. J. Addis (Headmaster, Brockley Secondary School), E. Cotgreave Brown (Amesbury School, Bickley), Miss B. E. Clay (Queen's School, Chester), Miss G. Clement (Godolphin and Latymer Girls' School), Miss M. A. Gilliland (Aske's School, Acton), and W. Jenkyn Thomas (Hackney Downs Secondary School). Representatives on the Executive Committee from the teacher training colleges included the Rev. S. Blofeld (St. John's College, Battersea) and A. E. Roberts (London Day Training College). Others ranged from university professors or former university professors such as A. C. Bradley, I. Gollancz, Sidney Lee and P. G. Thomas (Lecturer in English Language and Literature at Bedford College, London). Other members included P. J. Hartog, the Academic Registrar of the University of London, J. C. Smith from the School Inspectorate and Miss Linklater Thomson.

Of working officers, the distinguished philologist, Professor Sir Gregory Foster (1866–1931), was formally elected Chairman of the Executive Committee at the first General Meeting held in January 1907. Elizabeth Lee was elected to a major role as the Secretary and Assistant Treasurer. There were six women members in a twenty-three-member Executive Committee, a high proportion of women participants in a professional organization at this time. Indeed, of the initial membership of the Central Body of the EA there were 148 women, including ten on the General Committee. Most of the women members were schoolteachers, with far fewer women in academia in these early decades of the twentieth century. However, eminent women were recognized by the EA in its first decade. The sixth President of the EA was Anna Isabelle Thackeray (1837–1919), the eldest child of the great novelist, William Makepeace Thackeray. Lady Ritchie, as she was known after her marriage to Richard Ritchie, became President in 1912.[28] Also active in the EA and on its Executive from the earliest days was George Sampson (1873–1950), a senior educationalist, literary critic, and editor.[29] He served as the Honorary General Secretary of the English Association, on innumerable committees of the Association, and on the national Newbolt Committee. His involvement, and that of others like him, illustrates why the EA gained such prestige and influence in the years before and after the First World War; its participants, particularly at the level of committee membership, consisted of highly influential, well-connected figures across the educational and governmental spectrum.

Determining Strategy, 1908–18

As the EA became established, the Minutes of the Executive held at UCL on 20 February 1908 reveal the concerns of these early years. Additional committees were appointed to oversee the EA's growing business, including a Finance Sub-Committee (consisting of Elizabeth Lee, P. J. Hartog and Miss C. Linklater Thomson);[30] a Publications Sub-Committee with nine members of which Miss Thomson was Convenor. A 'Branch of the Association in the West Riding of Yorkshire' was formed, with the President, Sir Arthur Herbert Dyke Acland, undertaking the negotiations, though it was pointed out that 'At the same time it was to be made clear that no county borough need join the Branch unless it wished to do so'. As well as considering its relationship to its regional branches, the EA also dwelled on its close connection with schoolteachers. The Minutes reveal that 'The Representatives appointed to attend the meeting to arrange a Joint Educational Congress reported that the original proposal of the Teachers' Guild had fallen through. The representatives were desired to continue the negotiations'. And a third potential relationship also seems to have preoccupied the EA, and especially its secretary F. S. Boas, for some time. At the end of a lengthy discussion, Boas was charged 'to find out more definitely what was intended by the proposal of the *Modern Language Review*'. As the Minutes relate 'Opinion was greatly divided' relating to 'the

---

[28] An author in her own right, she published six works of fiction including *The Story of Elizabeth* (1863) and *Old Kensington* (1873). She also contributed a lengthy biographical introduction to the Centenary Edition of her father's works published by George Smith in 1898.
[29] See Reid, p. 93.
[30] Charged 'to consider the position of Associate members', among other aspects of business.

advisability of cooperating with the Modern Language Association in the publication of the *Modern Language Review*'. Why this should have been a bone of contention is difficult to discern from the formal Minutes, but already, it seems, suspicion between the associations and their respective activities was in evidence.

Charged to investigate a proposal by the newly formed *Modern Language Review* relating to cooperation with the EA, Boas reported to the EA Executive Committee meeting on 17 July 1908 that:

> *The Modern Language Review* has appeared in quarterly numbers since October 1906. It is edited by Prof. J. G. Robertson, and is printed at the Cambridge University Press. It has contained articles, reviews, and bibliographies bearing on English, French, German, Spanish and other modern languages. The articles have dealt with both literary and linguistic subjects, and have been largely devoted to research.
>
> The *Review* has not been the official organ of the Modern Language Association, but members of that Association have received it free on payment of the subscription of 10s. 6d. A new arrangement has just been made, by which the subscription to the Modern Language Association is reduced to 7s. 6d., and members will no longer receive the *Review* free. But in return of a guarantee of £50 by the Modern Language Association, it will be supplied to members at 7s. 6d. per annum instead of 12s. 6d., which will be the price to the public. Modern Language Association will also have a representative on the Board of Management of the Review for every £10 guaranteed.
>
> Prof. Robertson and the Syndics of the Cambridge University Press, who make a grant towards the support of the Review, have invited the English Association to guarantee the *Review* on the same footing as the Modern Language Association. That is to say, for a guarantee of £50 (which can be underwritten by members personally) members will be entitled to receive the *Review* at the reduced price of 7s. 6d., to nominate five representatives on the Board of Management, and to propose an editor to deal with the English publications in the *Review*, which will be increased in size.
>
> The deficit during the years of publication has been £50, £30, and £20; the last figure is an approximate estimate.
>
> The Syndics of the Press suggest as a new title 'The Modern Language Review of the English and Modern Language Associations', but would be willing to consider other titles that our Association might propose. They would agree to any arrangement with the Association being considered as a temporary one—say for three years.

This report appears to have caused extensive discussion. Boas moved to accept the invitation, with the provision 'that the title is changed to the English and Modern Language Review'. Sidney Lee moved an amendment: 'That while this Committee is anxious to encourage research and while it is of the opinion that members of the Association should privately do what they can to promote the welfare of the *Modern Language Review*, it is unable to recommend the Association's Corporate co-operation in the conduct of that periodical'. Such an emendation reveals the practical self-interest of the EA, emphasizing that research in English must be its top priority. The Minutes record that following a discussion, Lee's amendment was carried, although not unanimously. Percy Simpson then moved a motion that was to have important and far-reaching consequences for the EA. In 1907, it already had published three EA Pamphlets: *Types of English Curricula in Boys' Secondary Schools*; *The Teaching of Shakespeare in Secondary Schools*; and *A Short List of Books on English Literature to 1832 for Teachers*. All three, as their titles suggest, were aimed at secondary teachers. Steering the EA in the direction of research and academic university interests in the emerging world of university English studies Simpson's motion reads, 'it is desirable that the Association should issue either a Review of its own, or occasional collections (*viz.* articles of literary criticism [and] research [and] that this question be referred to the General Committee'. This motion was carried and a decision was taken for the General Committee 'to appoint a special sub-committee to consider ways and means by which it could be carried out'. This, of course, was to form one of the most, if not *the* most, important activities of the EA: its publications list, and sustained commitment to serving the English teaching community with high quality research and bibliographical tools.

As an illustration of this focus, even in 1908 the EA produced five pamphlets of thirty pages or so, selling to members at 6 d. or 1/–. These pamphlets were the main literary vehicle for disseminating pedagogic ideas, literary criticism, and practical advice to a wide audience. In *English Literature in Secondary Schools* J. H. Fowler argued against the use of Anglo-Saxon sources and the over-usage in schools of glosses or annotated editions.[31] G. Clement, Headmistress of Godolphin and Latymer Girls' School, was concerned with the issue of the teaching of formal grammar in a manner that encourages by expression;[32] and an Executive collaborative publication was sceptical about teaching Shakespeare to children younger than twelve years of age.[33]

Other publications included bulletins sent to individual members three times a year, which focused on EA activities. These circulated extracts of speeches, conference reports, and practical guides for teaching. Advertisements for textbooks were discouraged, as 'the intention to spread "right ideas" did not allow commercial motives to predominate'. For instance, an advertisement for Stuart Petrie Brodie's grammar textbook was twice rejected by the EA, but was accepted by the *Times Educational Supplement*.[34] Then, two years after Percy Simpson's emphasis on the need for the EA to be engaged in literary publication, the first volume of *Essays and Studies by Members of the English Association*, collected by A. C. Bradley, was published by the Clarendon Press, a series that continues to be published today with Boydell and Brewer. This first volume consists of seven essays directed largely at an academic and general audience. The first essay, on 'English Place-Names', was an expansion of a lecture delivered at the London Institute in January, 1907 by Henry Bradley, the distinguished philologist and lexicographer, who was an editor of the *Oxford English Dictionary*, and President of the Philological Society 1890–1893, 1900–1903 and 1909–1910.

---

[31] J.H. Fowler, *English Literature in Secondary Schools*, Pamphlet 5, 1908.
[32] G. Clement, *The Teaching of English in Girls' Secondary Schools*, Pamphlet 6, 1908.
[33] *The Teaching of Shakespeare in Schools*, Pamphlet 7, 1908. Prior to 1919, the year of the appointment of the Newbolt Committee, forty-three pamphlets had been published. Approximately half of these were directed at school as opposed to universities or adult students and teachers.
[34] G. Bellamy, 'The Genesis of the Newbolt Report on the Teaching of English in England: a Study of the Early Years of the English Association', (unpublished master's thesis, University of Leicester, 1977), pp. 9–10.

In the second essay, the distinguished poet Robert Bridges, who became Poet Laureate in 1913, writes 'On the Present State of English Pronunciation', while the remaining essays focus on literary concerns. W. P. Ker's 'Browning' is a reprint of his 2 March 1910 lecture at Queen's College, London; George Neilson's 'Blind Harry's *Wallace*' concentrates on a poem probably written between 1470 and 1488; George Saintsbury's 'Shakespeare and the Grand Style' was his Presidential address to the EA given in January 1910; Edith Sichel makes interesting observations on 'Some Suggestions About Bad Poetry'; and in the final essay, C. E. Vaughan writes on 'Carlyle and His German Masters'. The volume introduced the format which was to be followed for years; reprinted lectures juxtaposed with original commissions, essays on language and on literature covering a wide period with many perspectives. *Essays and Studies* appeared regularly in succeeding years.

Despite the lively activities of the EA in these early years, by their third year it was already clear that financial difficulties were occurring. The report presented to the third AGM of the EA, held on 15 January 1909, reveals the practical state of affairs of the EA, and while the three matters on the agenda—the adoption of the annual report, the adoption of the balance sheet, and the election of officers—occupied the meeting, the report of the special finance sub-committee might have been a disappointing surprise. It reveals that 'the year 1908–09 shows a loss of about £20', which careful calculations seem to attribute to the 'financial result of [having] associate (i.e., 1/–) members'. Through agonizing real and notional mathematics,[35] projected income and expenditure and analysis of membership figures, then 'the result would be to leave £84 to be divided among the 1300 members, or 1s. 32d. a head', the true cost of the Associate Membership. Remedies to offset the over-spend included the publication of the membership list biennially rather than annually, although, at the same time, the Secretary's salary was raised from £30 to a generous £50.

This attempt to put the EA's finances on an even keel was short-lived: at a meeting of the Executive on 27 May 1909, an emendation was made 'that while accepting the recommendation to print the full List of Members only every two years, a supplementary list should be issued in the alternate years'. Other matters at this time reveal the engagement of the EA in diverse activities such as examinations and publications, as well as cooperation with the Classical Association, itself founded in 1903. The EA and the Classical Association determined to cooperate 'on the matter of a Leaflet on Translations from the Classics'. The next item refers to 'a choice of subjects for discussion by the whole Association during the years 1909–10'. The subjects chosen were: 'Home Reading'; 'Syllabuses in English Literature'; and the 'Investigation of New Words [and] Forms of Expression'. There was a suggestion that this investigation 'might become part of the permanent work of the Association'.

---

[35] '[while] £166 out of the total expenditure of £233 might be set down as necessary expenditure even had no associates existed; and that by dividing the remaining £67 among the whole number of members & associates, the minimum cost of each extra associate might be roughly ascertained. The result would be 12a d'. Major expenditure resulted from the publication of the EA's leaflets (£58. 3. 2), postage (£25), and the Secretary's wages (£30 p.a.). Only slightly more than £2 was spent on dinners!

A. C. Bradley informed the Executive at this meeting 'that the delegates of the Clarendon Press, Oxford, agreed to publish the Association Annual' and, most importantly given the previous concerns with finances and printing costs, 'do take financial risk'. This discussion was followed by a debate on the publication of the Presidential address, one suggestion being that it be printed as a Leaflet, reflecting the way in which it 'was spoken at the meeting'. Then it would be published 'in an enlarged form as an essay' in the Annual. Others thought 'that the Presidential address ought to be available for all members, not only for those who would buy the Annual'. In the event Saintsbury's January 1910 Presidential address to the Association, 'Shakespeare and the Grand Style', was published as the fifth essay in the first *Essays and Studies*. The final matter noted in the Minutes for 27 May 1909 was the decision 'to send circulars of the Association to 100 Selected Professors of English in the United States'. This attempt to attract American membership was unsuccessful. By 1909 the Modern Language Association of America (MLA), which held its first annual conference in December 1883, was a thriving organization with a very large membership and a dynamic publication programme; the EA could not compete on the MLA's home territory.

The last General Committee before the First World War to be examined here took place on 23 February 1911. Acland was in the Chair and thirteen members of the General Committee attended. Amongst these were three figures who were to play an important role in the EA's activities subsequently. Two were newly elected to the Executive Committee: Professor Ernest de Sélincourt, the distinguished Wordsworthian and Professor of English at Birmingham; and the distinguished explicator of Shakespeare's image patterns and author of *Mysticism in English Literature*, Caroline Spurgeon. At the time of her election to the Executive Committee, she was Lecturer in English Literature at Bedford College, University of London, but in 1913 became the first woman Professor in the University when she was appointed Hildred Carlisle Professor of English Literature. The third influential and committed member of the Executive was John Bailey, who had served previously, and was to become Chair of the Executive from 1912 to 1915. President of the EA in 1926, he wrote numerous books and articles on seventeenth- and eighteenth-century literature.

Most of the meeting of 23 February 1911 was preoccupied with Committee co-options and elections. The last item noted by John Bailey, who signed the Minutes, was the announcement 'that Branches were in course of formation at Nottingham, Dublin, Belfast, Madras, Toronto, [and] South Africa'. In short, a few years after its formation, the EA had branches all over the world including Southern Asia. Membership had grown steadily since the initial meeting and by 1914 stood at around the 2000 mark. By 1914, such distinguished figures as the writer and statesman John Buchan and G. M. Trevelyan, the historian who would serve as President of the EA in 1951, were members of the Executive Committee. Vice-Presidents included the writer Edmund Gosse and Earl Curzon, who went on to have a distinguished political career. Power and influence was also reflected in the presence of twelve university professors, four heads of public schools (Eton, Merchant Taylors',

Wellington and Westminster), seven heads of other schools, and three principals of colleges. Other members who served on either Executive and/or General Committees included Stanley Leathes, a distinguished civil servant, who acted as Chair of the Prime Minister's Commission on Modern Language in the educational system in Great Britain, 1916–1918. Bellamy observes that 'such a distinguished membership was its own advertisement and the numbers grew steadily'.[36]

When WWI broke out in 1914, the EA 'had developed a group-consciousness'; its own 'way of working', a structured organisation, and a 'network of contacts'.[37] Bolstering its success and popularity, the EA held an Annual Banquet, and invited guests to the annual general meeting and its conferences. Speakers at the conferences exemplify the diverse interests the EA catered to: in 1911 Dr. W.H.D. Rouse, Head of the Perse School, Cambridge, lectured on 'The Place of English Composition in the Language Scheme of a Secondary School' and Miss E.A. Ford, a lecturer at the Clapham Day Training College for Teachers, spoke on 'The Teaching of Composition in Upper Classes'; in January 1914 Professor Frederic Moorman spoke on 'The Teaching of English on the First Year of a University Course'. During these years, Arthur James Balfour, Prime Minister from 1902 to 1905 and one of the founding members of the British Academy, followed his 1913 EA Presidency by agreeing to be Vice-President in 1914. The prominence of the EA's officers at this time is illustrated, too, by the Marquis of Crewe, who served as President in 1916.

---

[36] Bellamy, p. 6.
[37] Bellamy, p. 12.

III
From World War I to World War II

The Newbolt Report

The first, albeit imperfect, realisation of the aims of the EA was the *Report of the Teaching of English in England*, commissioned in 1919 by the President of the Board of Education.[38] The aims of the EA were the establishment of English Studies as a secure and intellectually respectable element in the curriculum of schools in Britain and in what were then known as the Dominions. The EA was instrumental in lobbying for a formal Committee and Report, culminating in the Newbolt Report. John Dover Wilson, the distinguished Shakespearean scholar and editor,[39] provides a fascinating account of the formation of the Newbolt Committee, with its members' conflicting personalities and temperaments. It is worth quoting at length this account from his autobiography:

> After the great Education Act of 1918 had become law, the subject that principally engaged the board of Education was the teaching of English Language and Literature in school. […]
> Accordingly a departmental committee for the investigation of this subject was appointed in May 1919 by the President of the Board, with the following terms of reference: "To inquire into the position occupied by English (Language and Literature) in the educational system of England, and to advise how its study may best be promoted in schools of all types, including Continuation Schools, and in Universities and other Institutions of Higher Education, regard being had to:
> (1) the requirements of a liberal education;
> (2) the needs of business, the professions, and public services; and
> (3) the relation of English to other studies".
> But it is clear, and I believe became generally acknowledged, that these terms had been drawn too broadly. It was understood from the beginning that the main function was to deal with the teaching of English, spoken and written, to young people in infant, elementary, and lower forms of secondary schools—for which reason the Secretary was an inspector of the elementary branch of the Board, and I was appointed as an inspector with a knowledge of evening classes and adult education, which comprised that part of the population which had somehow escaped proper instruction at the elementary stage.
> Moreover, the personnel of the committee was not selected with much reference to university teaching. It consisted in fact largely of the Executive Committee of the English Association. The only members of professorial rank besides Miss Caroline Spurgeon of Bedford College were Sir Charles Firth (who I think never attended) and Sir Arthur Quiller-Couch who, finding that nothing but soft drinks could be procured in the offices of the Board at which we held our meetings, absented himself after a single appearance.

---

[38] Board of Education, *Teaching of English in England*, 1921.
[39] In 1912, following a career in teaching, Wilson had become a Government Inspector of Education, a position he held until 1924 when he became Professor of Education at King's College, London.

The only other member of professorial rank was F. S. Boas, formerly professor in Northern Ireland and at that period an L.C.C. Inspector of Schools. I ought not, however, to omit to mention J. H. Fowler, the veteran and much-honoured teacher of English at Clifton College; and John Bailey, who though he held no official post was one of the pillars of the committee of the English Association and a very graceful writer, with delightful little books on Milton and Shakespeare to his credit. Other members included Miss Enright, the head teacher of the school at Rotherham, who had been put on the committee at my suggestion, and Mr. George Sampson who in the course of the committee's session published at the Cambridge University Press an excellently written and popular book, *English for the English*. This last, however, disconcerted some of us on the committee who were devoting strenuous hours in the public service to a report which would follow much the same lines as his book, a book that could hardly have been written without the evidence which a member of the committee had at his disposal.

The proceedings throughout were dominated by our chairman, Sir Henry Newbolt, the poet, a personal friend of mine—charming, suave, delighting to discuss at length the problems that confronted us. But he possessed little knowledge or sympathy with English scholarship and the teaching of the history of English literature in universities. And though about the time the committee was sitting, he had himself seen through the press a book on the history of English literature (to which I had been asked to contribute certain chapters) brought out by Nelson, his true attitude was well revealed in the fact that he insisted, despite my protests, on placing all the Old and Middle English literature chapters in a sort of appendix to the volume. This, I told him, was literally preposterous, but he would not retract.

This prepossession of the Chairman helps to explain the attitude of two important university witnesses. It was unfortunate that a morning had been set aside for evidence from the professors of the two principal colleges of the University of London. University College was represented by W. P. Ker, and King's College by Sir Israel Gollancz—it being apparently unknown to our organizers that the two professors were not on the best terms. Ker, perhaps the greatest scholar who has ever taught English literature in a university, with all the austerity and acerbity of a learned Scot, had little but contempt for his rather garrulous colleague at King's. Gollancz, a keen Shakespearian, thought his main duty was to impress upon the committee the importance of keeping Shakespeare's Day in the schools of England. Newbolt found this an engaging topic, and the two went on talking about it for some time, until suddenly our chairman realized that he had not yet heard anything from Ker. He therefore turned to him and asked him something about the teaching of English at University College. To this Ker tight-lipped replied, 'That is a domestic question'. These words constituted the whole body of evidence which he presented to the committee. Newbolt had him to dinner afterwards, we learned, but he refused to add anything more to the evidence or to countenance the committee in any way whatever; and when the Report appeared in print, he had it burned publicly in the courtyard of University College.

Thus an entirely erroneous conception of the aims and purpose of the committee became traditional in University College. Indeed, in a relatively recent controversy in the correspondence columns of *The Times* (on 18th November 1965), concerning the teaching of Anglo-Saxon, the then principal of University College clearly showed himself under the impression that the report of the committee (which incidentally sold like a novel when it appeared in print) was an attack on the teaching of Anglo-Saxon in universities.

Another university witness, Professor Saintsbury, had obviously been made suspicious by Ker. He had been succeeded in Edinburgh by Professor Grierson and had retired to Bath, but he was willing to appear before the committee. His purpose became clear almost immediately after he entered the room, for he began at once to harangue us on the importance of Anglo-Saxon. He continued this theme so persistently that at last I ventured to interrupt. "Excuse me, Professor Saintsbury", I said, "but the committee is mainly concerned with children—the English of boys and girls in the elementary schools and the lower forms of the secondary schools. At what age," I asked, "ought one to begin to learn Anglo-Saxon?" He turned that extraordinary face of his full upon me and, raising his fist, thumped the table. "Sir," he thundered, "you cannot begin Anglo-Saxon too early!"…

Despite the disapproval of W. P. Ker and a few other academic witnesses at the committee, the Report when published in 1921, two years after the first meeting, was at once welcomed by teachers in general. It sold, as I have said, like a "best seller", being widely read in business as well as educational circles.[40]

The committee thus described by Wilson had fourteen members, of whom nine were members of the EA, including Sir Henry Newbolt, the poet and historian, who was Chair of both the Department Committee and, in 1928, the EA itself. The other members of the Newbolt Commission with EA connections included J. C. Bailey; Miss K. M. Baines, a school inspector; F. S. Boas; Miss H. M. Davies, teacher in English at Bingley Training College, Yorkshire; Miss D. Enright who was head teacher at Rotherham and became Principal of the Selfridge Continuation School; Miss L. A. Lowe, who was Head Mistress of the Girl's High School, Leeds, and a member of the Committee of the Yorkshire branch of the EA; G. Sampson, an LCC Inspector and member of the EA Executive Committee; Caroline Spurgeon; and John Dover Wilson, then a School Inspector.

The Newbolt Report was published on 5 November 1921 in the *Times Educational Supplement*, which devoted a column leader to it, followed by a detailed account of the report including each of the Report's one hundred and fifty recommendations. These recommendations stressed the crucial primary importance of teaching English as a subject in its own right. Quintessentially, the Newbolt Report upheld the values that the EA stood for. The Report attached 'importance to the teaching of English in the earliest stages' of childhood. It stressed 'the necessity in the interest of national unity of a liberal education for all English children, based on the national language and literature'.[41] Generalized in nature it contained throughout its 400 pages abstract observations largely unsubstantiated by practical proposals; for instance, 'literature is not just a subject for academic study, but one of the chief temples of the human spirit, in which all should worship'.[42] The report expressed unease with antiquated teaching methods and criticized the presence of out-dated philological courses in the undergraduate curriculum. It proposed that language study should encompass syntax and semantics in addition to phonology especially when joined with both a critical and historical analysis of literature.

The report criticised the focus on literary history as a mere series of dates and factual information obtained from textbooks; emphasis, it dictated, should be on the reading of actual works of literature. It attacked the conception that 'the process of education is the performance of compulsory hard labour, a "grind" or "stiffening process", a "gritting of the teeth"' Its recommendations, embodying the intellectual

---
[40] John Dover Wilson, *Milestones on the Dover Road*, Faber & Faber, 1969, cap. 4.
[41] Nowell Smith, *The Origin and History of the Association*, 1942, p. 3.
[42] Margaret Mathieson, *The Preachers of Culture: A Study of English and its Teachers*, 1975, p. 69.

aims of EA members, stated: 'We have declared the necessity of what must be a however elementary a form, a liberal education for all English children whatever their position or occupation of life…we believe that in English literature we have a means of Education not less valuable than the classics and decidedly more suited to the necessities of a general and national education'.[43] A reduction of rote-learning, memorizing, and other antiquated teaching methodologies should be replaced by 'plain speech and writing, and practice given in talking and listening'. The report asserts:

> If we use English Literature as a means of contact with great minds, a channel by which to draw upon their experience with profit and delight, and a bond of sympathy between the members of a human society, as we shall succeed, as the best teachers of the classics have often succeeded in their more limited field.[44]

The authors of the Newbolt Report passionately believed in the necessity for improvements in English teaching, especially at the elementary level. These views were rigorously advocated by George Sampson, an influential member of the EA, in his *English for the English*. Sampson asserts 'Deny to working-class children any common share in the immaterial, and presently they will grow into men who demand with menaces a communism of the material'. Sampson also insists 'that it is the purpose of education, not to prepare children for their occupation, but to prepare children against their occupation'.[45] Such ideas stressing the primacy of English, the absorption in literature, in works of literature, are found in the anti-utilitarian tradition expressed, for instance, in the Victorian period by Dickens in *Hard Times* and Matthew Arnold's prose and poetry. In the twentieth century, the sentiments of the Newbolt Report are echoed with variations in the writings of F. R. Leavis, D. Thompson, and Raymond Williams to name but three major expositors of the values of English as a humane study.

In short, the Newbolt Report exemplified the influence of the EA and its members and embodied their values. Its vigorous advocacy of the primacy of English as a subject reverberates to this day. It demonstrated a concern with education and its crucial importance, with 'values', and with 'Englishness', indeed with an implicit attempt to create a national culture. To quote the Report again:

> The belief which inspires every paragraph of the present Report is that this much-desired spiritual unity in the nation and the equally necessary uplift in the whole level of the popular imagination can only come through a general acknowledgement of the paramount place which the native speech and literature should occupy in our schools and in the common life of our people.[46]

---

[43] Henry Newbolt, *The Teaching of English in England*, 1921, pp. 14ff.
[44] Newbolt, pp. 15ff.
[45] George Sampson, *English for the English*, 1921, pp. xv and 11 respectively.
[46] Newbolt, p. 277. For interesting assessments of the Newbolt Report from different perspectives, see D. J. Palmer, *The Rise of English Studies*, 1965, Appendix II, pp. 179–185; M. Mathieson, pp. 69–82; G. Bellamy, chapter 4; and B. Doyle, *English and Englishness*, 1989, pp. 40–67.

It is hardly surprising, perhaps, given the damage of the First World War that emerging from its trauma were beliefs in the curative and uplifting power of a native, English literary and linguistic tradition to unite and spiritually revivify the people.

Meetings, Business, Banquets

Two major social and business events dominated the EA calendar: the Annual General Meeting, which saw the Business Meetings and the delivery of the Presidential Address and which was followed by the annual conference; and in May of each year, the Annual Dinner. Each of these occasions fostered the sense of belonging to the EA, often encouraged new networks to evolve, and permitted considerable business to take place.

The formula for the AGM changed little. It met on a Friday and Saturday usually in May or June in London, often at Bedford College, or the Central Hall, Westminster. One example will suffice to demonstrate the common pattern: the 19th AGM that took place at the Central Hall, Westminster on Friday and Saturday, 12–13 June 1925. The Business Meeting was held on the Friday afternoon at 4:30 with the Treasurer in the Chair. The Report and Balance Sheet was scrutinized and adopted. This was followed by the notification of deaths–this AGM was different from others in that the President of the EA, Lord Curzon, had died during his Presidential year. Following this item, the state of the EA's membership and revenues was noted. Subsequent to this, the election of a new President (John Bailey), the re-election of Vice Presidents, and other committee elections took place. These proceedings, which took an hour, were then followed by an Address delivered by James Rennell Rodd (future EA President in 1933) substituting for Lord Curzon, and a vote of thanks from the Chairman. The speeches, and most of the proceedings, were printed in summary form in the *Bulletin*.

The other regular social/business event was the Annual Dinner of the Association, which took place at some of the most exclusive London restaurants. The venue for the Friday 12 June 1925 dinner was the Trocadero Restaurant. In the Chair was Sir Henry Newbolt: worthy guests of the association included Professor Denis Saurat, Professor of French at King's College, London; E. M Forster, the novelist; and Ethel de Sélincourt, wife of the 1936 EA President. Among the toasts (faithfully recorded in the *Bulletin*), was a jubilant recognition of companionship in Forster's statement that a 'delightful feature of the English Association was that is brought together not only all of its members but guests as well'.[47]

Often a Conference followed the Banquet. On Saturday 13 June 1925, the subject was 'The Appeal to the Eye and Ear in the Study of Literature', with Dr. Ernest Baker in the Chair. Papers were given on reading literature from a psychological perspective; other perspectives were provided by a Head Mistress, a retired Training College Principal, a representative of the British Drama League and the BBC.

---

[47] *Bulletin* 55, November 1925, p.11.

These are reported also in the *Bulletin*. The last annual dinner recorded before World War II followed the AGM in May 1938. It was held at the Holborn Restaurant with the President, Harley Granville-Barker, in the Chair. Lack of space in the new journal *English* led to a truncated report of the proceedings. In May 1939, a conference was held at Bedford College for which the topic was the consideration of government reports on education. The AGM was held on 17 June 1939 at St. Ermin's Restaurant at 12:30 p.m. The place of the president, the Archbishop of York who could not preside at the Business Meeting, was taken by F. S. Boas. An hour later, the Annual Luncheon took place with the Archbishop presiding and the usual toasts and speeches. The Presidential Address took place in the Hall of Westminster School at 4:30 p.m. A similar pattern occurred in 1940 except that the Presidential Address also took place at St. Ermin's Restaurant. This seems remarkable in the light of the full-scale war occurring all around, but perhaps assisted in giving an impression of continuity and the upholding of traditional English values.

Officers of the EA, 1918–1939

The twenty-three presidents from 1918 until the outbreak of the Second World War contained a mixture of politicians and statesmen, educational administrators, clerics, writers and academics. Political figures are represented by Prime Ministers such as Herbert Asquith, President of the EA in 1918, and Stanley Baldwin, President in 1927. Statesmen and politicians include Rowland Edmund Prothero, Baron Ernle who served during the First World War as President of the Board of Agriculture and Fisheries and was President of the EA 1920–1921. Viscount Grey of Fallodon was a distinguished Foreign Secretary and President of the League of Nations Union from 1918: he served as EA President in 1923. Another diplomat who became EA President in 1933 was James Rennell Rodd, the first Baron Rennell. John Sankey, EA President in 1935, as Viscount Sankey became Labour's First Lord Chancellor, 1929–1935. Another lawyer and judge who served as EA President in 1929 was Lord Chief Justice Howard of Bury.

Men of letters serving as President range from Sir Edmund Gosse (1922), who in common with Laurence Binyon (1934), worked in the British Museum, to John Galsworthy, the Nobel Prize winner (1924) and Sir Henry Newbolt (1928). Academics serving as President during the inter-war period range from C. H. Herford in 1919, Oliver Elton in 1932, Ernest de Sélincourt in 1936, and John Bailey in 1926. John William Mackail (1930) was a distinguished civil servant in addition to his literary activities focussing on Virgil, Shakespeare and others. Sir Edmund Chambers (1940) earned his living as a distinguished civil servant who produced works on Mediaeval and Elizabethan literature and Shakespeare which are still regarded as classics.

Of these twenty-three Presidents two did not receive a school or university education. Sir Edmund Gosse was privately educated and Harley Granville-Barker, the great actor, producer, director, dramatist and Shakespearean interpreter and EA

President in 1938 went on the stage. Only three Presidents, Herford (Trinity), Baldwin (Trinity), Inge (King's College), were from Cambridge. The great majority were products of Oxford: Asquith, Ernle, Grey of Fallodon, Curzon, Mackail, Lang, Rennell, Temple, were all Balliol men. Galsworthy and Bailey were at New College; Newbolt, Elton and Chambers at Corpus Christi; Hewart and de Sélincourt were products of University College; Binyon, Trinity; John Sankey, Jesus College. Most were also products of the Public School system (Clifton, Eton, Marlborough, and Winchester, to instance four). Two (Lang and Mackail) followed the Scottish route from either Edinburgh or Glasgow to Balliol College, Oxford. The pool of eligible serving Presidents for associations such as the EA or, for instance, the Classical Association must have been small: Lord Curzon, Asquith, Mackail, Baldwin, Hewart, Temple, Inge, serving in both capacities. Montagu Butler, the first EA President also served as President of the CA in 1913. A Wordsworthian empathy is reflected in the title of Viscount Grey of Fallodon's 1923 address to the EA, an oration on 'Wordsworth's 'Prelude''. The great Wordsworth scholar Ernest de Sélincourt, EA President in 1936, chose as the subject of his Address to the EA 'The Early Wordsworth'.

IV
World War II and Its Aftermath

1940–1967

The Second World War had a significant effect on education and academia, ranging from the aerial bombardment of London and other British cities, to the deployment of academics and schoolteachers in the armed forces.[48] The EA, its publications and ability to function, was obviously affected, and a curiously detached notice in *English* comments that: 'The competition for the award of a prize for the best essay has proved disappointing' citing 'the disorganizing effects of the war on the schools, especially those which have been evacuated'.[49] This stiff upper-lipped response (as if evacuees should be composing their essays on the trains) continued throughout the war.

The minutes of the Executive Committee meetings held during the war are revealing. Remarkably, in spite of the Blitz in London, the blackout and general wartime restrictions in the capital, meetings went on and were attended by those Executive members who, owing usually to their age, were not subject to military call-up. A meeting was held in South Kensington in October 1941 at which none of those present was eligible for war service. Ranging from Frederick Boas, who was born in 1862 to Sir Arthur Edward Hall in 1885, all were well beyond the age of enrolment. Guy Boas was the youngest, being born in 1896. The Chair from 1941 to 1943 was Nowell Charles Smith, and in the words of his Obituary notice in *English*, his 'term as Chairman of Committee coincided with the most difficult of the war years, but he fearlessly kept going the Association's committees and lectures in London'.[50] He also 'took a leading part in the publication of *England*, an anthology collected by Association members and published in 1944'. The all too brief notice concludes: 'He will be long remembered for his literary and scholarly distinction and his selfless devotion to high causes'.[51] In addition then to his 1942 address at the Annual General EA meeting on 'The Origin and History of the English Association', given at a time when origins were of great importance, his Chairmanship and leadership through the bleak London war years should not be underestimated.

Two other members of the executive committee played a prominent role in its wartime activities and in the post-war period: Rear Admiral Sir Arthur Edward Hall and Arundell Esdaile. From differing walks of life, both reflect the increasing diversification of the higher echelons of the EA. Hall was treasurer of the EA from

---

[48] Harold Perkin observes that 'The Second World War affected the universities and their staffs and students, as it affected British society as a whole, more directly and profoundly than the First'; 'Like the rest of the civilian population, too, the universities found themselves, in contrast with the First World War, in the front line'. See his *Key Profession: The History of the Association of University Teachers*, 1969, pp. 106–7.
[49] *English*, 3, 13, 1940, p. 44.
[50] *English*, 13, 76, 1961, p. 143.
[51] *ibid*

1939 to 1943 and 1950–1951, Vice Chair from 1944 to 1946 and Chair from 1947–1949 and from 1952 until his death in 1959. He became an EA member in 1913, served in key naval engagements in WWI and joined the Executive Committee in 1938. Of his Chairing from 1952 to 1959 the Obituary Notice observes:

> He was a firm and equable Chairman, gathering the committee round him as his personal friends. In addition to this most valuable quality he gave unremitting attention to our work in all its details, not only in committee but on those many occasions behind the scenes to which a chairman can give either more or less of his time. He always gave that much more, and only now one realizes how much he was giving in equal measure to other good causes. Under his guidance the Executive Committee enjoyed seven years of serene and successful effort.
>
> To members of the Association he was a welcoming figure at lectures at the Alliance Hall, from which he was seldom absent, and at the Annual Luncheon he presided with a quiet dignity and unaffected geniality which made the occasion as it were a pleasant at-home for ourselves and our guests, and it was universally regretted last year that for the first time his health prevented his attending.
>
> Dr. Johnson once said that no man is obliged to do all that he can. It was not a dictum which Arthur Hall accepted. The English Association may well think that he did all he could for its interests, and the memory of what he did and of his great gift for friendship will long remain.[52]

Esdaile, for his part, did not serve in the World Wars; as an employee of the British Museum during WWI, he was not called up and by WWII he was too old for active service. A prolific author and library historian, Esdaile helped to establish the first British school of librarianship at University College, London and played a prominent role during the 1930s in the International Federation of Library Associations, undertaking 'an ambassadorial tour of the United States and Canada in 1941' on behalf of the British Library Association, during which he also represented the EA. From 1944 to 1946, he served as Chair of the EA's Executive Committee.

The minutes of the Executive Committee for 15 October 1941 very occasionally reflect war-time preoccupations and interests; a member of the Committee, Dorothy Margaret Stuart, wrote to suggest 'that the Association should get into touch with the Headquarters of the Canadian Army in England with a view to organising Lectures and Talks for Canadian troops', which the EA was unable to do. And the Committee was sympathetic to the request from the Librarian of Birkbeck College, London, for the supply 'at a reduced rate' of new sets of *YWES* and *Essays and Studies* 'to replace the volumes that had been destroyed through enemy action'.

These minutes reveal that in spite of bomb raids on London and other cities in the United Kingdom, the affairs of the EA went on almost as normal. This pattern is confirmed by a scrutiny of the minutes of the first meeting for the next year, held at Cromwell Road on 28 January 1942 in the early afternoon (at a time early enough presumably to comply with the blackout regulations). Esdaile reported in a letter on his efforts in the United States on behalf of the EA, which revealed that neither the College English Association nor the MLA were interested in assisting the EA in the early years of the War, or forming any kind of liaison with it. The Executive

---

[52] *English*, 12, 73, 1960, p. 1.

Committee then turned its attention to other matters including donations and 'an application for membership from a prisoner of war in Germany, concerning which, however, the Committee agreed that no action should be considered until it had been found whether his family were able and ready to pay the subscription'. It is surely extraordinary that the Committee were so minded, and equally extraordinary that a POW would think of joining the EA in his years of captivity. Other remarkable issues included the arrangement of forthcoming lectures, and the suggestion that 'General de Gaulle should be invited to take the Chair on' 28 March when a fellow member of the French Free Force in London would be lecturing. These two items suggest that the War seemed not to be regarded as a hindrance to the efforts of the EA—in a manner replete with national defiance and resistance—and indicates that the Committee simply refused to engage in a serious contemplation of the War and its potential consequences.

The next meeting in February 1942 heard, unsurprisingly, that de Gaulle was unable to attend to chair the March lecture. The Executive also learned that St. Ermin's Restaurant in London, which had been decided upon for the Annual Luncheon, 'could not accommodate the Association…owing to the difficulty of food supplies'. It therefore 'agreed to cancel the Luncheon and postpone further arrangements for the Annual Meeting and Address until later'. War-time conditions and the uncertainty of the period eventually stymied the EA's efforts to retain a normal schedule.

War-time conditions are also reflected in the minutes for the meeting of the Executive Committee held on 24 November 1943. In addition to apologies for absence from four members, there had been refusals to serve on the Executive Committee from a number of people because of practical difficulties with travel and their inability to get to London for meetings. Other correspondences indicating war-time issues were also noted in the minutes illustrated, for example, by an exchange of letters and publications between the EA and 'the U.S.S.R. Society for Cultural Relations with foreign Countries', together with the receipt of copies of the *Moscow News* and *VOKS Journal* (the former in English, the latter in Russian).

At the close of the meeting, the out-going Chair, Nowell Smith, spoke of what he 'had been unable, for various reasons, during his three years of office to promote'. His ambitious aims indicate that he saw the EA not only as a promoter of a national heritage at a time when it was clearly under threat, but also that it was perceived by him as something of an arbiter and guardian of an entire English cultural aesthetic. He included the hope firstly 'that the Association should become a great nation-wide instrument both for dissolving class divisions in a common interest in our national heritage of language and literature'; secondly, the hope 'for raising and fortifying public taste and intelligence against the influences of mass-provided passive amusement of demagogic propaganda, and of mere vacuity'. Smith believed, too, in the objectivity of the EA, claiming that it 'had the advantage over political and religious organisations in having no inherent tendency towards division and strife'; his vision was that the EA's national message meant its adoption throughout the country, and that it 'should aim at having branches, groups of individual members in every town and village'. What the EA should not do, Smith believed, is to 'create the impression of being run by Schoolmasters and Schoolmistresses; on the contrary one of the divisions it should dissolve was that between teacher and parents, the teaching professions, and the rest of the nation', and that yet, and somewhat contradictorily, 'the interest and help of teachers through-out the country were indispensable as a first step, and to secure these should be the main endeavour of the Executive Committee in the immediate future'.

Such high (and, perhaps, unrealistic) ideals and hopes in the middle of the war may have been a bold response to outside threats to the national literary and linguistic heritage; that, in effect, the EA could form a home-guard of cultural values. Smith's belief in the status and authority of the EA to effect change on a national scale is explicit, and was, presumably, held by other active members of the Association. Its focus here, too, is upon the association's role in secondary rather than higher education, perhaps demonstrating its ostensible policy of egalitarianism; its emphasis on the availability of 'taste and intelligence' for all. None of these aims was effected, but at least Smith aimed high!

The subsequent meeting of the Committee was held in January 1944, and was attended by the largest turnout since the outbreak of hostilities in 1939. An exchange of publications with the University of Lund in Sweden, with the British Council acting as intermediary, perhaps signalled the hopeful anticipation of a return to peacetime conditions. A letter from Professor S.C. Deb, the Honorary Secretary of the Allahabad Branch in India, was followed by a proposal from Professor Ifor Evans that a Sub-Committee should be created 'possibly one on International Relations—to consider systematically [the EA's] contact with other countries'. Again this ambition suggests a sense that future plans were worth making, though the war's effects were felt in the report that Oxford University Press had advised the EA 'that the war increase for printing would rise from a token surcharge of 7 ½ % to 25%' and 'would come into force as from Jan. 1st 1944, and would affect future numbers of *English* and *The Years Work in English Studies*'. Guy Boas then reported on the progress of the anthology *England*. Finally, it was decided that more regular and frequent meetings would subsequently take place.

Similar issues preoccupied the next meeting on 23 February, 1944 when fifteen members of the Committee were again present. The main concern seems to have been discussion of the implications of 'the Norwood Committee on Secondary Schools to remove English Literature from the subjects of the School Leaving Examination'. Also the Committee report cast doubt 'on the value of Specialist English Teachers in Schools', which would, they oddly thought, result 'in its practical disappearance as a University Honours subject'. The EA decided to send a delegation to the Board of Education to obtain additional information, a delegation that consisted of Esdaile, Guy Boas, Professor Vivian de Sola Pinto, Dr. H. V. Routh, and Jenkyn Thomas. The EA Executive chose a delegation drawn from various constituencies—the Library world (Esdaile), the Universities (de Sola Pinto and Routh), and the schools (Boas and Jenkyn Thomas)—to represent them in discussions with the Government's Board of Education. Other matters discussed at this EA Executive meeting were more routine, though again, war-time work at OUP had its impact on the EA:

publication of *YWES 22* 'had been much delayed on account of Government printing to which the Oxford University Press had been obliged to give priority'.

Such was the flavour of subsequent EA meetings held at 3 Cromwell Place on the last Wednesday of the month, usually at three in the afternoon. The minutes from 1945 reflect a mood of buoyancy internationally resulting from the impending end of the war in Europe; overseas British Institutes in Cairo and Alexandria, for example, expressed a wish to become full members in January. The meeting of 28 March 1945 learnt that through the good offices of the British Council there were on-going attempts to create EA branches in Turkey, Sierra Leone and Trinidad. Sub-Committees became increasingly proactive and extensive reports survive from the Finance, Publications, Schools and newly formed Literary Advice Sub-Committees. The latter was an ambitious undertaking (that could never be feasible in the present-day academic world) to 'help Members by advising them on their work [and] manuscripts will be read by members of the Committee specifically qualified to deal with the nature of their contents'.[53] Only advice would be given, and appropriate fees would be charged, with an extra 50 percent added to those who submitted work and were not EA members. The EA clearly intended to underline its projected role as guardian of standards in English with genuine action.

There were other, numerous indications of the EA flourishing significantly in this post-War period. In February 1945, a request for an order of 630 copies of *Essays and Studies* from the Clarendon Press was agreed to by the Press which hitherto had been very involved with War time printing; the Executive Committee learnt at its May 1945 meeting that OUP was reprinting the most recent *YWES*, volume 23; and the EA secretary noted that a 'considerable increase in membership' during 1945 meant that stocks of *Essays and Studies* and *The Years Work in English Studies* might be insufficient to meet the members' needs. At the same meeting, the Committee heard that finances were in a very healthy position, and it was thus suggested that provincial members should be granted 'additional privileges…including the reviving of Branches that closed owing to the war, and the possibility of financing for the provinces lectures given to the Central Body'.

Immediate post-war EA minutes are not without interest, particularly for the 'aim high' policy of the Association. The April 1946 meeting was told that Winston Churchill, then out of High Government office, 'had declined the Committee's invitation to be President for 1947 on account of his already heavy commitments', but Sir Osbert Sitwell was able to accept that role. At this meeting, too, it was announced that Jenkyn Thomas and Dorothy Margaret Stuart had prepared the first EA Newsletter to be included with *English*; another new initiative was the appointment of S.E. Buckley, as EA Organizing Officer.

The difficulty of finding suitable accommodation and office space in post-War London had its effect upon the EA. A special meeting was called for 31 October 1946 at Sloane School where Guy Boas was Headmaster. The main concern was the need for the EA to move its office from the first floor of 3 Cromwell Place, with no

---

[53] *English*, 5, 28, 1945, p. 135.

feasible alternative in sight. A symptom of the gradual recovery from the War is the revival of the Rugby Branch of the EA announced at the meeting, and the institution of new branches at Blackburn, Coventry, Manchester, North West Kent, and Worthing, Sussex. There were also developments overseas in efforts to start a branch in Lahore in India.

Minutes of subsequent EA meetings held during 1946 and 1947 at a variety of venues in London show the burgeoning of membership and flourishing of regional branches; for example, 5,000 copies of a lecture given by F. S. Boas on 'Ovid and the Elizabethans' had been ordered and OUP were asked to print an additional 500 copies of the annual Presidential Address. Despite this growth in membership in the latter years of the 1940s, finances were not that strong: committee members could not claim travel expenses, and the EA could not afford to undertake the publication of a biography of W. P. Ker. Other difficulties were posed by continuing shortages after the War; these are reflected in the EA's willingness to co-operate with other learned societies in lobbying the government 'for an adequate supply of paper for educational books'.

In a bid to speak authoritatively for all aspects of British education, the 1950s saw a concerted effort by the EA to reflect educational changes brought about by the Butler Education Act in 1944, and by the post-War world more broadly. Membership of its Schools Sub-Committee was broadened to represent Primary Schools, Secondary Schools, and Teacher Training Colleges as well as the Grammar Schools, who were already well represented. At the post-18 level, in addition to the highly selective universities, there were the two-year Teacher Training Colleges. Expansion in these areas was deemed essential for the EA to carry out its work and increase membership.

The relative financial buoyancy of the EA reflected in the immediate post-War reports of the Finance Sub-Committee was probably over-optimistic, as has already been indicated. The post-War years in Britain were bleak ones, with ravaged national finances and whole areas of devastated landscape. Not only had the country experienced six years of bitter warfare, but it also then underwent the dismemberment of its empire. The expansion of EA branches in the later 1940s surely reflects a desire for stability, a return to normalcy and a need for cultural sustenance at a time of rationing and cut backs. The national goals of the EA might have seemed appealing, too, in the light of the threats during WWII. Reality returned abruptly for the EA in March 1950, when the Finance Sub-Committee reported that accounts for 1949 showed a deficit of £246, an increase on that for the preceding year, which reduced the EA's surplus to £73. The reasons for the deficit were not due to a reduction in EA membership, but resulted from a loss in Royalties from the major publications because of increased publication costs.

Such figures reveal just how financially dependent the EA had become on its publications; hence it attempted in the early 1950s to expand this area of activity through numerous publications. The minutes reveal the personalities who played a prominent part in EA activities during the period. Amongst these were Margaret Willy, and Sir Philip Montefiore Magnus, who chaired the 30 March 1950 EA Committee meeting. He reappears most prominently in a rare note of public discord recorded in the minutes of the March 1959 meeting outlining an objection by Rostrevor Hamilton to comments made by Magnus. No further details about the comments are forthcoming, thus one is left to ponder the unhappy nature of the meeting.

Of the members prominent EA affairs in the post-war years Willy and Hamilton were poets; and Magnus and Hamilton also worked as civil servants. There is, at this time, a noticeable diminution of academic involvement in EA Executive affairs. Vivian de Sola Pinto and Routh were frequently absent from the meetings, and the composition of the EA executive in 1950 shows a preponderance of retired, male, non-academics actively involved with university English studies. This is somewhat surprising and contrasts with the active academic membership during its early years. It should be placed in the context of a dramatically expanding post-war university system and a concomitant increase in lecturers and students. Clearly, university staff at all ranks were under greater work load pressure, but even this factor does little to explain the decrease in senior academic practitioners active at the highest level of the EA in the post-1945 period. Efforts were made to invite London-based academics to participate; for instance, Professor Geoffrey Tillotson, the eminent eighteenth-century scholar, was invited to become a Committee member, but declined, due to the pressure of work.

Other indications of the EA's difficult relationship with university English Studies are reflected in the Committee minutes of the April 1950 meeting. The Chair, Sir Ronald Storrs, reported that 'he had expressed on behalf of the Association its willingness to interest itself (though not financially) in the proposed Shakespearean Research organisation to be formed in connection with the English department in the University of Birmingham'. The fact that the EA had no money with which to invest in major projects is a major factor in its inability to participate effectively in national academic initiatives. An attempt to engage the EA in academe at an international level is seen in Professor Geoffrey Bullough's efforts to interest members in what became the International Association of University Professors of English.[54] Bullough suggested to the EA executive 'that particulars of the English Association' should be sent to the next meeting 'in order to interest Dominion and foreign Professors of English', though to what end is not made clear.

The early 1950s were a period of reflection and reorganisation for the EA. Minutes for 1951 reveal fissures emerging in the structure and administration of the Association; nominations and elections to the Executive Committee 'had got out of step during and since the war years'; clauses of the EA's Constitution were felt to be antiquated.[55] Three prominent executive members, Sir Arthur Hall, Jenkyn Thomas and Professor Vernon Herbert Blackman pressed for radical constitutional revisions. At the meeting there was agreement 'that the General Committee should not be resuscitated, that one-quarter of the members of the Executive Committee

---

[54] Its initial meeting was held in Oxford in August 1950 and the first President of the Association was the eminent C.L. Wrenn from Oxford.
[55] For example, it was recorded that there was supposed to be a General Committee, but it 'had not met for over ten years'.

should retire each year and that they should be eligible for re-election', to take office on October 1.

It was evidently urgent for the EA to review its activities and organisation, since at the same meeting it faced an increased deficit, attributed to the increasing costs of *English* and *YWES*. Economies were agreed upon relating to the publications; the size of *English* was restricted to 48 pages, with less spent on advertising the journal, *YWES* was to be cut by 10%. In addition, EA membership subscriptions were increased, together with the prices of the four major publications, *English*, The Presidential Address, *YWES*, and *Essays and Studies*. Additional income from 'an educational trust' was also to be considered in the remedying of the deficit. However, at the next EA meeting held in April 1951, considerable opposition to these proposals was voiced, chiefly from David Low[56] and Guy Boas, who both insisted upon 'rigid economies in the administration' prior to increasing subscriptions.

Further dissention is seen in the Committee minutes of 28 June 1951 from a meeting chaired by Low, at which only eight members from eighteen were present. There was an attempt to discontinue *English* (as being too expensive) and to replace it with pamphlets, but this was overturned. When it was reported that members noted the Annual Report did not offer membership statistics, 'The Committee held that it was better not to publish such figures at present', illustrating the precarious situation in which the EA found itself. Guy Boas sent a letter to the meeting criticising 'the after luncheon arrangements at the Annual Luncheon', and calling attention to other unnecessary costs to the EA, all underlining the difficulties faced by the Association during these years.

A year later, on 26 June 1952, evidence of discord emerges once more. At this meeting, lengthy minutes record a discussion resulting from the resignation of Low as Secretary of the EA. Low's reason for resigning is related to his omission from a proposed gathering to discuss London GCE Examinations. Low was concerned that the meeting 'might develop into an attack' on the specific London Examining Board. In spite of the Chair's attempts to reassure Low, both he and Professor Geoffrey Bullough, his colleague at King's College, resigned over the matter. Frederick Boas subsequently managed to persuade Bullough not to resign, but the discussion over these matters reflects the concerns of members of the EA at the time; Boas, for example, 'wished that the Universities would give more support to the work of the English Association as they had done in its early days'.[57]

A year later, in November 1953, other difficulties arose, particularly in relation to finance, principally because of the substantial rise of printing costs for the EA's publications. Although OUP agreed to a slight increase in royalties paid to the EA on sales, the published price of *YWES* was increased from 15/– to 21/–, and the price to members was raised from 12/6 to 15/–. As the editor, F. S. Boas, was over ninety years

---

[56] Chair of EA from 1959 to 1964, and faculty member at King's College, London.
[57] Minutes, 26 June 1952. Curiously, Low and Bullough were reappointed to sub-committees at the September 1952 meeting indicating their change of heart towards the EA. As it transpires, the contentious Examinations meeting had been postponed because all those invited to chair the meeting had refused to do so.

old, the Organising Officer was instructed to liaise with Dr. Beatrice White about the future editor's position of *YWES* 'should Dr. Boas at any time feel unable to continue'. F. S. Boas' impending retirement from *YWES* is recorded in the following September when the minutes also note the decrease of Guy Boas' EA activities. Guy had resigned from the editorship of *English* and refused to be co-opted as a member of the Executive Committee 'as there was little likelihood of his attending meetings'. He collected *Essays and Studies* for 1954, and Margaret Willy replaced him as editor of *English*.

These years approaching the Fiftieth Anniversary of the EA's foundation were a period of transition.[58] The passing of the older order is noted in the Minutes for 31 May 1956: the first item concerned the news that Arundell Esdaile had become too ill to undertake any further literary work; Guy Boas, too, had become unwell; in 1957 Jenkyn Thomas, after many years' service to the EA, decided to stand down from re-election to the EA Committee. Nominations for election to the Executive Committee for 1957/1958 made at the April 1957 meeting further reflect a transformation in the personnel of the EA, including the election of two academics from the University of London, William Armstrong and T. S. Dorsch, who were among those who would subsequently play an important part in the EA.

Underlying financial difficulties for at this time can be seen in the June 1957 Minutes, when an offer to compile an index to all back numbers of *English* and *Essays and Studies* was turned down because of the expense involved and the prospective lack of demand. Given the considerable importance of the EA's publications to its financial health and academic status, a great deal of emphasis was placed on this area of activity in the late 1950s up to the mid-1960s. Executive Committee Minutes reflect considerable time taken up with the Report of the Publications' Sub-Committee. In February 1958, Rostrevor Hamilton reported that *Essays and Studies'* sales were satisfactory; that 'nearly 17,000 copies of *English Essays of To-Day* had been sold in India during 1957', bringing in royalties of over £400; and copies of *YWES* were to be increased by 5%. And, by a policy of careful financial management and increased activity, by March 1960, the Treasurer, William Armstrong, was able to report that the 1959 Accounts showed a surplus of some £268, which was to be invested in low-risk stocks.

Five years later, the report of the Publications Sub-Committee took prime place on the EA Executive Committee agenda for the 14 July 1965 meeting, and included discussion of the publication of a *Guide to English Courses in the Universities* earlier that year, which sold 11,000 copies within a few months. Other business included the decision not to reprint *Poems of Today* because of low sales and high costs; the favourable response to the publication of a *Commonwealth Poems of Today* aimed at the schools market; discussion of the Autumn 1965 issue of *English*, focusing on a Commonwealth theme and published to coincide with regional Arts Festivals; and increased sales from the first series of *English Short Stories of Today*. The usefulness

---

[58] *Essays and Studies 1956 Jubilee Volume*, collected by Sir George Rostrevor Hamilton, was published to celebrate this anniversary year.

of *YWES* to the flourishing field of English was shown in the increase of numbers published from 2,500 copies to 3,000.

The demand for additional copies reflected the immense expansion of English Studies during the 1960s. This became known as the 'Robbins era' following the Report of the Robbins Committee on Higher Education, 1961 to 1963. Alongside this was the creation in the 1960s of the new universities of Sussex, York, East Anglia, Essex, Kent, Warwick, Lancaster, Sterling, and Ulster. How the EA reacted to this inevitable expansion in English Studies and the demise of Classical Studies will be examined in the final decades of its history to date.

Meetings, Business, Conferences

Conferences and the Annual General Meetings inevitably were curtailed, especially in London, during the Second World War. We have seen from the examination of the war-time Executive Committee Minutes that the St. Ermin's Restaurant was unable, due to food shortages, to provide a meal for the 1942 Annual General Meeting scheduled on 6 June 1942. Two years earlier, on Saturday 8 June 1940 at 12:30 pm, the AGM was held at St. Ermin's; Dr. F. S. Boas presided. At 4 pm the EA President, Sir Edmund Chambers, gave his presidential address entitled, 'The Timelessness of Poetry'. This was published subsequently by OUP and issued to all members of the EA with the autumn number of *English*. In 1940 meetings were still held in London; for instance, on 9 March at the Alliance Hall, Westminster, there was a talk on 'The End of Peaceful Travel'. In his address, A.G. Macdonell argued that with the advent of war travelling must be mental, with the assistance of books, rather than actual. This address was published subsequently by OUP and issued to all members of the EA with the autumn number of *English*.[59] A year later, on 7 June 1941, the AGM was held at St. Ermin's with the annual luncheon. The President, Viscount Samuel, gave his Address that same afternoon on 'Style'. At the same restaurant later that year, in October, an afternoon lecture on the poetry of Matthew Arnold, was attended by an audience of over seventy.

Three meetings of the EA were held at the Alliance Hall, Westminster, during the spring of 1942. On Saturday 10 October 1942 Arundell Esdaile 'spoke to a large audience on Dr. Johnson and the Young'. Under a month later, Harold Goad spoke on 'The International Future of English'. So, in spite of problems with the 1942 AGM and annual luncheon, in addition to the death of the EA President, George Gordon, half-way through his term, there was still notable EA activity even at the height of war-time. The 1943 AGM was held at the Alliance Hall Westminster on 29 May, although there seems to have been no luncheon before the AGM that afternoon, after which Harold Nicolson gave the Presidential Address on 'The Poetry of Byron'. Two meetings at the same venue took place in the autumn of 1943, one on the reviewer and poet Humbert Wolfe, and the other on Byron.

---

[59] *English*, 3, 14, 1940, p. 103.

The first major war-time conference took place at the Alliance Hall, Westminster on Wednesday 12 April 1944 with Nowell Smith in the Chair. The subject was 'Basic English', and an eight page report on the Conference was circulated with *English*.[60] Earlier, on 11 March, Lord David Cecil gave a talk to the EA before a full audience at the Alliance Hall on the subject of Fanny Burney as a novelist, and there were regular autumn talks, notably by C. S. Lewis on 24 November on Rudyard Kipling. The AGM took place on 3 June 1944, again with no formal lunch. The President, F. S. Boas gave his Presidential Address on 'American Scenes, Tudor to Georgian, in the English Literary Mirror', a tribute to the Anglo-American War-Time Alliance.

In spite of the 'V' Bombs let loose on London and elsewhere during the last months of the war, EA activities picked up in 1944 and 1945. In addition to spring lectures, on 28 April 1945, a conference on examinations in English was held at the Alliance Hall, which was particularly well attended by teachers.[61] The AGM took place on 10 July 1945 at the same venue after which the President, the Archbishop of York, Cyril F. Garbett, gave his Presidential Address on the subject of 'Reading in Wartime'. Then later in the autumn of that year, two further EA meetings were held at the Alliance Hall, a pattern continuing the following year. 1946's AGM at Central Hall, Westminster, saw the President, historian Sir Arthur Bryant, speak on 'The Art of Writing'.

Conferences of interest in these immediate post-war years reflect the educational concerns of the period and the consequences of the Butler Educational Act which created a three tier school system: Grammar Schools, Technical Schools and the Secondary Modern Schools, selection for which was determined by an examination at the age of eleven, the 'Eleven-Plus'. Generally, Secondary Modern School staff were not university trained, but were a product of the teacher training colleges, which expanded in the post-1945 period. The City Literary Institute in London witnessed an educational conference under the EA's auspices held on 4 January 1947 with Arundell Esdaile in the Chair. Speakers included W. R. Niblett, Professor of Education at the University College of Hull, who spoke on 'The Teaching of English in Secondary Modern Schools'. This was followed by A. E. Martin's account of the methods employed for training students for their future work; and H.G.W. Chapman, from the Camden Emergency Training College, also gave a talk on the problems to be encountered in the classroom in Secondary Modern Schools with large classes.[62] Emergency Colleges were created to deal with a teacher shortage and gave returning servicemen a two-year crash course in teacher training. The report of Chapman's comments in *English* reveals no criticism of the Butler Education Act. There is an observation on 'the large class, which wearies and frustrates the right kind of teacher. It often crushes and loses to the profession the sensitive kind of young teacher which the work in English especially needs'. Also noted by Chapman is the perception that 'pupils of Secondary Modern Schools are of different mental calibre from those entering…Grammar and…Technical Schools',[63] a perception

---

[60] *English*, 5, 26, 1944.
[61] *English*, 5, 29, 1945, p. 173.
[62] *English*, 6, 34, 1947, p. 220.
[63] *English*, 6, 34, 1947, p. 220.

which blighted the futures of millions of school children in the post-1945 period and condemned some to menial jobs.

Such then was the pattern for the EA's activities in the late 1940s and succeeding decades: annual conferences; the AGM followed by the Presidential Lecture; and frequent London meetings consisting of lectures on literary topics. Details are included in the regular 'Association Notes' found in the last pages of each issue of *English*. On 5 July 1947 and in 1948 the AGM returned to its pre-war venue, at St. Ermin's Restaurant in London's St James's Park; however, in July 1949, the AGM was held at the Caxton Hall, Westminster, perhaps because an expensive restaurant such as St.Ermin's was viewed as an unsuitable venue at a time when the British economy was in poor shape and when EA 'expenses exceeded income' and it had been necessary to raise the cost of subscription.[64] The following year the AGM and Luncheon was held at the New Hall of the Horticultural Society, Westminster. The formula up to this point seems to be that the AGM was followed by the Presidential Address (in this instance the President was the humorous writer Sir Alan Herbert), then lunch at which speeches were made by the guests. This particular AGM and luncheon, if the report in *English* is to be trusted, seems to have been especially 'raucous', concluding with a chorus of 'Auld Lang Syne'![65] In 1960 the venue changed to the Church House Westminster where it continued into the late 1960s.

A representative flavour of proceedings may be seen from the report in *English* of the 1965 AGM. This took place at Church House, Westminster on Saturday 26 June 1965. The sequence of events consisted of a business meeting at which the Chair of the Executive Committee presented the Annual Report, followed by the presentation and adoption of the Annual Accounts. The President, Vice-President, and Honorary Officers for 1965–1966 were proposed and seconded. Following the business meeting the presidential address was delivered. In this case in 1965, Richard Church spoke on 'A Look at Tradition'. A vote of thanks followed the luncheon with a toast to the guests and a toast to the English Association, each with replies.[66]

During the 1950s and 1960s, three meetings were organized by the EA in London during the Spring and three meetings in the Autumn. Detailed accounts were given in *English*. To take but one example, in the Autumn of 1960, there were lectures on William Blake, on 'An Approach to English Language Teaching' and on J. M. Synge. Annually the EA sent a representative to contribute to the Conference of Educational Associations usually held at University College, London. The EA also arranged conferences. In November 1953, for example, a conference arranged by the Association on the Teaching of English Grammar was held at the City Literary Institute. In the chair was Eric Wynne Hickie,[67] a classicist, who rose to become Inspector of Schools until his retirement in 1952. From 1953 until the early 1960s he served as Organizing Officer of the EA, and between 1953 and 1956 he organized five conferences focusing on differing aspects of English teaching.[68]

---

[64] *English*, 7, 42, 1949, p. 301.
[65] *English*, 7, 44, 1950, p. 108.
[66] *English*, 16, 89, 1965, p. 205.
[67] *English*, 10, 55, 1956, p. 37.
[68] *English*, 15, 87, 1964, p. 125.

Presidents

There were twenty-seven presidents from 1941 until 1967. Twenty five of these were men, two women: Dame Veronica Wedgwood, the historian, in 1956; Clemence Dane (Winifred Ashton), the dramatist, in 1961. George Gordon died in the middle of his Presidency in 1962. Of these twenty-seven Presidents, Gordon, Sir Herbert Grierson (1948), E. M. W. Tillyard (1958), Sir Maurice Bowra (1959), Sir Sydney Roberts (1963), G. M. Trevelyan (1951), and A. L. Rowse (1952), had academic careers. Gordon, for example, was President of Magdalen College, Oxford; Tillyard, Master of Jesus College, Cambridge. Grierson was a distinguished literary editor and scholar, who, in 1894, became the first Professor of English at Aberdeen University. In 1915 he succeeded Saintsbury as Professor of Rhetoric and English literature and Edinburgh University until 1935. When he became EA President in 1948—at the age of 82—Grierson had been retired for more than a decade. Amongst his prolific output, his edition of John Donne published in 1912 in two volumes is considered to be one of the most important literary publications of the twentieth century.

Sir Maurice Bowra, President in 1959, was associated throughout his life with Wadham College, Oxford, becoming Vice-Chancellor of the University in 1951. His scholarship was exceptional, especially in the areas of Greek studies, and he became not only a Fellow of the British Academy in 1938, but also served as its President. Another Master of an Oxbridge College, Sir Sydney Roberts, a distinguished Samuel Johnson scholar, became EA President in 1963. So, of these seven academics who served during the period as EA Presidents, four were College presidents, three—Gordon, Bowra, and Rowse—were connected with Oxford, and three—Tillyard, Roberts, and Trevelyan—with Cambridge. The exception was Grierson, who spent most of his academic career in Scotland. George Macaulay Trevelyan, President in 1951, is most famous for His *History of England* (1926), which was, in relative terms, a best seller. From 1927 to 1940, he was Regius Professor of Modern History at Cambridge, and from 1940 to 1951, he served as Master of Trinity College, Cambridge.

Presidents during the Second World War and after came from a variety of backgrounds and professions. The seventh academic to serve as President during the post-WWII period was A. L. Rowse in 1952. A prolific writer and researcher, and an often-controversial figure, his books included several on Shakespeare that caused quite a stir when published. As noted above, Cyril Forster Garbett, President in 1945, was Archbishop of York; in 1960 the President was another Archbishop of York, Arthur Michael Ramsey, who became Archbishop of Canterbury in 1961, serving in this capacity until 1974. Ramsey served as Professor of Divinity at the University of Durham from 1940 to 1950 and amongst other achievements, was for two years (1950–1952), Regius Professor of Divinity, at the University of Cambridge and Fellow of Magdalene College. Another Anglican clergyman who became EA President, was the theologian and Dean of St. Paul's, Walter Robert Matthews. EA President in 1955, Matthews went to King's College, London where he lectured from 1908 to 1918 in Philosophy, later becoming Professor of the Philosophy of Religion and subsequently, Dean of St. Paul's.

Two eminent lawyers served as Presidents during the period. Sir William Norman Birkett, who drafted the judgment at the Nuremburg Trials, was President in 1953. A great advocate, he earned a brilliant reputation in murder trials, and was twice a liberal MP. Another EA President with a great legal career was Lord Denning, President in 1964. Called to the bar in 1923, appointed a judge in 1944, from 1962 to 1982 he served as the Master of the Rolls, and he was widely renowned as one of the most significant judges in English law.

In addition to L.S. Amery, President in 1949, various politicians and statesmen served as EA Presidents during the 1961–1967 period. Herbert Samuel, or Viscount Samuel, the Liberal politician, was President in 1941. Leopold Stennet Amery was EA President in 1949. A prominent Conservative politician, he advocated imperial preference and tariff reform and did much to protect colonial territories. Like Amery, who was educated at Balliol College, Oxford, another Balliol graduate to serve as EA President (in 1943) was Sir Harold Nicolson, the journalist and erstwhile Conservative MP. The fourth politician to serve as EA President (1950) was Sir Alan Herbert. From 1924 onwards Herbert wrote for *Punch*, and from 1935 until 1950, the year he was EA President, he was an Independent MP, representing the Oxford University seat. Another EA President with a political career was Oliver Lyttleton, the first Viscount Chandos, who served as EA President in 1966, having been from 1940 until 1954 a Conservative MP. In Churchill's 1951 Government, he was Secretary of State at the colonial office and was involved controversially with defeating insurgents in Malaya and then in Kenya. From 1962 to 1971, he was the first Chairman of the National Theatre—the Lyttleton Theatre on the South Bank complex being named after him.

A number of writers were chosen as EA Presidents. These included Clemence Dane (1961), Richard Church (1965), Charles Morgan (1954), and Edmund Blunden (1967). In 1920, Blunden wrote for *The Athenaeum* and his collection of poems, *The Shepherd*, won the prestigious Hawthornden prize. He took up a number of Chairs in English, before retiring from academe to write full-time. He received the Queen's gold medal for poetry in 1956, and, in 1966, became Oxford Professor of Poetry, resigning from this position two years later. He was truly haunted by his experiences in World War I and at the battle of Passchendale. His powerful memoir *Undertones of War* (1928) conveys some of the consequences upon his imagination. His EA Presidential Address given at Church House, Westminster on 3 June 1967 was entitled 'A Few Not Quite Forgotten Writers?' As the other presidential addresses, it was published and distributed to EA members with the Summer 1967 issue of *English*.

Of these other writers, perhaps the least well known now is Charles Morgan. His first novel, *The Gunroom* (1919), recounted his experiences in the pre-war Royal Navy. In 1932, *The Fountain* gained him the Hawthornden prize and eight years later, his novel, *The Voyage*, was awarded the James Tait Black memorial prize. Sir Arthur Bryant, on the other hand, is still relatively popular. EA President in 1946, Bryant was an eminent historian and biographer noted for his *English Saga* (1940), *The Years of Endurance, 1793–1802* (1942), and *The Years of Victory, 1802–1812* (1944) drawing a parallel between England's role during 1934 to 1945 and its situation during the earlier Napoleonic Wars.

F. S. Boas, the long time editor of *YWES* and active member of the EA, served as its President in 1944. Another EA President, Sir Ernest Gowers (1957) was, like Boas, a civil servant. Sir Kenneth Clark (1962) had been keeper of the Department of Fine Art at the Ashmolean Museum, Oxford, before becoming Director of the National Gallery in London, and then from 1946 until 1950, Slade Professor of Fine Art at Oxford.

In short, the great majority of these EA wartime and post-war EA Presidents were from wealthy and elite backgrounds. Educated at either Oxford or Cambridge, many had experienced at first hand the traumatic experience of combat during the First World War. The EA chose for its Presidents men whose careers had been distinguished. Usually in their later years, the Presidents were figureheads, commanding respect for previous achievements, but playing little if any role in the actual affairs of the EA. Their function was to validate and authorise the Association, to impress by their name on the headed notepaper, adding stature to the EA. They did, however, give the annual address at the AGM in May or June in London, and this in itself was a valuable event. The closest the EA came to the Royal imprimatur was during the 1968 Presidency of HRH The Duke of Edinburgh. He addressed the AGM at the Church House Restaurant, Westminster, on 13 July 1968 on the subject of 'Communication'.

Seven former EA Presidents took the opportunity provided by the anniversary of the EA in 1956 to reflect upon its history, significance and achievements. Among these, Viscount Samuel, President in 1941, commented that 'clarity and sanity in poetry, dignity and grace in prose, are essential elements in good style. In present fashions they are often lacking. The English Association strives to restore and maintain them'. Sir Harold Nicolson, the President in 1943, commented on a perceived EA political faction: The EA, he countered, 'stands for close comprehension and co-operation between the English-speaking peoples, a conjunction which is essential for the safety of the free world'. F. S. Boas, President the year after Nicolson, remembered the 'hopes and fears' in the foundation of EA and thinks 'one may feel that we have justified our claim that English is worthy of a place of its own'. Lord Justice Birkett, President in 1953, pointed to the EA's 'continued insistence on the proper teaching of English as an essential element in the national education'. Charles Morgan, the 1954 President, in a wordy tribute, saw 'the task of the EA...to make men, women, and children aware of the opportunity which [the English language] offers them', and W. R. Matthews, President in 1955, echoed the optimistic and prescriptivist sentiment that the EA 'is one of the bulwarks against the corruption of our noble English tongue'.[69]

---

[69] *English*, 11, 62, 1956, pp. 50–51.

V
The 1960s and Beyond

Meetings and Business

The history of the EA in the last decades of the twentieth century is in many ways a reflection of the history of education during the period. Developments in tertiary education generally were very much a focus of government activity in the early 1960s, culminating in the Robbins Report[70] in 1963, which advocated the immediate expansion of Higher Education, through the significant and deliberate growth in student numbers and in the creation of new university institutions in the 1960s, such as Warwick, Essex, Lancaster and York. This was followed in the 1970s to 1990s by a gradual increase in student participation, but a concurrent gradual decrease of public funding from the HE sector and a contraction in posts. In 1992, the binary divide distinguishing between university and polytechnic was abandoned with the assumption that all HE institutions could better compete on equal terms. An examination of the EA during these years reveals concerns with internecine warfare within English Departments, particularly with regard to concerns about the parameters of the subject and its relationships with linguistics, media and cultural studies; and about the impact of critical theories upon the English curriculum and research agenda. Also important were the evolving ideas of what the study of English at secondary school level should entail, especially with the erosion of the Grammar Schools and tertiary system created by the Butler Education Provision of 1944, and the Labour Government's adherence (notionally!) to a Comprehensive Education system for all within the public sector.

Such elements are reflected indirectly in an examination of Executive Committee meetings during the period. Representative minutes over the period reflect a common thread of concerns. In April 1966, an Executive Committee meeting was held with T. S. Dorsch in the chair. In addition to the usual business, including a Report of the Publications Sub-Committee, there was discussion of the Annual Meeting and luncheon, the plans for Autumn Lectures and the election of new members. Though unable to attend the meeting Samuel Gorley Putt, a Cambridge scholar, and EA Chair from 1964 to 1972, and Vice-President from 1972 to 1978, sent a letter concerning 'his great concern at the poor attendance at lectures' arranged by the EA. He suggested that the Committee might have to consider the possibility of cancelling lectures during 1967, although three for the Autumn had already been arranged for the London area. Such a lack of attendance seemed symptomatic of a decline in interest in the EA and its activities, noticeable particularly during the late 1960s and subsequently.

---

[70] Lord Robbins, *Higher education: appendix one to the report of the Committee appointed by the Prime Minister under the Chairmanship of Lord Robbins, 1961–63: demand for places in higher education*, 1963.

This lack of interest was due to a number of complicated factors. Some of it may well have been due, according to Rob Colls, to what *The Times*—on the publication of the Robbins Report—perceived as a doubt 'whether the universities could continue with their preservation of the great cultural tradition. More students would mean lower standards'.[71] By the 1960s Cambridge, with the forceful, controversial presence of Dr. F. R. Leavis, perceived itself as replacing the metropolis as the centre upholding values. S. Gorley Putt admired Leavis and what he stood for, as is very evident in Putt's 'Technique and Culture: Three Cambridge Portraits' published in *Essays and Studies*,[72] and in his other work.

Gorley Putt chaired the Executive Committee meeting of 25 May 1966 at which attendance at the EA meetings and lectures was discussed fully. A compromise was reached after members of the Committee, who felt 'that the lectures were a vital part of the Association's work', also decided to cut back the number of lectures to two in the Spring and two in the Autumn of 1967. They were to be held not only as usual on a Saturday afternoon, but also—for a trial period—on a Wednesday evening.

By 1970 the EA Executive Committee had been enlarged and included the poet John Heath-Stubbs among others. A lecturer at Merton College, Oxford, and the recipient of many awards, including the Queen's Gold Medal for Poetry in 1973, Heath Stubbs produced over thirty-five volumes of poetry, in addition to criticism, translations and editing various works and contributing to many periodicals.

The June 1970 Committee meeting held at 8 Cromwell Place in London included discussion of the problem of office accommodation. New offices had been leased at Exhibition Road in London and problems had arisen, requiring three EA officers to deal with the issue (Beatrice White, the Vice-President; S. Gorley Putt, the Chair; and P.M. Yarker, the Treasurer, who played a prominent role in the EA Executive during the 1970s). When the EA Executive met in September 1970, the problem with the lease of the new premises had been temporarily resolved. Amongst the other items discussed at the meeting was the expenditure incurred in the move from one part of London to another. An indication of the financial plight of the EA is indicated by its need to save money at every opportunity; a minute pointedly observes the view that it 'seemed likely that the Association would be able to save approximately £60 per annum by using duplicating machinery in the present premises'. By the mid-1970s, financial difficulties had increased; in a Report appended to Minutes for 1975, it is stated that 'a brief examination of the published accounts for the year to December 1975, reveals that the Association is trading at a substantial loss'. In addition to a review of publications, branch membership was scrutinized to determine the best way forward for increasing income. The memorandum includes the observation that 'The ability of the Association to lose £4,000 a year and survive must be questioned, when its only reliable assets are its investments, which have a market value in September, 1975 of £4,400'.

---

[71] Robert Colls, *Identity of England*, 2002, p. 366, citing *The Times* from 4 December 1963.
[72] *Essays and Studies* 14, 1961, pp. 17–24.

By October 1975 the EA offices had moved from Exhibition Road to 1 Priory Gardens, Bedford Park, in west London where they remained until the move in the early 1990s to the University of Leicester. The agenda for the Executive meeting in October 1975 included the suggestion of the payment of expenses for Committee members to attend meetings although it was subsequently agreed 'that in the present financial circumstances no recommendation could be made but that the matter should be allowed to lie on the table for further discussion when more appropriate'. Similarly, the EA Committee was aware that 'In seeking to increase revenue from publication the need to increase the reward to contributors was not being forgotten'. In addition to the chair, Professor R. Sharrock, those present included Professor Beatrice White and John Heath-Stubbs and three other members of the EA who played a prominent role in its activities during this period: Geoffrey Harlow, James Redmond and Martin Dodsworth. The first two significantly contributed as editors of *YWES*. Martin Dodsworth, Professor of English at Royal Holloway London until his retirement in 2001, served as Chair of the EA from 1987 to 1992 and edited *English* from 1975 to 1987. A prolific scholar, Dodsworth edited *Essays and Studies* in 1989, devoted to the theme of '*English Economis'd*: English and British Higher Education in the Eighties'.

Despite the efforts of an active and engaged Executive Committee, the 1970s were a period of considerable political and economic instability. The financial assessment in 1975, together with a 'Self Help' memorandum from the Treasurer reveals that the EA was all too aware of its perilous financial situation. It needed, among other things, to ensure that its overdraft banking facilities were appropriately arranged and that its liabilities to creditors should not exceed a fixed limit. Perhaps the most important issue facing the EA Executive was the financial problems associated with the rapid rise in inflation at the end of the 1970s. In this the EA was not alone amongst Associations.[73] It is hardly surprising that the EA Minutes for the second half of the 1970s are replete with financial statements, financial projections and memoranda designed to permit the EA to work its own way out of its tribulations. That which accompanies the 10 December 1975 Minutes, asks: 'How do we recruit more Ordinary and Full Members? How do we recruit more schools into membership?' and 'How do we get more libraries to place orders for *English*, *Essays and Studies* and *YWES*?' These questions, precisely, were to occupy the EA Executive from this period until very recently.

At the meeting of the EA in April 1979 held at 1 Priory Gardens there was a detailed report from the Finance Committee with an accompanying draft 'Income and Expenditures Account for the Year Ended 31st December 1978'. The Hon. Treasurer 'called attention to the outstanding improvements in the financial position of the Association and indicated that from this position of stability it was now suitable for the Executive Committee actively to consider ways of increasing the activities of the Association for the benefit of members'. Further, 'It was not now beyond

---

[73] Compare, for instance, W.G.V. Balchin, *The Geographical Association: the First Hundred Years 1893–1993*, 1993, p. 63.

the finances of the Association to establish some bursaries or grants for the benefit of students of scholars of English'. In this optimistic picture of the financial situation the EA differed from similar associations, such as the Geographical Association, which were operating on a deficit budget. It was recommended that there would be 'no increase in subscription rates for 1980' and 'a loosening of the tight reins by which expenditures had been held back for many years'. Most of the expenditure went on Issues 127 to 129 of *English*, the production of *Contemporary Approaches to English Studies*, and the 4th series of *English Short Stories of To-day*. At the same June meeting in 1979, the discussion for new activities noted that 'the amount of publicity about the Association within universities was not nearly as great as was desirable'. There was also a sense that the EA should promote greater activity in the regions outside London, where numerous branches were still in operation. Another idea at that meeting was not to come to fruition until the beginning of the twenty-first century: the foundation of a Fellowship. Beatrice White raised again at this June meeting her previous suggestion for the institution of a form of Association Fellowship. Further, her intention was that such a Fellowship would be given as an 'honour' only to persons of outstanding merit; and that it should be purely nominal, 'though the occasion would be marked by a suitable ceremony as was done by the Royal Society of Literature and the Royal Society of Arts'. Although there was subsequent discussion of her suggestion at EA Executive meetings, it was only in 2000 that the EA created a new category of membership by instituting a Fellowship scheme.

At the Executive Committee meeting in June 1979 were numerous other stalwarts of the EA, including Raymond Chapman, Professor of English Studies at LSE, who served as a Committee member from 1977 to 1989. As well as a prolific scholarly career, including the editorship of the 1984 *Essays and Studies* volume, Chapman also published under the pseudonym Simon Nash, writing a number of thrillers during the 1960s. And during the early 1980s other committed new members were to be brought on board the Executive, including Laurel Brake, Professor of Literature and Print Culture at Birkbeck, London. An Associate Editor for *YWES*, Brake was co-opted to the Publications Sub-Committee in 1981, and then to the Executive Committee. She subsequently played an important role both as an Executive member and from 1984 to 1991 editor of *YWES* (Volumes 62–69); indeed, she is one of the longest-serving contributors to *YWES*. She wrote first as co-author with James Ogden the chapter on 'The Later Seventeenth Century', from Volume 54 (1975), and then contributed to the Nineteenth-Century chapter from Volume 55 until Volume 74 (1996), a run of twenty volumes. Brake also edited and contributed to *Essays and Studies 1995* (1995) devoted to 'The Endings of Epochs'.

Others prominent in EA activities and its Executive Committee during the last years of the twentieth century include the nineteenth-century scholar, Miriam Allott, whose deep commitment to the EA is reflected in the establishment in 1996 of the Miriam Allott Lecture Fund used to finance a series of peripatetic lectures on the language of literature. In 1950 she married the poet, and critic, Kenneth Allott who subsequently became A.C. Bradley Professor in Modern Literature, a position she occupied following her husband's death in 1973. Six years later she took the

Chair of English at Birkbeck College, London, and in 1988 edited *Essays & Studies*, a volume devoted to Matthew Arnold on the centenary of his death.

Other members of the EA Committee in the 1980s who played prominent roles in its activities included Sandra Clark, Professor of Renaissance Literature at Birkbeck, and David Daniell, the Tyndale scholar who spent his career at University College, London, retiring in 1996 as Professor of English. Daniell was very active on the EA Committee, as Associate Editor of *YWES* from 1976 until 1986, and as a contributor to the Shakespeare chapter from Volume 54 (1975), for almost two decades. Others of course were active on the Executive Committee and some contributed to YWES. Warwick Gould, now Director of the Institute of English Studies, and a distinguished Yeats scholar and editor, was active in the EA in the 1980s and 1990s. Andrew Lincoln, also an Executive Committee member, contributed the Blake section to the Romantics chapter of *YWES*. He edited the *EA Newsletter* for a period, and also contributed an essay on 'Blake and the Natural History of Creation' to *Essays & Studies* in 1986.

During the 1980s, Executive Meetings began to be held at the Keynes Library in Garden Square, London. The meeting in July 1987 was Geoffrey Harlow's last in the chair. Matters on the agenda included a discussion of the EA's input on the Kingman Committee of Enquiry into the Teaching of English Language, membership subscription rate, and the proposal by Geoffrey Harlow of a Beatrice White Prize. In relation to the first item, the presentation of evidence to the Kingman Committee illustrates the EA involvement with the teaching of English Language to those aged 7 to 11 and beyond. Appended to the minutes of 29 July 1987 is an extensive seven page report on behalf of the EA headed 'Evidence for the Kingman Committee of Enquiry into the Teaching of English Language'.

Also included as an appendix to the same Minutes is a detailed 'Proposal for a Beatrice White Prize' drawn up by Geoffrey Harlow as a response to a bequest Beatrice White left the EA. The Beatrice White Prize, it was decided, 'shall be awarded for the best scholarly article noticed in *YWES* in the fields of Medieval and Early Renaissance English Literature written by a person under the age of thirty'. Following discussion at a subsequent EA Executive Committee meeting, the age limit was extended and monographs in addition to articles were included: judging was undertaken by the *YWES* editor(s) after input and recommendation of *YWES* contributors in the relevant fields.

Martin Dodsworth chaired the Executive Committee meeting held in April 1990 in the main building of Birkbeck College, London. He introduced Gordon Campbell, now Professor of Renaissance Studies at the University of Leicester, and a noted Milton scholar, as the new editor of *YWES*. Campbell has subsequently played a critical role in the Association's affairs. He served as the *YWES* co-editor for Volume 69 published in 1991, and as editor for the next two volumes; he has been General series editor for *Essays and Studies*, Volumes 49 (1996) to 55 (2002). He served as Chair of the EA and, in 1995, as its President, and was instrumental in facilitating the move of the EA's office in 1993 from London to Leicester. In 2006, he is still a member of the Executive Committee and a major force in EA concerns, including the constant scrutiny of its finances and operations.

Indeed, in terms of finances, the Minutes of the April 1990 meeting reveal that in contrast to some previous years, the EA was operating at a surplus, largely due to the minimizing of office expenditure and to the profits made on School Conferences. Still, as ever, there was no room for complacency, for as these Minutes reveal there were major matters of concern for the Association. These range from: (1) 'the difficulties experienced in gaining growth in membership'; (2) issues concerning the internal structures of the EA, 'especially the roles and sizes of the Executive and Chair's Committee'; (3) the issues of 'the association's objectives' [such as] whether or not it 'should become a more professional organisation'; (4) how much it can learn from the experience of other similar organizations such as the Historical Association or Geographical Association; and (5) 'how it might develop a strong regional structure'. In order to discuss these issues a 'Think Tank Day' was organized by the Executive for all of its members to be held in July 1990 at the British Academy in London.

The short-term consequences—in relation to governance and administration—can be seen in the Minutes of the Executive Meeting held in October 1990. Essentially, 'terms of office for officers of the Association' were agreed upon which would be presented to the next Annual General Meeting in June 1991. It was proposed at the meeting that the Chair should serve 'a three-year term, renewable for one further three-year term only'. However, the Treasurer could serve 'a three-year term renewable as many times as may seem appropriate'. The Chair's Committee was dissolved and the Executive was subsequently to meet at two-month intervals on the last Wednesday afternoon of September to July. In addition, it was decided that the Membership Committee should be dissolved, and that a *Newsletter* would appear three times a year.

However, the important longer-term consequences of the 'think tank' session are reflected in the Minutes of the September 1993 Executive meeting, with Gordon Campbell as Chair and Martin Dodsworth as President. It had been agreed at the previous meeting, following a lengthy discussion, to move the EA office to the School of Education at the University of Leicester. This decision proved to be so controversial that three members of the executive 'registered their strong opposition to the move', and there were resignations from the Executive. The position of Secretary of the EA changed from Ruth Fairbanks Joseph to Helen Lucas, an archaeologist and industrial librarian, and, with effect from 1 November 1993, the EA's new address was to be at the University of Leicester. Thus ended eighty-seven years of the EA as a London-based organisation. However, as subsequent Minutes show, the move of the Association's offices did not result in any real movement for the Executive Committee Meetings, all of which are still held in London either at the University or at the British Academy.

In September 1996 Helen Lucas collated a brief history of the EA from the perspective of the celebration of its 90th birthday. She wrote:

> The English Association today is an international organization with some 2,500 members in 76 countries and flourishing branches in South Africa and Australia…

At a luncheon in June 1996, celebrating its 90th birthday, the Association reviewed both its history and its role today and in the future. In many ways the present decade has been one of expansion for the Association. Its journals have increased in number and broadened in range, as have its conferences. It has played an increasingly active part in the national debate about the teaching of English, most particularly in the area of the National Curriculum. This it will certainly continue to do as we approach yet another period of consultation leading to a further revision of National Curriculum English in the year 2000. The Association may reasonably be said to be meeting the second of its constitutional 'objects': 'Furthering the due recognition of English as an essential element in education at all levels and participating publicly in any national debate on the subject on any level'. (The Executive committee of the Association reviews its work in terms of these 'objects' at each of its meetings.)

The English Association is a very active organization. Its publishing programme, for example, includes the two annual volumes of *The Year's Work*, the series of *Essays and Studies* and the journal *English*, all primarily aimed at readers in the world of higher education, whilst for schools it produces *The Use of English* and *Primary English*, as well as the series of *Bookmarks* designed to stimulate and guide reading by middle- and upper-school age children. Some of these publications are well established, but others are new: *The Year's Work in Critical and Cultural Theory* and *Primary English* have come into being only in the last five years and *The Use of English* only transferred to our wing in the nineties. The range reflects both the diverse academic strength of the Association and its qualifications for participating in public debate. In recent years participation has taken two principal forms: in conferences and in consultation on the National Curriculum. Both at Primary and Secondary levels the Association has arranged conferences addressing matters of principle and practice within the National Curriculum (papers from these conferences have appeared in our journals), Conferences have traditionally been held in London and Oxford, but recent Primary English conferences have been held in Southampton and in Chester and the Autumn 1996 Teachers' Conference will take place in Manchester. Similarly the Association hopes to replicate the perennially successful London Sixth form conference in Leicester in the Spring term of 1997. Next year should also see the first of a series of annual peripatetic lectures on the theme of the language of literature—each year the lecture will be held in a different institution. The new venues will, we hope, both help to establish the Association as an active presence across a broader area of the country and enable it to draw upon and influence the work of a much larger number of educational institutions and individuals. The Association, that is, is not only active, but has been increasing its activities, and is still doing to.

This expansion in the Association's activities has co-incided with a period of unprecedented change and controversy in the teaching of English at all levels. In the schools the pressures upon teachers have often been cruel: changes, whether at GCSE level, in the format of SATs or in the National Curriculum itself have frequently been bewildering. The centralization of the curriculum has both discouraged individual initiative and made it difficult to retain the critical sense of an alternative. Here is where the work of the Association is so important. Through its journals, its activities and its public pronouncements the Association will continue to engage with these and other issues. Within the range of the journals there is an appropriate forum, whether it be for the discussion of National Curriculum English, standards at 'A' level, modularized courses in the universities, or anything else. The best kind of Association is one in which its associates are active; where the lines that connect its executive with its members and sympathizers are of a kind to encourage them to participate in its work. The debates that take place in the Association's journals are open to everyone.

The account concludes with the observation that in a time of great educational turmoil, especially as the secondary school level, in deciding what should be studied as school, 'it is up to us to help' (in the words of Martin Dodsworth):

> And help we will. The Association has for ninety years drawn on the talents and energy of its members with a view to enhancing the study of English Language and Literature, especially in educational contexts. We look forward to continuing that work for generations to come.

The EA became a Company Limited by Guarantee, and its Trustees directors, in January 2001. In 2004, the EA appointed a Patron—the eminent English Language scholar, Professor the Lord Quirk of Bloomsbury, CBE, FBA. In 2006 its Officers, Professor Elaine Treharne, President, Professor Peter J. Kitson, Chair of the Executive Committee, Roger Claxton, Honorary Treasurer, and Helen Lucas, Chief Executive and Company Secretary, maintain a well-organized and influential Association. Its financial situation fluctuated dramatically in the early years of the twenty-first century as the EA sought to increase its administration, in 2000 employing three members of staff to oversee the day-to-day operations of the Association. Worryingly, by 2002 the Association's expenditure exceeded its income by £19,618, and a deficit continued until 2005, when a number of financial expediencies remedied the situation. The number of full-time members of staff was reduced from three to two in September 2003; the costs of subscribing to the EA's publications were increased in line with other publishers' increases; and the weakened dollar, with its detrimental consequences for membership and subscriber income from the USA, was offset by introducing new income streams.

During 2005 the EA was responsible for seven publications, two conferences, four awards and prizes, and the expanding Fellowship scheme. These and other activities will be examined in the sections that follow.

Conferences

Conferences have consistently been an active part of the EA's activities during the period, and the years 2003–04 are representative. The Annual Report for 2003 noted that four conferences were held during the year, of which two were held in March. The first, 'A Level One Year On', was a conference for Secondary Schoolteachers held at St. Catherine's College, Oxford, with four speakers. The second, 'Shakespeare for Students', a conference for sixth-form students of English took place at Birkbeck, and had three speakers. An October conference was held at St. Catherine's College, Oxford, on 'Bridging the Gulf: the English Literature Syllabus from A-Level to University': a conference for English Teachers and University Admissions Tutors, there were eight speakers. Between 3–7 November an undergraduate course was held in conjunction with the Shakespeare Centre, Stratford-upon-Avon, on 'Shakespeare and Stratford: Text and Theatre'. In 2004 there were four conferences, of which one was held at Stratford—on 'Hamlet in Stratford', which coincided with the Royal Shakespeare Company's final performance of *Hamlet*.

Occasional publications produced during the period include collections such as that edited by Michael Baron on *Larkin With Poetry: English Association Conference Papers* published in 1997. This includes seven essays based on papers given at conferences on 'Philip Larkin' and 'Poetry in the Classroom, the Media and the World' held by the English Association in 1994 and 1995.

A new publishing venture raising important concerns for English Studies within Higher Education started in 2001. The first *Issues in English*, called *Doctor! Doctor!: Doctoral Studies in English in 21st Century Britain*, deals with the question 'How well are doctoral students served by the current degree?' The authors, Annabel Patterson at Yale, and Judie Newman from the University of Nottingham, both produced provocative and thoughtful essays outlining the practices, problems and prospects for PhD education in British universities. Other *Issues in English* have followed, including ones on Medieval Studies from an international perspective,[74] and most recently, on creative writing in the academy[75] and the issues in studying English at A' Level.[76]

Recognising the pressures faced by authors in publishing academic monographs at precisely the time when a good number of publishers are withdrawing from specialist publications of this kind, the EA announced in 2004 a major new monograph series entitled 'English Association Studies', to be published by Boydell and Brewer. The series, comprised of one or two research monographs in any field published annually, will be formally launched in 2006. This series, together with the numerous other occasional publications, illustrates the highly focused approach to different target markets for the books and pamphlets produced by the EA, and the movement from texts and materials produced for the wider public to a largely educationally-based one.

The Presidents

From 1936 to 1987, the annual lectures given by the EA Presidents were published in the Presidential address series. Since Edmund Blunden's 'A Few Not Quite Forgotten Writers?', the 1967 address, there were to 1987 twenty Presidential addresses. S. Gorley Putt in his *Wings of a Man's Life* provides an interesting and amusing (and arguably patrician!) account of the 1968 address and President. At the time Gorley Putt had returned to teaching at Christ's College, Cambridge:

> In the summer of 1968, as Chairman of The English Association, I had 'received' the Duke of Edinburgh at our Annual Luncheon—having pointed out in my invitation that although his public statements had been mainly on the scientific or technical side, he had usually managed to express himself in such trenchant English that we hoped that he would

---

[74] Elaine Treharne, ed., *Vital Signs: English in Medieval Studies in 21st Century Higher Education*, Issues in English 2, 2002. This contains excellent essays by Wendy Scase, Robert Bjork, and Richard K. Emmerson.
[75] Maureen Moran, ed., *Write or Wrong?: Creative Writing in the Academy*, Issues in English 3, 2005.
[76] Adrian Barlow, *Second Reading*, Issues in English 4, 2005.

become our President for a year and make the annual Presidential address. He agreed, and his talk on 'Communication' was the most vivid Presidential statement during my eight years as Chairman. He told me that he had written his own speech as usual (perhaps on naval signal pads?). A press photographer had taken a snap of the occasion, but it was not until I was well established in my first Michaelmas Term that a proof photograph arrived at my breakfast table. My bedmaker at that time was a lady of considerable bulk who dusted a foot or so above and a foot or so below her ample waistline, talking without respite while I tried to eat a boiled egg and open my mail. On this particular morning she was in full flight while I opened the envelope containing a photograph showing only two persons: the Duke making his speech and myself sitting laughing beside him at one of his jokes. Striving to stem her flow of commentary, I held up the proof-copy and said:

"Do you recognize anybody here?"

She studied the two faces.

"Oh, sir," she said, leaning backwards upon the invisible shooting-stick which seemed to lend support to her massive figure when relaxed; and rolling her eyes upwards to the ceiling.

"Oh, sir! What a nice gentleman he is! What a nice gentleman! He don't mind who he mingles among."[77]

In 1987 the association stopped inviting external dignitaries to become President as it was becoming a thankless task and taking up too much time. Instead it was decided that the retiring Chair of the Association, after serving a term of office for three years, would become the President. There have been twenty-five presidents from 1958–2006, twenty two of these men, and three women: Dame Rebecca West, the author, President in 1969; Rachel Trickett, the Oxford academic, President in 1982; and Elaine Treharne, a medievalist at the University of Leicester and the first woman to be both Chair and President, from 2004–2007. Other Presidents have included Nevill Coghill (1971), Lord David Cecil (1973), George Steiner (1975), I. A. Richards (1978), Robert W. Burchfield (1979), John Sparrow (1980), and Kenneth Muir (1987). These, together with all the Presidents since 1989—Derek Brewer, 1989–1992; Martin Dodsworth, 1992–1995; Gordon Campbell, 1995–1998; Roger Knight, 1998–2001; and Martin Blocksidge, 2001–2004—had academic or teaching careers.

Other Presidents have emerged from literary backgrounds more generally. Dame Rebecca West published her first novel in 1918, and is perhaps best known for her journalistic studies of the Nuremberg trials, *The Meaning of Treason* (1947) and *A Train of Powder* (1955). Two publishers, plus an academic journal publisher, and a journalist/publisher, have served as Presidents: Sir Basil Blackwell, President in 1970, spent most of his life in Oxford, founding the Shakespeare Head Press in 1921, and taking over the Chair of the family firm upon the death of his father. John Murray, President in 1976, was a London-based publisher, and for many years his firm published *YWES* amongst other EA publications. The medieval scholar, Derek Brewer served as EA President twice, the first time in 1982–1983 and then again from 1989–1992. Educated at the Universities of Oxford and Birmingham, he taught at the latter until 1965 when he moved to Emmanuel College, Cambridge where he

---

[77] S. Gorley Putt, *Wing's of a Man's Life*, 1990, pp. 293–294.

was both a Fellow and a Master of the College, the latter until his retirement in 1990. In 1972 he founded D.S. Brewer Ltd., which has since become part of Boydell and Brewer Ltd. This internationally renowned publishing house has been a stalwart supporter of the EA, publishing the series *Essays and Studies*, as well as being the most significant press for Medieval Studies. Sir William Rees-Mogg became President in 1984. Educated at Oxford where he was Brackenbury Scholar, he became a distinguished writer and scholar, and edited *The Times* from 1967–1981. Since 1983 he has been Chairman of Pickering & Chatto (Publishers) Ltd. He was succeeded as President in 1985 by Bernard Levin the journalist, author, television personality, and music critic. Educated at Christ's Hospital and the LSE, Levin principally wrote for Rees-Mogg's *The Times*, and *The Manchester Guardian*, in addition to many other newspapers and journals, and as well as serving as President, from 1985 to 1988, he also served as Vice-President.

Fewer politicians than previously served as EA Presidents during the last quarter of the twentieth century. The President in 1972 was the Rt. Hon. Jo Grimmond who led the Liberal Party through a very fallow period in British political life, between 1956 and 1967. The last diplomat and author to serve as EA President, in 1981, was Conor Cruise O'Brien. O'Brien worked for the Irish Department of External Affairs from 1944 to 1960, before taking up university posts, including a Chair at New York University in the 1960s. He also served as a member of the Irish parliament, as an editor of the London *Observer*, and has had a prolific career in journalism and writing. In 1974 General Sir John Hackett, the military historian and author of *The Third World War* (1978), was President. After leaving the army in 1968 he became principal of King's College, London until 1975. Sir V. S. Pritchett, the distinguished writer and critic, served as EA President in 1977.

Two EA Presidents, both academics, were not born in the UK. Robert W. Burchfield, the renowned lexicographer and linguist, was President in 1974, during which term of office he gave an Address on 'The Fowlers: Their Achievements in Lexicography and Grammar'. A New Zealander by birth, Burchfield was educated at Victoria University College, Wellington, though his studies were interrupted by war service in the Royal New Zealand Artillery. In 1949 a Rhodes Scholarship to Magdalen College, Oxford gave him the opportunity to study English Language with J. R. R. Tolkien and C. S. Lewis, and he spent his academic career at Oxford. In 1957 he was appointed editor of the Supplement to the *O.E.D.* According to his obituary in the *Daily Telegraph* 'the University Press reckoned he would need seven years and 1,275 pages to do the job. It took him 29 years, and the four-volume supplement covered 6,000 pages'.[78] The President in 1975, George Steiner, a distinguished author and journalist, was born in Paris in 1929 to Austrian and Bohemian Jewish parents who immigrated to the United States in 1960. Steiner obtained his doctorate from Oxford, and was on the staff of the *Economist*, later becoming Professor of English and Comparative Literature at the University of Geneva.

---

[78] *Daily Telegraph*, 6 July 2004.

The last EA President to serve for a single year, before Chairs of the Executive Committee automatically progressed to a three-year Presidency, was Kenneth Muir in 1987, Muir had been more than very active in the EA's affairs for a number of years, contributing, for instance, on several occasions to *Essays and Studies* (in the volumes for 1966 and 1973) and collecting *Essays and Studies* for 1977. A noted Shakespearean critic and scholar, Muir was educated at St. Edmund Hall, Oxford, subsequently taking up academic positions at Leeds and Liverpool, where he was King Alfred Professor of English Literature. At Liverpool, as Head of Department and Dean of the Faculty of Arts from 1958 to 1961, he encouraged many of his colleagues to participate in EA activities and to contribute to *YWES* and *Essays and Studies*. The author of over fifty books, Muir was a prolific and immensely influential Shakespearean, and a great contributor to the work of the EA.

Roger Knight was President from 1998 to 2001 when Martin Blocksidge succeeded him. Blocksidge and Knight had both served formerly as Chairs of the EA Executive. Blocksidge was educated at St. John's College, Oxford, and taught at Abingdon School, Dulwich College, the Royal Grammar School, Guildford, and from 1990 at St. Dunstan's College, London. Throughout the 1980s and 1990s Blocksidge was very much involved with examining and national examinations policy. A member of the Independent Schools Inspectorate from 1995 onwards, his publications include *The Sacred Weapon: An Introduction to Pope's Satire* (1993), *Teaching Literature 11–18* (2000) and *Shakespeare and Education* (2004). Roger Knight edited *The Use of English* from 1982 until 2002. He was a Professor of Education responsible for the Post-Graduate Certificate of Education at the University of Leicester until his retirement in 2003. Educated at Magdalene College, Cambridge, Knight's publications include numerous books on English Studies nationally, as well as *Edwin Muir: An Introduction to his Work* (1980).

An innovation evident during the EA Centenary year in 2006 is the position of Patron, held by Professor the Lord Quirk of Bloomsbury, CBE, FBA. This distinguished role was introduced in order to bring an external dignitary back into the senior honorary role in the Association. Educated at University College, London, where he obtained his doctorate, Charles Randolph Quirk, the distinguished grammarian and English Language expert was President of the British Academy from 1985–1989, Professor of English Language and Literature at University College, London, and subsequently, Vice-Chancellor of the University of London. Awarded a CBE in 1976 and knighted in 1985, he was raised to the peerage in 1994 and has influenced the development of English Language studies worldwide with his prolific publications and public service.

VI
Publications: Annuals

Essays and Studies

In 1908 the Association's Executive Committee agreed on the desirability of publishing occasional collections of literary criticism and research. Two years later the first volume of *Essays and Studies by Members of the English Association* appeared. In the 1956 Jubliee Volume Arundell Esdaile observed that in *Essays and Studies* 'effort is devoted to building up in each a series of short (but not therefore elementary) papers by scholars expert each in some period or aspect of English language or literature, care being taken to make the range of each volume wide and representative'.[79] Esdaile also noted that 'The Collector, appointed afresh for each year's volume, is always a leading and active member of the Association'. The Collector was given this title, since she or he 'does not edit the [contributors'] work, or usually write a paper',[80] a practice continued until 1987 when volume 4 of the new series, begun in 1950, adopted an editor.

The first volume was collected by A .C. Bradley and consisted of seven essays directed largely at an academic and general rather than a school audience. The collection featured essays by Henry Bradley on 'English Place Names' and future Poet Laureate Robert Bridges 'On the Present State of English Pronunciation'. The remaining essays focus on literary concerns: W.P. Ker on 'Browning', George Neilson's 'Blind Harry's *Wallace*', George Saintsbury on 'Shakespeare and the Grand Style', Edith Sichel's 'Some Suggestions About Bad Poetry' and C.E. Vaughan on 'Carlyle and His German Masters'.

The second volume, edited by Henry Charles Beeching, opened with A. C. Bradley's 'Jane Austen: A Lecture', followed by F. S. Boas on 'Richardson's Novels and their Influence'. Two disquisitions on individual eighteenth- and early nineteenth-century practitioners of fiction were followed by contributions focusing on other genres. C. E. Montague's examination of 'the Literary Play' began with Henry Arthur Jones and William Butler Yeats. The fourth essay by A. Clutton-Brock focused on 'Description in Poetry', while John Bailey discussed 'The Grand Style: An Attempt at a Definition'. F. W. Moorman's 'A Yorkshire Folk-Play and its Analogues' focuses on the source of medieval drama. The final essay in the second volume appealed to EA members interested in place-names: Henry Alexander's piece on 'The Particle *Ing* in Place-Names'.

In 1912 the third volume, collected by W. P. Ker, consisted of seven contributions but decreased in size from the 196 pages of the first volume to 152 pages. Its lead

---
[79] *E&S*, ns 9, 1956, p.4.
[80] *Ibid.*

essay is from an address to the EA delivered on 17 November 1911, entitled 'What English Poetry May Still Learn from Greek', by Gilbert Murray. It reveals that the Classical backgrounds, interests and concerns of many of the members had not diminished. The third essay, 'Some Childish Things' by Adolphus A. Jack, reflects upon children's literature. J. W. Mackail assesses 'The poem entitled *A Lover's Complaint*, printed at the end of the volume of Shakespeare's sonnets' when published in 1609. The other four essays are largely focused on individual poets: T. S. Omond's 'Arnold and Homer' concentrates on Arnold's lectures *On Translating Homer* published in 1861; David Watson Rannie's 'Keats' Epithets' examines closely and in considerable analytical detail one aspect of his poetry; Saintsbury's 'Dante and the Grand Style' publishes an address he gave to the Dante Society on 3 May 1905; and 'Blake's Religious Lyrics' are the subject of the final contribution, by H. C. Beeching.

While five of the seven contributions in this third volume were by academics, not all essays in these early volumes were confined to university teachers. As with the EA membership, some submissions represented a much broader base. The sole female contribution to these early volumes, however, was Edith Sichel's piece in the first publication. A prolific contributor of short stories and articles to journals such as *The Cornhill* and *The Spectator*, she also wrote on French history. A contributor to the second volume, Arthur Clutton-Brock, practised at the Bar before becoming art critic for the *Times* from 1908, a frequent contributor to the *Times Literary Supplement*, and a writer.

The fifth volume was collected by Oliver Elton, who had been EA President in 1932. The six contributions are diverse and represent the eclectic interests of the EA membership. Subjects range from an analysis of rhythm in poetry and prose, an essay on place names and sagas, one on a romantic poet, two on Victorian writers, and an essay on translation. The opening essay by Douglas Sutherland MacColl, 'Rhythm in English Verse, Prose and Speech', is by far the longest at some 15,000 words, and offers a criticism of elements in George Saintsbury's *A History of English Prosody from the Twelfth Century to the Present Day*. MacColl takes issue with Saintsbury's concepts of 'feet', 'foot', 'short', 'long', 'accent' and other fundamental issues, and draws his illustrations from Greek, Latin and English examples, with many quotations from Milton, and *Paradise Lost* in particular. Curiously, his extensive analysis is ignored in Derek Attridge's definitive *The Rhythms of English Poetry* (1982).

Two essays focus on different productions of the Victorian period: A. E. Taylor's 'The Novels of Mark Rutherford', a tribute to the fiction of William Hale White [Mark Rutherford], was originally a lecture delivered before the Dundee branch of the EA in June 1913. J. C. Smith's 'Emily Brontë—A Reconsideration' draws upon the 1910 publication of her *Complete Poems* to make a case for the power of her poetry and for the greatness of *Wuthering Heights*. F. Melian Stawell's 'Shelley's 'Triumph of Life" is an extensive exposition of Shelley's poem. F. W. Moorman, who contributed to the second volume of *Essays and Studies*, in this volume writes on 'English Place-Names and Teutonic Sagas'. Moorman's 'is an attempt to discover what light is thrown on upon the origin, or growth of certain great Teutonic sagas by an investigation of English place-names'.[81] The eclectic nature of *Essays and Studies* is further exemplified by A. Blyth Webster's 'Translations from Old English: A Note and an Experiment', the final essay in the fifth volume. Webster considers Rossetti's observations on translation in the Preface of his *Early Italian Poets* before moving to Edward Fitzgerald, Robert Bridges and William Morris. Webster specifically considers Morris' attempts to translate *Beowulf*, which he considers to be a failure.

Not surprisingly perhaps, *Essays and Studies* failed to appear during the 1914–1918 War. The sixth volume was thus published in 1920 and put together by A. C. Bradley, retaining what by now had become a traditional formula of six essays on a wide range of subjects. Henry Bradley's essay on 'The 'Caedmonian' Genesis' opens this volume, with the second contribution being W. P. Ker's 1919 address to the English Association in Oxford on 'The Humanist Ideal'. Ker's purpose is not 'to define the humanities; rather otherwise, to show in a few examples how hard or even impossible it is to define the humanistic ideal so as to include all its manifestations'.[82] Ker is followed by a sustained consideration of a Victorian novelist in George Saintsbury's 'Trollope Revisited'. This study resists the temptation to cite at length and instead focuses upon analysis. For Saintsbury, Trollope's 'greater-books [are] *Barchester Towers*, itself, *Framley Parsonage, Orley Farm* (not quite throughout), *The Small House, Can You Forgive Her?* and the *Chronicle*'.[83] George Sampson's consideration of the prose of Robert Louis Stevenson takes issue with Saintsbury's dismissive assessment of Stevenson's prose style; the essay following Sampson's is devoted to an evaluation of a living writer, Joseph Conrad by Florence Melian Stawell. Her 'Conrad' argues that Conrad's achievement should be regarded as one of the most significant among English novelists. She pays particular attention to *Lord Jim*, *Under Western Eyes*, Conrad's first novel *Almayer's Folly*, and what she regards as Conrad's most ambitious work, *Nostromo*. The sixth and final contribution focuses not on a specific novel or poet but on 'South-Eastern and South-East Midland Dialects in Middle English'. Divided into five sections, Henry Cecil Wyld's account is replete with illustrative details and tables, as indeed, was his subsequent book, *The Universal Dictionary of the English Language* published in 1932.

These *Essays and Studies* exhibit a wide range of subjects. They also reveal the diversity of professional backgrounds displayed by its contributors, only some of whom are professional academics. An analysis of the twelve authors in volume 5 (1914) and volume 6 (1920) reveals a pattern that the two collectors had both retired from their positions; the contributors were a judicious mix of the senior professional academic, the professional educationalist, journalists and literary figures. A detailed analysis of contents from volumes 5–25 (1914–40) illustrates that all have either six or seven contributions, though three have additional material in the form of a 'Preface', a 'Prefatory Note',[84] and an obituary tribute, written by the EA Committee, in volume 9, which was collected by the 'Late W. P. Ker', and published

---

[81] *E&S*, 5, 1914, p. 75.
[82] *E&S*, 6, 1920, p. 30.
[83] *E&S*, 6, 1920, p. 43.
[84] *E&S*, vols. 8 (1922) and 10 (1924) respectively, edited by John Bailey and E. K. Chambers.

in 1924. The unattributed 'Preface' to volume 10, 'which completes the first decade of *Essays and Studies*, is dedicated to its distinguished Vice-President, and President for 1911, Dr. A. C. Bradley', and concludes with the observation that 'If the *Essays and Studies* have made for themselves a modest place in English Letters, it is largely due to Dr. Bradley's inspiration and counsel'.[85]

From the perspectives of form, historical chronology and genre, most subjects, periods, major authors, and critical greats make an appearance in *Essays and Studies* in these earlier decades. In the area of English Language, as well as Wyld's contribution mentioned above, in volume 9 Dorothy M. E. Dymes wrote on 'The Original Language of the *Ancren Riwle*',[86] seeking to establish the linguistic genesis of the prose guide, and J. H. Grattan discussed the complexities of grammar in 'On the Teaching of Case'.[87] In volume 14, in an essay entitled '*Ancrene Wisse* and *Hali Meidhad*', J. R. R. Tolkien's concern was a 'linguistic' one. He begins 'with the conviction that very few Middle English texts represent in detail the real language in accidence, phonology, often even choice of spellings, of any one time or place of person',[88] a view that despite the proliferation of corpora linguistics and scribal profiling has yet to be substantially disproved.

Other contributions to *Essays and Studies* during the 1920s and 1930s in the broad 'language' category include J. M. Wattie on 'Tense'[89] and A. Mawer on 'English Place-Names and their Pronunciations'.[90] The novelist Rose Macaulay drew upon examples mainly from letters written over three centuries to reflect 'On Linguistic Changes'.[91] An interesting subject, still in need of further exploration, appeared in 1937 with M. S. Serjeantson's essay on 'The Vocabulary of Cookery in the Fifteenth Century'.[92] Serjeantson notes that 'the overwhelming proportion of French technical terms is very noticeable'. Also that 'the words which denote methods of cooking, and the names of the finished dishes are almost exclusively French',[93] though perhaps, given the French aristocracy's dominance in high culture, even in this late period, these loanwords are not surprising.

W. A. Craigie's 'The Language of the *Kingis Quair*', uses an analysis of the poem to discuss the issue of its attribution, concluding that 'the evidence of the language is entirely in favour of the attribution to King James VI of Scotland, I of England.[94] Ronald Brunlees McKerrow's contribution to the 1922 volume is a response to the Newbolt Report, which 'directed attention anew to the teaching of English Grammars'.[95] McKerrow focuses his attention on the opinion that there was too much formalism in the teaching of grammar. In company with A. W. Pollard and

---

[85] *E&S*, 10, 1924, p. 5.
[86] *E&S*, 9, 1923, pp. 31–49.
[87] *E&S*, 9, 1923, pp. 115–125.
[88] *E&S*, 14, 1928, p. 104.
[89] *E&S*, 16, 1930, pp. 121–143.
[90] *E&S*, 17, 1931, pp. 90–105.
[91] *E&S*, 20, 1934, pp. 108–122.
[92] *E&S*, 22, 1937, pp. 25–37.
[93] *E&S*, 23, 1937, p. 37.
[94] *E&S*, 25, 1940, p. 38.
[95] *E&S*, 8, 1922, pp. 148–167.

W. W. Greg, McKerrow 'was one of a remarkable trio who between them were most responsible for the founding principles of modern biographical studies'.[96] In 1925, he launched the quarterly journal from Oxford University Press, the *Review of English Studies*, the first issue of which opened with R. W. Chambers on the *Ancren Riwle*.[97] Indeed, *Essays and Studies* and McKerrow's journal drew upon some of the same contributors; for instance, C. H. Herford, Percy Simpson, John Dover Wilson, R. W. Chambers, R. W. Chapman and Ernest de Sélincourt, among others.[98]

A further article of interest in the broad category of 'Language' was also written by a non-academic. In volume 13 the prolific Anglo-Irish poet and writer of fantasy fiction, Lord Dunsany, in a brief seven page essay, writes on 'English Language Conditions!'. He reflects upon the fact that 'several good useful English words have dropped out of the language', such as 'hostile', 'Roman', and 'English' used as adjectives.[99]

There are a number of interesting contributions on general subjects in *Essays and Studies*. Mario Praz is one non-native contributor to the series, representing an international dimension to the influence of the EA and the reputation of its publications. Volume 15 contains an extensive essay by Praz on 'The Italian Element in English', which ranges over many Italian loanwords in English from a broad diachronic perspective.[100] Other continental contributors include French academics such as André Maurois, who wrote 'Proust et Ruskin' published in French in volume 17,[101] and, four volumes earlier, Émile Legouis, who wrote 'La Réaction Contre La Critique Romantique de Shakespeare'.[102]

As well as Maurois' contribution, two general essays are found in the 1931 volume collected by W. H. Hadow, a volume which has, in contemporary academic lingo, a cutting-edge interdisciplinary aspect.[103] The lead contributor in this volume is William Ebor, the Archbishop of York, who writes on 'Poetry and Science'. J. A. Fuller-Maitland continues this mode of investigation in 'Music and Letters', which speaks of a chasm between professional writers and musicians. Interestingly from the perspective of the reception history of individual writers he refers several times to George Eliot; these are perhaps the only isolated references to the writer in *Essays and Studies* between 1919 and 1940, since her reputation was in eclipse during the inter-war period. Fuller-Maitland's contribution is also interesting towards the conclusion of his essay when he refers to 'Broadcasting programmes' as an element contributing to a healing process between music and letters. Broadcasting had just begun in Britain by the time of the publication in 1932 of this essay, and already

---

[96] David McKitterick, 'Introduction', in Ronald B. McKerrow, *An Introduction to Bibliography for Literary Students*: 1994, p. xi.
[97] *RES*, of course, currently edited by Gordon Campbell, a former Chair and President of the EA, and long-standing Trustee, is now published five times a year.
[98] David McKitterick, 'Introduction', p. xvi.
[99] *E&S*, 13, 1927, p. 138.
[100] *E&S*, 15, 1929, pp. 20–66.
[101] *E&S*, 17, 1931, pp. 25–32.
[102] *E&S*, 13, 1927, pp. 74–87.
[103] *E&S*, 17, 1931.

pre-empts the importance that the media would go on to develop through the course of the twentieth century.

Essays and Studies was not averse to critical debate of the strongest nature. In 1935, in volume 21, C. S. Lewis's 'Open Letter to Dr. Tillyard' evinces the controversy between Lewis himself and E. M. W. Tillyard.[104] Argument broke out after Tillyard responded to Lewis's 'The Personal Heresy in Criticism'[105] in which Lewis took issue with Tillyard's book on *Milton*.[106] For Lewis in his earlier piece, 'the concealed major premise [of Tillyard's book] is plainly the proposition that all poetry is about *the poet's state of mind*'.[107] In the following *Essays and Studies* Tillyard's 'The Personal Heresy in Criticism: A Rejoinder' clarifies at length what he means 'by personality in literature'.[108] Such critical controversies between academic critics somewhat anticipate the intense, and at times, vitriolic conflicts in academic journals such as *Scrutiny* (founded in 1932) which became a common feature of academic discourse.

In terms of periods and genres of English Literature, these volumes of *Essays and Studies* represent a reasonably equitable distribution. No one genre or period predominates. Old English is represented by at least eleven essays; Middle English by twelve with Chaucer only forming the focus of one essay. The sixteenth century, including Renaissance drama but excluding Shakespeare, is represented by six essays, with one on Spenser's *The Faery Queene*. Somewhat surprisingly, perhaps, Shakespeare is the subject of just five essays. The seventeenth century, excluding Milton, is represented by twelve contributions, with seven essays on facets of Milton. The eighteenth century has fifteen essays on its prose, poetry, and fiction. Similarly the nineteenth century, including the Romantics, is well represented. There are essays on Keats (two), Shelley (two), Wordsworth (two), Coleridge (three, including his critical terminology), three on Hazlitt, two on Scott. Both of the Scott essays are comparative: J. C. Smith writes on 'Scott and Shakespeare';[109] and H. J. C. Grierson on 'Scott and Carlyle'.[110] It seems fair to say that Hazlitt and Scott are far less canonical in the twenty-first century than they were in these early decades of the twentieth century. Other authors covered by these volumes of *Essays and Studies*, but seldom appearing as well-covered writers now, are Thomas Love Peacock, whose *Prose* and later correspondence receives attention, and Charles Lamb. There is, somewhat surprisingly, only one essay on aspects of Tennyson's poetry (in this instance his travels to Wales and 'Knowledge of Welsh Literature and Tradition');[111] and one on Robert Browning's reputation.[112] Volume 25 opens with H. W. Garrod's essay on 'Houseman: 1939'.[113] This is a consideration of the 1939

---

[104] *E&S*, 21, 1935, pp. 153–168.
[105] *E&S*, 19, 1933, pp. 7–28.
[106] E.M.W. Tillyard, *Milton*, 1930.
[107] *E&S* 19, 1933, p. 8.
[108] *E&S*, 20, 1934, pp. 7–20.
[109] *E&S*, 24, 1938, pp. 114–130.
[110] *E&S*, 13, 1927, pp. 88–111.
[111] *E&S*, 14, 1928, pp. 71–103.
[112] *E&S* 15, 1929, pp. 124–152.
[113] *E&S*, 25, 1939, pp. 7–21.

publication of Houseman's *Collected Poems* and shows the rapid response of the critic to newly published work.

In terms of the modern literary canon, there are notable omissions from the subjects selected for investigation in the pre-1940 period. There is nothing on George Eliot, Charles Dickens, William Thackeray, Charles Reade, or Wilkie Collins. The Victorian novel is represented by essays on Charlotte Brontë, Emily Brontë, Anthony Trollope, and Mark Rutherford. There is one essay on Jane Austen, by Mary Lascelles, in which the author's style is scrutinised.[114] Stevenson's prose receives attention, as does that of Surtees/Jorrocks, which is the subject of an ambitious dialogue and parody published by W. L. Renwick, where we are told the scene is set in 'a room in the ancient city of New Castle-upon-Tyne. It is late, but through the tobacco-smoke AELIUS and BARBARUS may still be discerned'![115]

In terms of the other essays in these earlier volumes of *Essays and Studies*, they demonstrate the then-canon of literary and linguistic study, which can be very much contrasted with the fields today. While there is an outline and assessment of 'Canadian Literature: the Beginnings' by Archibald MacMechan,[116] American Literature and other literatures in English, are very much neglected, demonstrating unequivocally the Anglocentric focus of scholarly contributors during these decades. While global literatures seem of little concern to researchers, Contemporary Literature of the first forty years of the twentieth century forms a considerable focus. The late Victorian and Edwardian essayist and novelist, W. H. Hudson, is thoroughly assessed by R. H. Charles.[117] Hardy's poetry and fiction are considered alongside Shaw, Doughty, Hudson and Conrad in Barker Farley's 'The Modern Consciousness in English Literature'.[118] Prophetic talent-spotting is displayed in H. J. C. Grierson's 'The Problem of the Scottish Poet'.[119] At the end of his disquisition, Grierson devotes four lengthy paragraphs to Hugh McDiarmid, noting that he 'is a true poet, though a wild one, with more of passion and thought, more fire in his belly, than of recent Scottish poets'.[120] And Louis MacNeice writes on 'Subjects in Modern Poetry', focusing on Auden, Spencer, and W. B. Yeats among others.[121]

In relation to the outbreak of war in 1939, there is a noticeable diminishing in pagination of *Essays and Studies*, as one might expect. The 1939 volume, collected by Laurence Binyon, extends to 131 pages, while the 1940 volume has 115 pages. Contemporary events and the Nazi anti-Jewish terror had already been reflected in volume 23, collected by S. C. Roberts. C. J. Sisson's 'A Colony of Jews in Shakespeare's London' draws upon London's 'Court of Chancery' in order to show how it 'treated a dispute between a London citizen and an alien Jew, a known Jew,

---

[114] *E&S*, 22, 1936, pp. 61–85.
[115] *E&S*, 17, 1931, pp. 76–89.
[116] *E&S*, 12, 1926, pp. 87–99).
[117] *E&S*, 20, 1934, pp. 135–151.
[118] *E&S*, 9, 1923, pp. 126–46.
[119] *E&S*, 21, 1935, pp. 105–23.
[120] *E&S*, 21, 1935, p. 120.
[121] *E&S*, 22, 1936, pp. 144–58.

who came to seek its protection and its help, and not in vain'.[122] This contrasts with 'the trial scene in *The Merchant of Venice* [which] is completely alien to [this] spirit'.[123]

Scholarly articles in the earlier volumes of *Essays and Studies*, then, sometimes reflect contemporary events, but always reflect (and presumably help solidify) attitudes towards and investigations of the contemporary literary canon. Contributors, as has been demonstrated, are not confined simply to male academics though. Notable female contributors, subsequently to become distinguished academics, include Helen Gardner, Mary Lascelles[124] and Helen Darbishire who, notably, collected the volume in which these colleagues' work appeared. This trend, of a woman collector promoting other women academics, is also illustrated in the earlier volume 13, collected by Caroline Spurgeon. This included three female contributors: Bertha S. Phillpotts[125] opens with 'Wyrd and Providence in Anglo-Saxon Thought';[126] Helen Waddell, author of *The Wandering Scholars*, focuses on the twelfth-century scholar and writer John of Salisbury;[127] and 'Shelley's Mental Progress' is the subject of a contribution from Marjory Amelia Bald, the author in 1923 of *Women-Writers of the Nineteenth Century*.[128]

1940–1956

Essays and Studies was published throughout WWII. Arundell Esdaile collected volume 26 (1942) and also the 1952 volume. Oxford University Press, at the Clarendon Press, continued to publish *Essays and Studies* until volume 32 for 1946, published in 1947. The first volume of the new series appeared in 1948 and was published by a new publisher, John Murray. The title changed to *English Studies* in 1948, but after three volumes reverted back to *Essays and Studies*. George Rostrevor Hamilton collected the 1950 volume (the third one to be published under the title *English Studies*) and also the jubilee volume published in 1956.

The number of essays included varied over the years. Naturally, those appearing during the war years were somewhat thinner in size than those published subsequently. Esdaile's volume 26 has 112 pages and six contributions. Volume 27, collected by Nowell Charles Smith for 1941 (published in 1942), was slimmer, with seventy-five pages but also with six contributions. R. W. Chapman, the distinguished Johnson, Boswell and Jane Austen scholar and influential publisher from 1920 to 1942 at Oxford University Press, collected volume 28, published in 1943 with seven contributions and 83 pages. Una Ellis-Fermor collected volume 29 published in 1944. This volume had six contributions occupying 100 pages of text. A well-known Oxford personality during the earlier part of the twentieth century, C. H. Wilkinson, collected volume 30, published in 1945, which has six contributions;

---

[122] *E&S*, 23, 1937, pp. 38–51.
[123] *Ibid*, p. 51.
[124] *E&S*, 22, 1936, pp. 103–27 and pp. 61–85, respectively.
[125] later to become Dame Bertha Surtees Newall.
[126] *E&S*, 13, 1927, pp. 7–27.
[127] *E&S*, 13, 1927, pp. 28–51.
[128] *E&S*, 13, 1927, pp. 112–37.

and of similar size was V. de Sola Pinto's volume 31, which also had six contributions with 106 pages of text.

These six war-time *Essays and Studies* reveal a diversity of contributors and subjects. Half of the contributors to volume 26 published in 1940 are women. Katharine A. Esdaile writes on 'The Real Thomas Amory'. She attempts to disentangle the fact from the fiction on the life and work of the eighteenth-century novelist and author of *The Life of John Buncle, Esq.* (1756–66). Dorothy Margaret Stuart draws upon examples from poets as diverse as Thomson, William Somerville, Thomas Blacklock, and others in her 'Landscape in Augustan Verse'. A poet from an earlier century concerns Evelyn Mary Simpson, who, having assisted her husband with their great edition of Ben Jonson (volumes published from 1938 to 1952), draws upon extant manuscripts on her 'The Text of Donne's 'Divine Poems''. The late seventeenth century and early years of the next century is the subject of Hugh Macdonald's 'Some Poetical Miscellanies, 1672–1716'. Chronologically, the latest period of literature to receive attention in this volume is the mid-Victorian, as the volume opens with William R. Rutland's 'Tennyson and the Theory of Evolution'. Finally, the 1940 volume also contains Henry Cecil Wyld's still-valuable 'Aspects of Style and Idiom in Fifteenth-Century English'.

Volume 27, collected by Nowell Charles Smith, begins with C. S. Lewis' consideration of the relationships between 'Psycho-Analysis and Literary Criticism'. This is followed by 'Lord Herbert of Cherbury: A Spiritual Quixote of the Seventeenth Century' by Basil Willey, King Edward VII Professor of English Studies Literature at Cambridge. Willey himself collected volumes 32 (1946) and new series 8 (1958) of *Essays and Studies*. The third essay, by Catherine Macdonald Maclean, the eminent eighteenth- and nineteenth-century specialist, is on 'Lewesdon Hill and Its Poet'. The subject is William Crowe, an obscure clergyman whose poem 'Lewesdon Hill' first appeared anonymously in 1788 and was praised by Wordsworth. Her essay is followed by R. W. Chapman's 'A Problem in Editorial Method', pointing out the fallibility of the printed word and anticipating subsequent editorial controversy by Greg, Bowes, Tanselle, McGann, and others. The remaining two essays are by W. H. D. Rouse on 'Style', and a short discourse by S. C. Roberts, 'At the Heart of the Nineties'.

Of particular interest is volume 30 for 1944, published in 1945, and collected by Cyril Hackett Wilkinson. Wilkinson himself had a distinguished military record and this *Essays and Studies* has the most military flavour of any of the war-time issues. It opens with 'The Naval Officer in Fiction'. The author, Admiral Sir Herbert William Richmond, had a highly meritorious university and military career, before becoming a naval historian. His essay ranges widely over more than two centuries of fiction, focusing especially on Ned Ward's description of the 'the rough seaman or brutal bully type' in *The Wooden World Dissected in the Character of a Ship of War* (1707). He then moves into Smollett's depictions in *Roderick Random* (1748) and *Peregrine Pickle* (1751), as well as those in Jane Austen and Captain Marryat. Richmond's essay is followed by F. Maurice's 'The History of Total War'. Appointed Professor of Military Studies at the University of London in 1927, Maurice's chief concern is the problem of creating war histories: what to select and not select. Other interesting contributors include Percy Simpson on 'The Art of Ben Jonson'; C. F. Bell, who writes on 'Thomas Gray and the Fine Arts', drawing upon Gray's unpublished manuscripts at Eton in order to thoroughly assess Gray's aesthetic perceptions. Bell's essay is followed by one on 'Naturalists' by journalist and author Sir William Beach Thomas, whose 'idealization of rural Britain…became a central theme in his life and writing'.[129] His *Essays and Studies* contribution ranges from Blackmore and W.H. Hudson, to Richard Jefferies, Gilbert White, and Lord de Tabley. The final contribution to volume 30 is by Sir William A. Craigie, the lexicographer and philologist, from 1916 to 1925 Rawlinson and Bosworth Professor of Anglo-Saxon at Oxford.

Vivian de Sola Pinto's volume 31 for 1945, published in 1946, is arguably more focused. Five of the six essays focus specifically on works of literature and authors rather than on broad topics. In the first essay, the Cambridge academic H. S. Bennett writes on 'Medieval Literature and the modern Reader'; there are essays on two Shakespeare plays, *The Merchant of Venice* and *Antony and Cleopatra*; Ethel Seaton writes on 'Comus and Shakespeare'; Beatrice White contributes 'Mary Coleridge: An Appreciation'; and in the final essay, L. A. Strong discusses a modern author in 'James Joyce and Vocal Music'.

Basil Willey's volume 32 for 1946, published in 1947, is notable: it was the last *Essays and Studies* to be published for a considerable period at the Clarendon Press, and the diversity of its subjects and contributors is interesting. Of the six essays, four deal with general subjects and two with specific authors. The historical timeframes covered are broad: I. A. Richards, who served as EA President in 1978, writes on the 'Responsibilities in the Teaching of English', while 'Banter in English Controversial Prose after the Restoration' is the subject tackled in a lengthy contribution from Hugh Macdonald. W. L. Renwick's very short 'Comic Epic in Prose' explores the implications of the phrase 'in prose' and the words 'Comic' and 'Epic'. In the final essay the Swiss-German Eugene Dieth provides an extensive analysis, with map illustrations, of 'A New Survey of English Dialects' during which he laments the closing of the English Dialect Society, after its sponsorship of the publication of eighty volumes. Two contributions focus on specific authors: M. G. Lloyd Thomas writes on Hopkins' prose in 'Hopkins as Critic' and Geoffrey Tillotson writes on 'Pater, Mr. Rose and the 'Conclusion' of *The Renaissance*', ranging in his incisive discussion from W. H. Mallock, to the *New Republic* and Pater's *The Renaissance*.

John Murray took over the publication of the volume from 1948, and the title changed for two collections before reverting back in 1950 to *Essays and Studies*. The first collection under Murray's imprint, *English Studies 1948* had as its sub-title, *Being Volume One of the New Series of Essays and Studies Collected for the English Association by F.P. Wilson*. The collector was Frank Percy Wilson who became Merton Professor of English Language and Literature at Oxford. *English Studies* 1948 contains many distinguished academic contributors and topics range from 'Hickes's 'Thesaurus':

---

[129] Derek Hudson, 'Thomas, Sir William Beach (1868–1957)', rev. Marc Brodie, *Oxford Dictionary of National Biography*, 2004.

A Study in Oxford-Book Production' to 'Marlowe's *Tamburlaine*'. Of the six contributors, two are women: Dame Helen Gardner, who, like her editor, Wilson, later became Merton Professor of English Language and Literature at Oxford. She writes on 'Milton's 'Satan' and the Theme of Damnation in Elizabethan-Tragedy'. Agnes May Christabel Latham, the Raleigh scholar, writes on 'Satire as Literary Themes and Modes in Nashe's 'Unfortunate Traveller".

English Studies 1949, collected by Sir Philip Magnus, contains seven rather than the six essays of the previous volume. Subjects range from Palgrave's *'Golden Treasury'* to 'Edmund Burke' and 'The Prose of E. R. Addison' Contributors represent a wider range than the narrowly academic focus of the volume collected by F. P. Wilson. The 1950 volume collected by G. Rostrevor Hamilton reverts back to the *Essays and Studies* title. The contributors include academics such as Geoffrey Tillotson writing on 'Arnold and Pater: Critics Historical, Aesthetic and Otherwise' and Nevill Coghill. F. P. Wilson's successor to the Merton Chair at Oxford, Coghill (who served as EA President in 1971) writes on 'The Basis of Shakespearean Comedy: A Study in Medieval Affinities'. Other contributors are the novelist, Pamela Hansford Johnson, discussing 'Three Novelists and the Drawing of Character. C. P. Snow, Joyce Cary, and Ivy Compton-Burnett'. She married C.P. Snow in 1949. Another contributor, Owen Barfield, writing on 'Greek Thought in English Words', was a solicitor. Gilbert Lancelyn Green writes on 'Stevenson in Search of a Madonna'.

This combination of a treatment of diverse subjects and authors from wide ranging periods from the medieval to the contemporary with contributors drawn not exclusively from academic world is a pattern repeated in subsequent issues of *Essays and Studies*. Thus the 1951 volume collected by Geoffrey Tillotson contains essays on Sir Walter Raleigh by Agnes Latham[130] and two on different aspects of Dr. Johnson. An essay on Dickens by John Butt and Kathleen Tillotson serves as a prelude to their important book, *Dickens at Work*, published in 1957.[131] This was Kathleen Tillotson's third and final contribution to *Essays and Studies*.

Arundell Esdaile's 1952 collection of seven essays ranges historically from sixteenth-century Biblical translation—the subject of Hugh Sykes Davies's 'Sir John Cheke and the Translation of the Bible'—through essays on *The Tempest*, and other Shakespearen topics to contemporary poetry. Women contributors, for once, predominate: Katharine Esdaile writes on 'Some Fellow Citizens of Shakespeare in Southwark'; Margaret Willy writes on Lilian Bowes Lyon; Beatrice White discusses 'Frederick James Furnivall'; and Jocelyn Bell writes 'A Study of Arthur Morrison', the neglected late Victorian novelist. Another contributor to the 1952 Collection was Bonamy Dobrée, who, according to F. R. Leavis, 'had one foot in university circles and one in the fashionable world of metropolitan literary journalism'.[132] Dobrée frequently wrote for his close friend T. S. Eliot's *The Criterion* during the 1930s, and

---

[130] 'Sir Walter Raleigh's Gold Mine: new light on the last Guiana Voyage', *E&S*, 4, 1951, pp. 94–111.
[131] 'Dickens at Work on *Dombey and Son*, *E&S*, 4, 1951, pp. 70–93.
[132] Jason Harding, *The Criterion: Cultural Politics and Periodical Networks in Inter-War* Britain, 2002, pp. 127–128.

following significant work on Restoration drama, became Professor of English Literature at the University of Leeds in 1936.

Geoffrey Bullough collected volume 6 of the new series published in 1953. Unusually, 'Notes on Contributors', all of whom are academics, are included. Subjects range from J. R. R. Tolkien's opening essay, which is on 'The Homecoming of Beorhtnoth Beorhthelm's Son' to Edward Meryon Wilson's 'Family Honour in the Plays of Shakespeare's Predecessors and Contemporaries'. Herbert Gladstone Wright, the Chair of English Language and Literature at the University College of Wales, Bangor from 1919 until 1954, writes interestingly on 'Some Sixteenth and Seventeenth Century Writers on the Plague'. Vivian de Sola Pinto contributes an essay on 'John Wilmot, Earl of Rochester, and the Right Veine of Satire'. This is followed by 'The Augustan Pantheon: Mythology and Personification in Eighteenth Century Poetry'. The writer, Rachel Trickett, lectured from 1946 to 1954 at University College, Hull and served as President of the EA in 1982. The author of six novels, her *The Honest Muse: A Study in Augustan Verse* (1967) is regarded as a definitive study of Augustan verse. The most recent period of literature studied in Bullough's collection is early nineteenth century: 'The Integrity of *Biographia Literaria*' is the subject of George Whalley's contribution. And the final essay in this issue is 'Language, Style, and the Anglo-Welsh' by Gwyn Jones, Professor of English Language and Literature at the University College of Wales, Aberystwyth. He founded and edited the *Welsh Review* from 1939 to 1948 and translated the *Mabinogion* (1948).

The 1954 volume collected by Guy Boas is somewhat thin, containing only five contributions, one of these being by the collector. Boas' subject, 'Great Englishmen at School', takes up more than a third of the total content and is far from academic, acting, one might imagine, as a filler for the volume as much as anything. In addition to a contribution from Margaret Willy on 'The Poetry of Donne: Its Interest and Influence Today', there are essays by two academics, Bertram Joseph and R. A. Foakes, both of whom wrote profusely on Shakespearean drama. The former was Professor of English at City University of New York. His *Essays and Studies* contribution is on Chaucer's '*Troilus and Criseyde*'; however, Joseph's preoccupation was with the 'gap between Shakespeare in education and in the theatre'[133] a subject on which he published extensively. Foakes' preoccupation is also with Shakespeare and Renaissance studies; he produced distinguished work on Coleridge and Romanticism and edited *Henry VIII* (1968) and *The Comedy of Errors* (1962) for the second of the Arden Shakespeare series and *King Lear* (1997) for third series. His contribution to the 1954 *Essays and Studies* volume, 'The Player's Passion: Some Notes on Elizabethan Psychology and Poetry' well reflects these interests.

D. M. Low's collection for 1955 includes six essays by a new generation of scholars, some of whom became highly influential in subsequent discourse and debate in English Studies and Education in the latter years of the twentieth century. The first contribution, on the other hand, is representative of a passing generation. John

---

[133] *Contemporary Authors*, 6, 1982, p. 257.

Crow's 'Editing and Emending' focuses on selected Shakespearean cruces and concludes with a joke on the word 'brandies'.[134] Contributors destined to have more influence in determining the tone and substance of subsequent debates on the future direction of English Studies and the study of English in schools are found in the 1955 volume. Charles Brian Cox, who became Professor of English Literature at Manchester University from 1976 to 1993, writes on 'Henry James and Stoicism'. Another contributor to this volume is Edward Dyson, who writes on 'The Interpretation of *Comus*'. Cox and Dyson co-founded the *Critical Quarterly* in 1958, which occupied a prominent place in the landscape of English Studies in the last decade of the twentieth century. Other contributors include John Lawlor, writing on 'Radical Satire and the Realistic Novel'. In 1950 he was appointed Professor of English Language and Literature at the University of Keele, and played a prominent role in the International Association of University Professors of English, serving as its Secretary-General and Treasurer from 1971 to 1995.

The eclectic nature of the EA's *Essays and Studies* and its contributors is well exemplified by the Jubilee volume collected by George Rostrevor Hamilton. Here, Arundell Esdaile writes on 'A Half Century of the English Association'; Kate O'Brien the dramatist and novelist, writes on 'Writers of Letters'; Martin Armstrong contributes 'The Art of Listening', which essentially deals with the medium of radio rather than the written word; Helen Gardner writes about 'Milton's First Illustrator'; Bonamy Dobrée is concerned about 'On (Not) Enjoying Shakespeare'; T. R. Henn writes on 'The Accent of Yeats' "Last Poems"'; E. M. W. Tillyard contributes 'The Novel as Literary Kind'; and R. M. Wilson, Professor of English Language at Sheffield, writes about 'Three Middle English Mystics', limiting himself to the most famous medieval mystical authors, Richard Rolle, Julian of Norwich, and Margery Kempe.

Examination of *Essays and Studies* volumes 10 to 20, from 1957 to 1967, reveals a greater diversity of contributors and subjects treated. For instance, volume 10, collected by Margaret Willy, consists of seven contributions, the first from Sir Ernest Gowers, who became EA President in 1957, on 'Some Thoughts on New Words'. George Rostrevor Hamilton's 'Poetry's Claim to Truth' ranges from Pope's *The Dunciad* to Wordsworth's 'The Solitary Reaper', while the remaining five contributions deal with specific writers. Of these, Margaret Willy writes on 'The Poetry of Emily Dickinson', which follows Howard Sergeant on the poetry of Roy Campbell. The other essays focus on 'Milton's Poetic Language',(Helen Darbishire), 'How 'Robert Elsmere' Struck Some Contemporaries' (Basil Willey), and 'Coleridge on a Distant Prospect of Faust' (John Nosworthy).

Only one other essay on Coleridge appears in *Essays and Studies* during the next decade, in the 1958 volume.[135] Romantic writers are not ignored, however. In the 1962 volume Robert Gitting writes on 'Keats and Cats'[136] and the theatrical historian Sybil Rosenfeld, discusses 'Jane Austen and Private Theatricals'.[137] Four years

---

[134] *E&S*, 8, 1955, p. 19.
[135] George Whalley, *Coleridge's Debt to Charles Lamb*, *E&S*, 11, 1958, pp. 68–85.
[136] *E&S*, 15, 1962, pp. 52–58.
[137] *E&S*, 15, 1962, 40–51.

later, the biographer Marghanita Laski writes on 'The Language of the Nightingale Ode':[138] and in the 1967 volume, 'Scott's "Chronicles of the Canongate"' is the subject of John Traill Christie's essay.[139]

Between 1957 and 1967 there are, in addition to Willey's *Robert Elsmere* essay, a number on nineteenth-century literature. It is hardly surprising, perhaps, that Dickens should be the subject of three essays. C. B. Cox writes 'In Defence of Dickens' in the 1958 volume,[140] in essence a continuation of Chesterton's 1906 defence of Dickens, especially in the light of F. R. Leavis's omission of Dickens in the pantheon of the most significant novelists in his *The Great Tradition* (1948). Kathleen Tillotson's 'Oliver Twist' assesses the importance of Dickens' 'Preface' to the novel and its 'complicated history of publication'.[141] Amongst other elements of the novel, 'The Image and Structure of *Our Mutual Friend*' is the subject of Kenneth Muir's consideration in 1966.[142] In this volume there are three other essays on nineteenth-century literary topics. In addition to Laski's essay on 'The Language of the Nightingale Ode', and Robert Sharrock on 'Carlyle and the Sense of History', Henry Gifford writes on 'Thomas Hardy and Emma'. Other essays on nineteenth-century topics include A. L. Rowse writing on a fellow West Country Oxford man and poet, 'Robert Stephen Hawker of Morwenstow: A Belated Medieval'.[143] In the 1961 volume, Edmund Blunden, who became EA President in 1967, writes 'On Regency Fiction: A Fragment', an essay revealing his comprehensive reading in the highways and byways of the literary prose of the 1820s and 1830s.[144] In the same volume Derek Hudson, the journalist, biographer and editor, writes 'A Study of Algernon Blackwood'.[145] Other contributions on the nineteenth century during the 1957 to 1967 period include Muriel St. Clare Byrne on 'What We Said about the Meiningers in 1881', a lengthy essay that focuses upon 'the company of players maintained by Duke George of Saxe-Meininger from 1874 to 1890, who at the height of their international reputation gave a six week season at Drury Lane in 1881'.[146] Also in this volume there is a contribution on 'Nature and Art in Oscar Wilde's 'The Decay of Lying" by Hilda Schiff.[147] Other nineteenth-century related subjects during these ten years include one on 'Frances Adams, 1862–1893: A Forgotten Child of the Age'.[148]

Three contributions traverse the centuries and the genres. These range from Beatrice White's 'Ultima Thule: Some English Travellers to Iceland' covering the years 1772–1878.[149] Roger Lancelyn Green's 'The Golden Age of Children's Books' in the 1962 volume collected by Beatrice White moves from Catherine Sinclair's

---

[138] *E&S*, 19, 1966, pp. 60–73.
[139] *E&S*, 20, 1967, pp. 64–75.
[140] *E&S*, 11, 1958, pp. 86–100.
[141] *E&S*, 12, 1959, pp. 87–105.
[142] *E&S*, 19, 1966, pp. 92–105.
[143] *E&S*, 12, 1959, pp. 106–132.
[144] *E&S*, 14, 1961, pp. 52–65.
[145] *E&S*, 14, 1961, pp. 102–114.
[146] *E&S*, 18, 1965, pp. 45–72.
[147] *E&S*, 18, 1965, pp. 83–102.
[148] *E&S*, 20, 1967, pp. 76–103.
[149] *E&S*, 14, 1961, pp. 81–101.

Holiday House (1839) to the work of J. M. Barrie published in the early decades of the twentieth century.[150] A very brief contribution traverses both the nineteenth and twentieth century: 'The Fascination of the Paranoid Personality: Baron Corvo'.[151] The focus here is on 'a paranoid personality' rather than on historical perspective, and the author, Pamela Hansford Johnson, the novelist and dramatist, confesses to having 'used [Rolfe] as a starting point for the hero of one of [her] own novels' (13).[152] In "Back to Methuselah': The Poet and the City' attention is upon what the author Margery M. Morgan claims to be the most 'strongly disliked' of all Shaw's plays, *Back to Methuselah* (1921).[153] With the exception of Shakespeare, whose tercentenary was celebrated in 1964 and to whom the 1964 *Essays and Studies* was devoted, the nineteenth-century and early decades of the twentieth century represent the most extensive contributions during this decade. They reflect the growth of interest in the period as a subject of academic and general study.

Essays and Studies from 1967 to the Present

Essays and Studies from 1967 onwards is as diverse as the earlier volumes. There were four publishers of *Essays and Studies* during the period 1908 to 2005: Oxford University Press from 1908 to 1947; John Murray from 1948 to 1989; Basil Blackwell in 1990; finally, D. S. Brewer, an imprint of Boydell, took over publication with volume 64 for 1991.

Other changes over a thirty or so year period are minor. *Essays and Studies* 1986 was the last to be 'Collected' instead of 'Edited'. Gerald Alfred Wilkes, Challis Professor of English Literature at the University of Sydney, was the collector of the 1986 volume. The 1987 volume, edited by Michael Green, also evinces a thematically based publication, rather than an eclectic collection, a practice that has subsequently continued into the twenty-first century. *Essays and Studies* in 1987 focuses on *English and Cultural Studies: Broadening the Context*. In Green's Introduction, 'Points of Departure "New" Subjects and "Old"', he comments that when Richard Hoggart was invited to co-edit this collection he suggested that the essays 'might in different ways discuss or exhibit the impact of cultural studies on the work of English departments'.[154] Following, then, are eight essays ranging in topic from Peter Brooker's 'Why Brecht, or, Is there English after Cultural Studies?' to two essays on various aspects of Dickens. One by Paul Hoggart, 'Travesties of Dickens', focuses on derivatives of *The Pickwick Papers*; the other, by Carolyn Brown on "Great Expectations': Masculinity and Modernity', examines 'masculinity and modernity as motives' in the novel.[155] The final essay in the collection, David Lusted's 'English Teaching and Media Education: Culture and the Curriculum', concentrates on

---

[150] *E&S*, 15, 1962, pp. 59–73.
[151] *E&S*, 16, 1963, pp. 12–15.
[152] *E&S*, 16, 1963, p. 13.
[153] *E&S*, 13, 1960, pp. 82–98.
[154] *E&S*, 40, 1987, p. 1.
[155] *E&S*, 40, 1987, p. 60.

curriculum transformation in the schools. The notes on editors and contributors reveal diversity in the twelve people involved with the volume. One of the essays, for example, 'Different Starting Points: A View of Teaching 'English etc' from Further Education' is the product of three collaborative authors all of whom were teaching in various West Midlands Colleges and schools for about ten years. *Essays and Studies* collected by Suheil Bushrui in 1982 was one of the first to focus on a theme for its contributions. Bushrui, Professor of English and Anglo-Irish Literature at the American University of Beirut, Lebanon, chose the theme 'The Poet's Power', divided into seven ages, from Chaucer, Shakespeare, Milton and Pope through to Blake, Tennyson and Yeats. The seven contributors include Bushrui writing on 'Yeats: the Poet as Hero', Kathleen Raine, the poet and critic, on 'Blake: the Poet as Prophet', and Robert Burchfield, English Association President in 1979, on 'Realms and Approximations: Sources of Chaucer's Power'.

There are other volumes illustrating the diversity of *Essays and Studies* during the latter half of the twentieth country and the beginning of the twenty-first. The volume for 1983, collected by Beatrice White, has seven essays, ranging from Elizabeth Maslen writing on 'Yorick's Place in 'Hamlet'' to the final one in the volume by Alicia Percival on 'The English Association and the Schools'. Her essay is one of the very few which examines the specific ways the EA attended to the teaching of English in schools.

Martin Dodsworth's *Essays and Studies* in 1989, *English Economis'd: English and British Higher Education in the Eighties*, contains eight contributions on an overtly political subject. 'These essays show the way thinking about English in higher education is going', Dodsworth writes in his Introduction.[156] Dodsworth's contributors commenting on change are largely drawn from faculty in English and Welsh Universities. One, Daniel Lamont, was the then Head of the School of Language and Literature at Lancashire Polytechnic; another, Roger D. Sell, was Professor of English Language and Literature at Åbo Akademi, Finland. The former writes on 'English across the Binary Line: an Institutional View'; the latter on 'English Departments in British Higher Education: A View from Abroad'.

The extent of *Essays and Studies*, like its themes and contents, has varied considerably. Beatrice White's 1983 volume is one of the shortest at 100 pages. Tom Shippey's *Essays and Studies* for 1990, *Fictional Space*, is the longest with two 224 pages of text and eight essays. Shippey's own Preface, 'Learning to Read Science Fiction', is more than thirty pages in length, an essay in itself. He also contributes to the volume an essay, 'The Fall of America in Science Fiction'. The six other contributions range from two essays focusing upon William Gibson's novel *Neuromancer* (1984), exemplifying the 'cyberpunk' movement, to an essay focusing on 'The Language and Languages of Science Fiction'. The volume concludes with an alphabetically arranged Bibliography. With the exception of the editor, Tom Shippey, then teaching at the University of Leeds, and Alasdair Spark from King Alfred's College, Winchester, the remainder of the contributors held positions in

---

[156] *E&S*, 42, 1989, p. 5.

American universities, illustrating clearly the differences in critical work between the USA and the UK.

Other *Essays and Studies* volumes of interest are those for 1996 and 2000. The former, edited by Katie Wales, who became Professor of English Language at Leeds University, focuses on *Feminist Linguistics in Literary Criticism*. The eight contributors are all English women academics—with one exception: Clara Calvo, writing on 'In Defence of Celia: Discourse Analysis and Women's Discourse in *As You Like It*', taught at the University of Grenada. The other *Essays and Studies* to be used as a representative example of the multiplicity of diverse areas, locations, historical periods and genres treated in these annual volumes of essays by various scholars, is that for 2000, *Reading the 'New' Literatures in a Postcolonial Era*. Edited by Susheila Nasta, then at the Open University, the volume contains nine essays, including the editor's 'Introduction: Stepping out. *Reading* the 'New' Literatures in a Post Colonial Era'. Focusing upon 'Reading the 'New' Literature in a Postcolonial Era', the contributors write on diverse areas including 'Notes Towards Reading the 'New' Literature in Nineteenth-Century Bengal' and 'Shamanism in Oceania: The Poetry of Albert Wendt'.

The Year's Work in English Studies

1921–1940

A decade following the first appearance of *Essays and Studies* in 1910, another EA annual publication aimed at an academic rather than a school or general audience was launched. The first editor of *YWES*, the great Shakespearean scholar and biographer Sir Sidney Lee, comments in his Preface to the first volume on its history that 'on the eve of the outbreak of war the English Association designed the annual issue of a descriptive and critical record of the published facts of English scholarship at home and abroad'. He adds that 'The fulfilment of the design has been inevitably delayed' because of the war. However 'it has at length been found practicable to issue the first volume of the projected series, covering the year November 1919–November 1920'.

The first volume was published by the Oxford University Press in 1921.[157] By the editor's own admission, a number of continental publications failed to materialise for review, though some books published prior to the year concerned (1919) were reviewed. *YWES*'s rationale as an evaluative narrative divided into chapters remains in place today. Its continuation was largely due to the EA's commitment to the volume and the lengthy editorial stints of some colleagues; F. S. Boas, for instance, served as editor from the fifth volume, when he succeeded Sidney Lee, and continued for over thirty volumes until 1955. *YWES* was always distributed by subscription

---

[157] A year prior to the MLA's first published *Bibliography of Books and Articles in the Modern Languages and Literatures*, from its inception a chiefly enumerative compilation.

mainly to libraries and distribution expenses were from the outset expensive. Its major function is succinctly expressed by John Bailey, the Vice-Chairman of the EA Executive Committee, at the AGM for 1923 held on 25 May at Bedford College, London. Bailey told the attendees he 'thought the reception given' to the publication of *YWES* 'in the circles best qualified to judge, showed that it met a need. It aimed at doing in English what *The Year's Work in Classical Studies* had done in Greek and Latin, and was of great service to anybody working on any particular writer or period, as to what had been published recently and what was most worth reading, could be seen at once. There had been a corresponding increase in influence' of the EA at the national level.[158]

As the Preface to the Jubilee volume of *YWES* in 1969 affirms 'The size of the volume from year to year reflects both the history of the work and the development of English studies'.[159] It had indeed grown exponentially through the decades: the initial volume was 140 pages of which seven were the Index; the second volume (1922 covering 1920–1921) was 192 pages in total; the third volume (1923)[160] extended to 272 pages. The fifth volume published in 1926 covered the year 1924. It was the first not edited by Sidney Lee: F. S. Boas edited it with C. H. Herford, and it contained the notices of 488 publications, 274 of which were books and 241 articles. Pagination ran to 318 pages in total.

It is hardly a surprise that the years leading up to the Second World War illustrate a diminution in the length of the volume and the comprehensiveness of its reviews. What is surprising is that it continued to be published at all. Volume 17 (1938), covering books produced in 1936, has 311 pages of evaluative text, with volume 18 (1939), running to 290 pages. The next volume, 19 (1940), reviewing works produced in 1938, contains notices of 232 books and 628 articles.

In the Preface to *YWES* 21 (1942), F. S. Boas surveys the series' development since its inception. He notes the four editors (Sir Sidney Lee, C. H. Herford, Mary S. Serjeantson, and himself), and that 'it has enlisted forty-three specialist contributors' who are 'connected with twenty-six Universities, University Colleges, and Learned Societies and Institutions'. He further comments that during a period in which 'magazines of a general literary type have become fewer, there has been a considerable increase in periodicals of a specialized and academic character'. Consequently 'the scope of [*YWES*] survey has thus been widened' and publication from 1939, for instance, has been included in the 1940 volume.[161] Boas pinpoints a problem, which has become infinitely greater in the present day of demands for research output by Higher Education Institutions and national audits: how to keep coverage current and representative given the vast increase in scholarly publications worldwide.

With the exception of the years of WWII, during which Boas noted the need for changes in personnel, consistency of contributors leads to a degree of uniformity of

---
[158] *Bulletin* 49, December 1923, p. 3.
[159] *YWES*, 50, 1969, p. 5.
[160] Where a date in brackets follows the volume number, it is the date of publication. *YWES* has generally been published two years after the year of publication of the books it reviews.
[161] All quotations from the Preface, *YWES*, 21, p. 3.

content. The first volume (1921) covered the years 1919–1920, and consisted of ten chapters: the first, 'Literary Criticism and History: General Works', was still found in the Jubilee volume 50, published in 1971 and covering 1969. Robert Dewar contributed this chapter to the first three volumes, and in his initial survey, he evaluated seven monographs, including Edmund Gosse's *Some Diversions of a Man of Letters* (1920), W. P. Ker's *The Art of Poetry*, and C. M. Gayley and B. P. Kurtz's, *Methods and Materials of Literary Criticism—Lyric, Epic and Allied Forms of Poetry*. This initial chapter concludes with a critical review of Stopford Brooke's *Nationalism in English Poetry* (1919). By the time of Dewar's last contribution, his chapter extends to the assessment of fifteen monographs. The second chapter in the first volume of *YWES* was divided into two sections: in the first, Hilda M. R. Murray reviewed selected general works of philology; in the second, Lillian E. Armstrong and I. C. Ward assessed work in the field of phonology. In volume 3, that noted textual editor, E. V. Gordon wrote the whole chapter assessing 'Philology: General Works'. His successor in volume 4, covering publications appearing in the year 1923, was another great medievalist, J. R. R. Tolkien, then Professor of English Language in the University of Leeds. Tolkien's assessment of works published was longer than that of his predecessors, and included works on Semantics. In volume 5 (1926), Tolkien, who had become Rawlinson and Bosworth Professor of Anglo-Saxon in the University of Oxford, wrote a forty-page evaluation (five times the size of Gordon's chapter) of items published in 1924. Tolkien wrote for one more volume. This chapter continued in place until WWII: among Tolkien's successors was C. L. Wrenn, one of the most significant editors of *Beowulf*. He was supposed to contribute the chapter for volume 20, covering 1939, published in 1941. By the late 1930s, Wrenn had become Chair of English Language and Literature at King's College, London, which was evacuated to Bristol during the early years of the War. As such, Boas explains in his 'Preface' to volume 20 'other circumstances have obliged [Wrenn] to postpone his contribution till volume twenty-one'. In the event, the second chapter became 'English Language: General Works' written by one of the greatest Anglo-Saxonists of the twentieth century, Dorothy Whitelock. The section on philology, interestingly, became a victim of the Second World War.

By the appearance of volume 21 in 1942, *YWES* had grown from its initial ten chapters to fifteen. In the first volume, chapter three was devoted to 'Anglo-Saxon Studies', in addition to the chapter on Philology. By the fifth volume (1926) covering items published in 1924, Chapter 3 became 'Old English Studies' under its new writer, E. V. Gordon. He opened his assessment with the bleak observation '1924 was a lean year in Old English Studies: few books and articles were produced, and none of these was of first importance'[162] before writing more than eleven pages anyway. The next year, 1925, witnessed the publication of 'more books and articles on Old English subjects…[than] for some past time',[163] even though few were up to the standards expected by Gordon. This chapter saw a variety of contributors through

---

[162] p. 66.
[163] *YWES*, 6, 1927, p. 67.

the 1920s and '30s, including Mary Serjeantson and C. L. Wrenn, who wrote the chapter on 'Old English' in volume 19 (1940) covering 1938. During WWII, Old English was covered by G. N. Garmonsway, translator of the *Anglo-Saxon Chronicle* among other numerous and notable scholarly works, who subsequently became a regular *YWES* contributor.

A similar pattern may be seen for chapter four, 'Middle English' the province for many years of Dorothy Everett. She took over the section in volume 6 (1927) covering 1925, and remained associated with it until after the Jubilee volume. In Volume 16, published in 1937, the 'Middle English' chapter became two chapters: the one on 'Chaucer, Gower, and Lydgate', whilst another contributor became responsible for the rest of the work in Middle English, under the heading 'Before and After Chaucer'. Subsequently, the fifth chapter in the first volume on 'The Renaissance' became in volume 16, the sixth chapter. The chapter in the second volume covering 1920–1921 was written by Arthur William Reed. He was obliged to relinquish the chapter after volume 8 (covering 1929). In his Preface to volume 9 in 1932, Boas stated that he himself filled 'what, it is hoped, will be a temporary vacancy', and was still writing the chapter a decade later.

Arundell Esdaile, the eminent bibliographer, librarian, and historian of the EA contributed the final chapter on 'Bibliographica' from volume 3, published in 1923. This 'inclusion of notes on the new bibliographical knowledge added in the twelve months, whether revealed in bibliographies and catalogues or in the sale-room'[164] was written by Esdaile until the volume 8, published in 1929, when it was taken over by another employee of the British Museum, Harry Sellers, who worked on the catalogue of English books, 1641–1700. Sellers contributed 'Bibliographica' from the eighth volume until the 'increasing pressure of official duties' compelled 'him to relinquish the volume'.[165] He was replaced by another British Musuem employee, his colleague John Southgate who wrote the section until being replaced in volume 23 (published in 1945 reviewing items produced in 1942) by Strickland Gibson, Oxford archivist and librarian.

In terms of late Renaissance Drama, the first volume, reviewing the publications of the years 1919–1920, has a chapter on 'Shakespeare and Elizabethan Drama' by Sidney Lee. Subsequently, 'Elizabethan Drama' became a separate chapter. Lee's initial chapter runs for twenty-five pages and Frederick S. Boas' separate chapter covers nonexclusively Shakespearean items, such as work on Massinger and others. Work noticed by Lee ranges from H. H. Furness, Jr. 'New Variorum Edition of' *King John* (1919) of which, on the whole, Lee is positive, to M. A. Bayfields' *Study of Shakespeare's Versification* (1920), to which Lee gives short shrift. He also assesses Alfred W. Pollard's *Shakespeare's Fight with the Pirates* (1920), where he finds that Pollard's 'detailed argument embodies much plausible speculation where one yearns for categorical evidence'.[166] Lee's coverage in the second volume runs for nearly fifteen pages and begins with the rather dismissive remarks that: 'Shakespearean

---
[164] *YWES*, 3, 1923, p. 208.
[165] *YWES*, 19, 1940, p. 3.
[166] *YWES*, 1, 1921, pp. 63–64.

criticism and research have engaged a considerable amount of energy during the year 1921, but nothing of first importance has been achieved'.[167] Among the books reviewed by Lee are the first three volumes of the New Cambridge Shakespeare project published in 1921 and Sir Arthur Quiller-Couch and John Dover Wilson's *The New Shakespeare*. Lee was not enthusiastic about the edition or what became known as the 'new' bibliographical editing of Shakespeare, and devotes nearly four pages of his survey to displaying a great deal of scepticism towards the new project; indeed 'too many of [Dover Wilson's] bricks are made without straw. Before one can positively determine the accuracy with which a printed text follows an author's manuscript, one must have access to authentic specimens of the author's writing, at any rate ample enough for the purpose'. Lee then adds that 'the long-cherished dream of discovering a play by Shakespeare in his autograph has not yet been realized'.[168] Lee is much more sympathetic to work by W.W. Braines who 'authoritatively', in Lee's view, establishes in his *The Site of the Globe Playhouse, Southwark* (1921), the 'precise site of the Globe'.[169] In hindsight Lee's judgement of Braines' study is remarkably prescient, though the New Cambridge Shakespeare remains an important landmark in the history of twentieth-century editing of Shakespeare. Lee's final contribution of over twenty pages was published in volume 3, covering the year 1922, and began with an essentially negative assessment of two new volumes in Quiller-Couch and Dover Wilson's *New Shakespeare* edition. Lee's highest praise is reserved for the now unjustifiably forgotten scholarship of Professor Leon Kellner, whose '*Shakespeare-Wörterbuch*, supplies German equivalents of the whole of Shakespeare's vocabulary…On every page there are signs of ripe Shakespearean scholarship and unsparing industry'.[170] Lee's chapter includes assessments of work on Shakespeare produced in France, Spain, Germany, Austria, the new Czech Republic, Serbia, and Armenia, in addition to work in English. A brief paragraph is devoted to the publication of a third revised edition of the enlarged version of Lee's own seminal *Life of Shakespeare* (1922).

Analysis of the annual Shakespeare chapter in *YWES* provides an invaluable springboard for the history and evaluation of twentieth-century Shakespearean criticism, scholarship, scholars and critics. 1923 witnessed the tercentenary of the publication of the First Folio, when Lee was probably too ill to contribute, although his name remains as editor with F. S. Boas of volume 4 of *YWES* published in 1924. In this volume the chapter on Shakespeare by A. W. Reed covers nearly twenty pages and includes A. W. Pollard's *The Foundations of Shakespeare's Text* and new volumes in *The New Shakespeare* edition. Reed is much more sympathetic to these products of 'the new bibliography' than his predecessor. Volume 6 (1927), reviewing material that appeared in 1925, is edited by Boas and C. H. Herford. Their 'Preface' pays tribute to Sidney Lee following his death, adding that 'it has fallen to Sir E. Chambers,

---

[167] *YWES*, 2, 1922, p. 66.
[168] *YWES*, 2, 1922, pp. 68–71.
[169] *YWES*, 2, 1922, p. 80.
[170] *YWES*, 3, 1924, pp. 62–63.

who has now undertaken the Shakespeare section of this survey, to give expression to the sense of loss felt by scholars everywhere'.

For Chambers, in his first set of reviews, 'the finest contribution of the year to the higher criticism of Shakespeare is undoubtedly to be found in…Granville-Barker's British Academy lecture on '*From Henry V to Hamlet*'.[171] Chambers continued to produce the annual *YWES* chapter on Shakespeare for a further four volumes. He was succeeded by John Ramsey Allardyce Nicoll[172] who had contributed the chapter on the Restoration since 1923. Nicoll now took over the 'Shakespeare' chapter, which became his own until attachment to the British Embassy in Washington in 1942 forced him temporarily to hand it over to Tucker Brooke, a colleague of his at Yale. Brooke's first contribution was to volume 22 covering the year 1941 and published in 1944. Nicoll resumed his coverage with volume 25 and continued until volume 30. In 1950, the year he became editor of the *Shakespeare Survey*, his *YWES* Shakespeare chapter was taken over by Muriel C. Bradbrook. During his tenancy of the chapter, Nicoll had made a major contribution covering numerous works of immense significance to Shakespeare Studies, including publications on Shakespeare's tragedies by G. Wilson Knight, Lily B. Campbell and Caroline Spurgeon.

Nicoll's remarkable insight in selecting the critical and scholarly works that will stand the test of time is representative of the evaluative qualities of *YWES*. The scholarly stature achieved by *YWES* realised the aim of the EA 'to maintain a high standard and its own literature and scholarship [produced] by highly qualified and often highly distinguished authors'.[173]

YWES 1940–1965

In the Jubilee volume of *YWES* its editors, Geoffrey Harlow and James Redmond noted in their Preface that 'The Second World War left its mark on the volume in several ways: "[The section on] Shakespeare was lost…through enemy action" in 1939'.[174] Such a loss in the days before being able to save multiple copies must have been a blow indeed to its author. Rather less seriously, Harlow and Redmond observe, 'a comment in the preface to 1943 on "the lengthening list of abbreviations" for periodicals—thirty one in number—would bring a wry smile to the face of any recent editor'.

F. S. Boas edited the volume up until 1955, which saw *YWES* 33 published. He edited or helped to edit more than thirty volumes of *YWES*—from its second volume onwards. From 1952, Boas had been assisted by Beatrice White, who became his successor, editing it for a further ten years from 1956 to 1965 (volumes 35 to 44). White observed in the 'Preface' to her first sole-edited volume that her predecessor 'devoted himself with tireless energy and ardour through the major difficulties of the

---

[171] *YWES*, 6, 1927, p. 135.
[172] Later, the founder and director of the Shakespeare Institute at Birmingham University.
[173] The Origin and History of the Association, Nowell Smith, Chairman's Address, 1942, p. 9.
[174] *YWES*, 50, 1971, p. 6.

Second World War to the responsibilities of assembling and encouraging a team of scholars competent to produce an authoritative statement on the annual work in the many fields of English studies'.[175]

Some of the transformations undergone by YWES during the war years and after are reflected in its format and contributors. In volume 20 (1941) there were thirty abbreviations of journals reviewed; fourteen chapters; and the volume ran to 204 pages, with an alphabetical Index of ten pages. Volume 21 (1942) had two more abbreviations and forty-three contributors (one of whom, for the first time, was Beatrice White, who wrote the 'Restoration' section, rather than the sections on Medieval and Renaissance Studies, which she specialised in later). It was larger than its predecessor, running to 257 pages, plus a ten-page Index. There was an additional chapter, on the 'Late Tudor Period, Excluding Drama', contributed by Arnold Davenport, a Lecturer in the University of Liverpool.[176] Volume 21 also altered the title of the second chapter from 'Philology: General Works' to 'English Language: General Works', contributed by the great Dorothy Whitelock.[177]

War-time conditions continued to affect the personnel who contributed to YWES, as Boas noted in his Preface to volume 22, covering the year 1941 and published in 1943. With the assistance of Dorothy Whitelock, and eleven other contributors, he managed to publish a volume with fifteen chapters. He himself contributed two chapters, as did Leonard Cyril Martin, King Alfred Professor of English Literature at the University of Liverpool. A prolific contributor from volumes 12–31, he wrote the chapter on 'The Poetry and Prose of the Early Stuart Age and the Commonwealth', Martin also contributed 'The Elizabethan Period: Poetry and Prose I'.

Volume 23 maintained the general size of its immediate predecessors, though the Index expanded and, for the first time, there was the insertion of a leaf of advertisements for Booksellers at the end. In this volume, published in 1945, Boas notes in his Preface that 'the influence of wartime conditions is evident in the relatively small number of books requiring notice, some of them from overseas published before 1943 and delayed in arrival, and others not yet arrived'. Still, as he comments, 'The full flow of articles in periodicals has continued'.[178]

There is a slight preponderance of female contributors at this time, many male academics having been called up, but they still only make up just over 50%. Of the thirteen writers in volume 23, seven are women. These include Una Ellis-Fermor,

---

[175] YWES, 35, 1956, p. 3.
[176] With a hiatus for war service from 1940–1 until 1947/8, Davenport continued to contribute not only the chapter on the 'Late Tudor Period, Excluding Drama', but also the chapter on 'Earlier Stuart and the Commonwealth Period, Excluding Drama' until volume 37 in 1958.
[177] Whitelock (1901–1982), one of the most distinguished Anglo-Saxonists of the twentieth century, may be regarded as representative of many academic women and women contributors to *YWES* during this period. Simon Keynes writing in the *DNB* (2004) comments that it 'was not easy in the 1930s and 1940s for a woman to make a successful career as an academic, and it was some time before Whitelock achieved the advancement that she so richly deserved' (pp. 692–93). In 1945 she applied for the vacant Rawlinson and Bosworth Professorship of Anglo-Saxon at Oxford, which went to another *YWES* contributor, C. L. Wrenn. This was a terrible disappointment for Whitelock, but in 1957 she became Elrington Bosworth professor of Anglo-Saxon at the University of Cambridge.
[178] *YWES*, 23, 1945, p. 3.

Dorothy Whitelock, Dorothy Everett, Gladys D. Willcock, Beatrice White, Edith J. Morley, and Dorothy Margaret Stuart. Of special note amongst these, is the redoubtable Edith Julia Morley, the first female Professor of English in a British university.[179] From the first volume of *YWES* in 1919, she wrote the chapter on 'The Eighteenth Century' until volume 38 (1960). Her run of upwards of forty years is the longest in the history of *YWES*. Her first contribution in 1919, nearly fourteen pages in length, encompassed 15 books including reprinted lectures, but no articles. Her accounts are largely descriptive, but on occasion, her views are made clear. In volume 24, for example, she includes a detailed account of the value of Edward N. Hooker's edition of *The Critical Works of John Dennis*. Hooker's edition 'for the first time enables the modern reader to judge for himself the worth and the standpoint of that much-abused and little known author'.[180] Her final chapter in volume 38 (1959), although curtailed by illness, proves further evidence of a generosity of spirit and a remarkable awareness of which works will stand the test of time. Amongst the books she describes is Ian Watt's *The Rise of the Novel: Studies in Defoe, Richardson and Fielding*. Morley concludes her account by remarking that 'the book is full of interesting suggestions…[and] will have to be consulted by all those who wish to study the development of fiction as an outgrowth of changed social conditions and the new importance of a middle-class audience in the eighteenth century'.[181]

A quarter of a century of *YWES* was marked in 1946 by the appearance of volume 25, which very much follows the general appearance of earlier volumes, though no advertisements are included. Notable among the contributors is Vivian de Sola Pinto, Professor of English Literature at the University of Nottingham from 1938 until 1961, who contributed the chapter on the 'Restoration Period' from volume 25 until volume 43 (1964). An experienced editor, Pinto's output also includes biographical and critical studies and his own *The City that Shone: An Autobiography*, which is dedicated to the memory of his former captain, Siegfried Sassoon in the Royal Welsh Fusiliers, with whom he served from 1915 to 1919 in Gallipoli and on the Western front.

Volume 27, published in 1948 and reviewing material produced in 1946, is the first true post-war *YWES*. In length 264 pages with a fourteen-page Index and advertisements, there is, as Boas, the editor, comments 'a marked increase in the number of books published and available for notice', some of these being retrospective.[182]

Succeeding volumes follow a similar pattern to this, and maintain a comprehensive level of coverage, including notices of all the major publications, series, and

---

[179] She became Professor of English Language in 1908 at Reading, a Chair that was not replaced on her retirement. Morley was a great champion of women's rights, and a renowned editor and writer. Rather shamefully, when at the EA Executive Committee meeting in May 1949, a letter from J. M. Nosworthy, then a lecturer at the University College of Wales, Aberystwyth, was read asking whether a volume of Essays to celebrate Morley's 75th birthday could be published under the auspices of the English Association, the Executive Committee 'were unanimous in placing on record their Appreciation of her services to the Association', especially with regard to *YWES*, 'but regretted that owing to the financial position of the Association it was not possible to comply with [this] request'.
[180] *YWES*, 24, 1946, p. 171.
[181] *YWES*, 38, 1959, p. 196.
[182] *YWES*, 27, 1948, p. 3.

journals in the field. Volume 29 (1950), with its new cover design, reviews the publication of the first volume of *Shakespeare Survey*, edited by Allardyce Nicoll, the contributor to the annual Shakespeare *YWES* chapter. Boas, the editor, assesses the first *Shakespeare Survey* and concludes it is a 'well planned and executed scholarly enterprise'.[183] Another annual publication to stand the test of time, which also appeared in 1948 and was reviewed in volume 29, is the first issue of *Studies in Bibliography*, then the *Papers of the Bibliographical Society of the University of Virginia*, edited by Fredson Bowes. It is referred to in Strickland Gibson's chapter 15, 'Bibliographica', as 'the most interesting bibliographical publication of 1948' and 'finely printed'.[184]

It was in the 1950s that major changes to *YWES* took place. In volume 30 (1951), for example, there are some notable changes of contributor. Thus, Dr. H.V. Routh, the author of 'The Nineteenth Century and After', died in May 1951, having written his chapter since the journal's inception. Routh had been a member of the EA since 1913, and served on its Executive Committee from 1944.[185] In addition to contributing to *YWES*, he frequently contributed to *English* and *Essays and Studies*. Although on the whole his *YWES* assessments were positive ones, he could also make critical judgements, as was the case with his observations on Allardyce Nicoll's *A History of Late Nineteenth Century Drama, 1850–1900* (published in1946). Routh admonishes Nicoll, a regular *YWES* contributor, for overlooking one of the most important elements shaping the theatre: Nicoll 'tells us nothing…about the succession of artists who did so much to make the drama live and often brought to light the spirit and significance of plays which the literary critic considers worthless'. Routh evinces Irving's production of *The Bells* and Herbert Beerbohm Tree's production of *The Vandyke*, and concludes that that 'drama is an art which lives on the stage in collaboration with the cast'.[186]

Other noticeable changes from volume 30 onwards include the appearance of chapters from Geoffrey Bullough and Herbert J. Davis. The former contributed the first chapter 'Literary History and Criticism: General Works' until volume 32, taking over chapter thirteen, 'The Nineteenth Century and After, I' in volume 33. Bullough, Professor of English Language and Literature at King's College, London,[187] author of the seminal eight volume *Narrative and Dramatic Sonnets of Shakespeare* (1957–1975), was forced through the pressure of work to stop contributing to *YWES*, with Volume 37. Herbert J. Davis, Reader in Textual Criticism at Oxford University and editor of the *Complete Prose Works of Jonathan Swift*, took over Chapter Fifteen, 'Bibliographica', from Strickland Gibson in 1953. He continued for three volumes until being replaced by John Crow of King's College, London who was unable to produce the chapter in time for the publication of volume 36 in 1957. The coverage of 'Bibliography and Textual Studies' then lapsed for many years until the tradition of coverage, unbroken from the first volume until volume 35 was

---

[183] *YWES*, 29, 1950, p. 144.
[184] *YWES*, 29, 1950, p. 277.
[185] The first Byron Professor of English Literature and Institutions at the University of Athens, and from 1938–1939, the founder and Director of the first Institute of English Studies in Greece.
[186] *YWES*, 27, 1948, p. 244.
[187] Instigator of the first American Literature undergraduate degree in a British institution.

revived in a different incarnation with volume 66 published in 1988, and reviewing books from 1986. During these years, both Davis and Bullough represented an international perspective in their scholarship that was (and indeed, still is) typical of *YWES* contributors; such a perspective is reflected in the pages of the journal's coverage, and in the introduction in volume 35, of a chapter devoted to American Literature, covering publications for the year 1954, published in 1956.

It was in 1955 that F. S. Boas finally stepped down as editor. He had been assisted by Professor C. H. Herford, by Dr. Mary S. Serjeantson for seven years, and for the last five years by Professor Beatrice White. Succeeding Boas in 1956, Professor White had individual responsibility for changes reflecting an innate conservatism in Boas' later years as editor. A decrease in the type size and moving to two columns made the work a better size, a format continued until volume 55 (1976). Perhaps a more important change, and a reflection of changing times, was the introduction of a separate chapter on American literature. Previously there had been some coverage of American literature in the chapter, 'The Nineteenth Century and After'. For instance, P. M. Yarker in his survey of periodical literature published during 1953 notes articles on Washington Irving, James Fenimore Cooper, and Hawthorne.[188] However, earlier American writers, and others such as Whitman, Wharton, or Emerson received scant treatment and twentieth-century authors hardly merited a mention. Marcus Cunliffe, a pioneering figure in the history of American studies in the United Kingdom was the first contributor to the chapter on American Literature. Professor of American History and Institutions at Manchester University initially, from 1965 until 1980 Cunliffe became Professor of American Studies at the University of Sussex, and then moved to George Washington University, Washington, D.C. His first *YWES* contribution occupied sixteen pages. Cunliffe continued to contribute the chapter until volume 38 published in 1960. He was succeeded by his colleague at the University of Manchester, G. H. Moore. More than forty years later the chapter instigated by Beatrice White had grown to two large chapters. In volume 84, published in 2005, the chapter covering 'American Literature to 1900' has three contributors running to twenty pages of text; the chapter on 'American Literature: The Twentieth Century' has eight contributors and extends to over seventy pages of text.

Beatrice White's editorship over a ten-year period represents the culmination of fifteen or more years of association with the EA, and a period of growth for the journal. White, a specialist in the late medieval and early Renaissance periods, was an academic at Westfield College, London University, where from 1961 to 1966 she was Vice Principal of the College, and in 1967, two years before her retirement, Professor of English Language and Literature. Significantly, in 1956 she was the first woman to lecture to the Medieval Academy of America at Harvard University.[189] Dorsch, in the Preface to the 1964 *YWES*, writes of the expansion of the journal, which occurred

---

[188] *YWES*, 34, 1955, pp. 288–89.
[189] Margaret Connolly, 'White, Beatrice Mary Irene (1902–1986)', *Oxford Dictionary of National Biography*, Oxford University Press, 2004 *DNB* (2004).

under her editorship and of her encouraging and outstanding work as editor.[190] As part of her work for the EA, White also brought out issues of *Essays and Studies* for 1962 and 1983, and made numerous other contributions to that series. In 1972, her erstwhile co-editor, Dorsch, oversaw the edition of an *Essays and Studies* volume, brought out in her honour. Apart from Dorsch himself, there were nine other contributors including overseas colleagues; the bibliography of her work comprised more than four pages of items, testimony to her own scholarship, as well as her work on behalf of the EA. Indeed, following her death in 1986, *YWES* 65 (1987) was dedicated to her. In addition, the English Association instituted the Beatrice White Prize, which is awarded every year through *YWES* for the most impressive article or book on a pre-1590 literary topic.[191]

In her Preface for volume 37 (1958) covering publications from 1956, White announced that 'material once incorporated in the chapter "Bibliographica" is now disseminated through the various chapters concerned'. The growth of *YWES* during the two years she edited it single-handedly 'has been so vigorous and lusty that the Editor can no longer deal with the material' alone, and thus T. S. Dorsch, lecturer and her junior colleague at Westfield College, joined her as assistant editor.[192] The growth in academic publications is easily illustrated by the list of Abbreviations contained within *YWES*: when White initially assisted Boas with volume 31 (1952), there were thirty-eight Abbreviations listed; volume 37, six years later enumerated seventy-one regular journals covered by *YWES* reviewers. In addition, there were now sixteen chapters; as one might expect, Chapters 13 and 14 in Boas' final volume (the unimaginatively entitled 'Nineteenth Century and After I' and 'Nineteenth Century and After II') became, with White's first volume, 'The Nineteenth Century', 'The Twentieth Century', with a separate chapter on American Literature.

By the publication of volume 41 (1962), covering items from 1960, the size of the volume had grown to over 300 pages of double column text with 17 pages of triple columned Indexes.[193] By the time that T.S. Dorsch, Professor of English at Durham University, succeeded Beatrice White in 1966, *YWES* had grown to 340 pages, and when Geoffrey Harlow took over as Editor in 1969's volume 48, he noted that during Dorsch's years of editorship of *YWES*, 'the volume has grown in size by more than half as much again, a growth that reflects both the swelling flood of English Studies and the widening scope of the volume'.[194] Dorsch's association with the EA didn't cease with his retiring from *YWES* editorship; he had, for a number of years, contributed to significant chapters on 'Literary History and Criticism: General Works' and 'Shakespeare'; he continued to contribute to *YWES* until volume 61, covering publications for the year 1981. In the autumn of 1989 he was still on the EA Executive Council, after some forty years of work on the Association's behalf.

---

[190] See Connolly, *DNB*, *ibid*.
[191] The first recipient was Rosalind Field for 'The Heavenly Jerusalem in *Pearl*', *Modern Language Review* 81, 1986, pp. 7–17, announced in the Preface to *YWES* 67, covering the year 1986.
[192] He was editor from 1966–1968.
[193] Volume 42 was the last published by OUP for many years. It moved first to John Murray with volume 43, then to Blackwell Publishers with volume 62.
[194] *YWES*, 48, 1969, p. 5.

1967–2005

In the last thirty-five years, the size and scope of *YWES* has grown enormously, and the bare statistics are extraordinary. The Jubilee volume, 50, produced in 1971, reviewing publications from 1969, was edited by Geoffrey Harlow, with Elizabeth M. Bennan and James Redmond as Assistant Editors. In their Preface, Harlow and Redmond pay tribute to their predecessors. They note that the first volume 'contained a modest 133 pages' and that the fifth volume reviewed 274 books and 214 articles. They also remark that there was a decrease in the number of books and articles reviewed during the later 1930s, which resulted, of course, in the volume becoming smaller. While the Second World War made an impact in a number of different ways, as has been discussed, since that period, the journal has essentially grown year-on-year. The Jubilee volume itself includes coverage of 1,000 books and 1,600 articles, and it is observed that not only did American Literature require two chapters, but also 'other literatures in English' were in need of much fuller review space than had previously been given over to the field.

The editors judiciously sum up a dilemma still facing *YWES*: 'We may soon reach a parting of the ways, where the choice lies between division into two volumes, or much greater selectivity. Cost militates against the first'.[195] Increased selectivity, they add, 'would shift the balance from description to evaluation' and make numerous additional demands upon contributors already under great pressure. The Jubilee volume covered, as a matter of course, 313 series or journals (noted in the Abbreviations). There were 452 pages, sixteen chapters and two indexes, the latter extending to 32 pages of triple columns. Twenty volumes later, *YWES* 70, covering the year 1988 and published by Blackwell for the EA, had grown to an unwieldy 926 pages.[196] It was edited by Gordon Campbell, with the assistance of six associate editors each responsible for several of the seventeen chapters. The Index extends in double columns from pages 836–926. Abbreviations reflect the enormous growth in coverage: these extend from pages xi–xxxvii for Journals, Series and Reference works; to pages xxxviii–lxi for the publishers' listing. There are nineteen chapters, including the final chapter on 'New Literatures in English', and sixty-seven contributors, the largest number contributing to 'Twentieth-Century Literature'. During the early 1990s, indeed, it became manifestly clear that *YWES* could not be sustained in that same form: the volume of publications to be reviewed, the large numbers of contributors to be organised and edited, and the vast increase in 'Literary Theory', in particular, all mitigated against maintaining the single-volume format. The result was the formation of a separate publication, *The Year's Work in Critical and Cultural Theory*, to be discussed below.

The tremendous expansion of material covered by *YWES* is a reflection not merely of a vast explosion in English Studies, and, in the 1990s, British Studies, American Studies, and Cultural Studies, but also the result of institutional expansion of the universities and the need to publish professionally or to perish. An insight into

---
[195] *YWES*, 50, 1971, p. 5.
[196] But published late, so great was the pressure on contributors to cover immense amounts of material.

the growth of the subject is reflected in the size of a standard guide such as M.H. Abrams, *A Glossary of Literary Terms*, a book that defines and discusses terms, critical theories, and points of view that are commonly used to classify, analyse, interpret, and write the history of works of literature'.[197] The first edition completed by Abrams was published in 1957. It was itself a revision of D.S. Norton's and Peter Rushton's *Glossary* first published in 1941 and in January 1956 in its twelfth printing. In 1957, Abram's *Glossary* had 105 pages; by its eighth edition in 2005, this range had extended to 370 pages.

The growth in English Studies reflected in a broad sense by Abrams' terminological definitions, and indicated by the expansion in *YWES*, is itself part of the explosion in the production of knowledge since the Second World War, especially in the fields of sciences. An important aspect of this phenomenon has been the increasing production of research by teams of scholars and *YWES* is no exception to this. The age of the single editor like Sidney Lee (1921–25), F. S. Boas (1926–68), Beatrice White (1956–65), and T. S. Dorsch (1966–68), has gone, and probably forever. Geoffrey Harlow, who edited the Jubilee volume in 1969, had two Assistant Editors. Three volumes later, with the coverage for 1972 published in 1974, the editor, James Redmond, worked with four associate editors. The sense that even greater teamwork was a necessity is seen in volume 69, covering 1988, and published in 1991, where two editors, Laurel Brake and Gordon Campbell, plus an executive editor and three associate editors worked to get the volume out. Volume 84 covering work published in 2003 has two editors and eight associate editors, each responsible for different chapters.

The involvement of greater numbers of contributors and editors has become essential to completing the vast amount or reviewing and organising. The sixteen chapters in the Jubilee volume were the product of individual hands and teams of collaborators. The first three chapters, and chapters 5, 8, 9, and 16 were the products of individual reviewers, covering, respectively 'Literary History and Criticism: General Works', 'English Language', 'Old English Literature', 'The Earlier Sixteenth Century', 'English Drama 1550–1660, excluding Shakespeare', 'The Later Sixteenth Century, Excluding Drama', and 'American Literature: The Twentieth Century'. In volume 84, none of the eighteen chapters is written by a sole author, indicating that all areas of literary and linguistic studies have required teamwork to complete the reviews, so greatly have numbers of publications grown.[198] Joint authorship by two people is the minimum within chapters and applies to five areas, while the vast chapter covering 'Modern Literature' has ten authors, and the first, covering the substantial field of 'English Language', has eleven.

Other important expansions and adaptations in the history of the volume reflect not just the growth of English Studies, but its widening remit and the changing nature of the field. Volume 63 of *YWES* published in 1985 introduced a new chapter

---

[197] M. H. Abrams, *A Glossary of Literary Terms*, 8th ed., 2005.
[198] Both the North American tenure-track insistence on major publications and the United Kingdom's Research Assessment Exercise, with its emphasis on written scholarly output, have inevitably created an enormous expansion in the numbers of journals, journal articles, books, and edited books, of very varying quality, but most requiring review.

on 'African, Caribbean, and Canadian Literature'; a year earlier, volume 62 included for the first time a separate chapter on Literary Theory. It reviewed current theoretical work in the constituent disciplines of Hermeneutics; Structuralism/Post-structuralism; Poetics; Semiotics; Psychoanalysis and Criticism; Rhetoric and Deconstruction, and Historical Materialist Criticism which included Literary History, Marxism and Feminism. This new chapter included 'a more discursive review of the state of the subject in 1980, at the beginning of the decade'.[199] Written by Robert Young, then a lecturer at the University of Southampton, the chapter extended for fifty pages. Young continued to write the chapter until volume 63 covering 1982 published in 1986. In subsequent volumes, three others assisted Young, and the chapter continued to be a collaborative effort until volume 71, covering 1990 and published in 1993. The chapter had by then expanded to seventy-seven pages written by seven different hands. It became obvious that this whole area of Theory required more space of its own, and thus in 1994, the EA published the first issue of *The Year's Work in Critical and Cultural Theory* expanding extensively the material previously covered in *YWES*. The editor of the new volume was Stephen Regan who edited the first two volumes.[200]

Other changes over a thirty-five year period involve publishers. John Murray published the Jubilee volume in 1971 for the EA, and continued to publish *YWES* until volume 60, covering the year 1979. Volume 62, the first edited by Laurel Brake with a team of four associate editors, was published for the EA by John Murray based in London and by the Humanities Press in New Jersey. Other innovations, besides the changing publishers and consequent changing covers of the volumes, was the short-lived practice of listing the 'Best Books and Articles' in the given year; in the first instance, this was the best of 1985.[201] With volume 68, covering 1987 and published in 1990 by Basil Blackwell and the Humanities Press, footnotes indicating books and articles referred to in the text were eliminated, and incorporated into the text itself to clear the page and save space and a section of Books Reviewed appeared at the end of each chapter.

Volume 69 covering the year 1988 published in 1991 was edited by Laurel Brake and Gordon Campbell, with an executive editor and three associate editors; volumes 70 and 71 were edited by Gordon Campbell with Deborah Madsen as executive editor and five associate editors; volume 72, which came out in the same year as volume 71 in order to try to get the reviews back on a two-year schedule of publication, was edited by Stephen Regan and Elaine Treharne with five associate editors. Elaine Treharne edited volume 73 covering the year 1992: this was the first of a sequence of volumes produced by Blackwell Publishers alone. Peter J. Kitson and Elaine Treharne edited volume 74, with three associate editors; Peter J. Kitson became the sole main editor until volume 78 published in 2000.

---

[199] *YWES*, 62, 1984, p. v.
[200] He also edited with Elaine Treharne Volume 72 of *YWES* and served as an associate editor for Volumes 69, 70, and 71.
[201] *YWES*, 66, 1988, pp. 771–74.

In 2001, publication reverted from Blackwell's to Oxford University Press with volume 79, covering books and articles from 1998. Volume 80, also published in 2001, witnessed a series of innovations, including two new editors, both in American universities, William Baker and Kenneth Womack who worked with a team of eight associate editors. This volume was the first whose contents went online as well as appearing subsequently in the usual hardcopy format.

The proliferation of documentation and knowledge caused by the Internet during the 1990s has created a revolution in communications and publications. In the early 1990s, most academics and their students used index-card catalogues in university libraries, bibliographies in print, and traditional print books and journals for their research. Reviewers for *YWES* relied on the provision of dot-matrix bibliographic printouts from the Modern Language Association of America,[202] which today, of course, is available in searchable form online. In this centenary year of the EA, bibliographies abound on the Internet; books can be ordered electronically; most libraries subscribe to electronic resources that include Ingenta and JSTOR, with their vast holdings of digitised journals; and traditional resources like books are themselves available in digital form; or easily purchased from bookshop websites. The electronic revolution has transformed the academic world. Some journals are published exclusively on-line, indeed, and do not appear in hardcopy format at all, and numerous, new electronic journals are launched regularly. *YWES* has taken advantage of the Internet, yet retains its traditional mode of publication simultaneously with electronic publication. The electronic access to journals and email notifications of their content has proved to be of considerable benefit to *YWES*, giving its contributors far greater access to a wider, more comprehensive range of journals. While access to the information is much quicker or almost immediate, the increase of material to be sifted and read makes up for any potential time the Internet might save. Moreover, archiving such electronic material has proved a problem, and is likely to become a major issue in publications in the immediate years to come: JSTOR has proved a successful and lasting method of storing digital information such as past journals.[203] *YWES* remains, at present then, an annual narrative bibliography which aims to cover all work of quality in English Studies published in a given year. It exists in both hardcopy and online versions, though one might ponder the future longevity, for all such publications, of the traditional 'book' version.

Before moving on to review other EA publications it would be useful to briefly pay tribute to those who contributed for a significant length of time to *YWES* during these latter decades. Mention should be made of the textual editor, Elizabeth M. Brennan, who served as an Associate Editor to the Jubilee Volume 50 covering 1969 published in 1971 and six subsequent volumes through to volume 56 covering 1975 published in 1977. Richard Middlewood Wilson contributed the English Language chapter from volume 25 covering 1944 published in 1946 until volume 52 covering

---

[202] Which arrived, like the Medieval Rolls Series, in a huge long print-out, to be separated along the perforations and sent out to individual contributors by the editor(s).
[203] For the history of electronic publication and in the Internet, and for the implications of these new media, see Roger C. Schonfeld, *JSTOR: A History*, 2003, especially on this latter point, p. xv.

1971 published in 1973. Others such as B.E.C. Davis contributed to *YWES* for at least a decade; Davis wrote The Renaissance chapter for over a decade in the 1960s to early 1970s. Joyce Bazire wrote the Chaucer chapter from volume 34, published in 1955, until volume 47, published in 1968, when she was joined by her colleague, the medieval drama specialist, David Mills. They continued to write the chapter jointly until volume 60. David Mills continued to contribute to the Chaucer chapter until volume 69 covering 1988 published in 1991. Both these long-serving valued contributors lectured in English Language at the University of Liverpool, where many *YWES* contributors worked. Indeed, Bazire was introduced to *YWES* by the then Head of the English Language Department at Liverpool University, Professor Simeon Potter. Others who completed ten year stints as *YWES* contributors include Helen Wilcox who began to co-author The Seventeenth Century chapter from volume 61 (1982), which covered material published in 1980, and continued writing this chapter until volume 70.[204] However, even her length of service cannot compare with that of James Ogden, a member of the English Department at Aberystwyth, who first contributed to *YWES* with volume 56 published in 1975: thirty years later he is still contributing to the chapter on The Later Seventeenth Century. Ogden's run is probably the third longest in the history of *YWES*, with only F. S. Boas and the redoubtable Edith J. Morley, writing for a longer length of time.

Chapters produced by various contributors allow both for continuity and change. Amongst those who provided continuity in the chapter on English Language are Richard Coates from the University of Sussex and Wim van der Wurff at Leiden. Coates provided the account of the year's work in Onomastics from the 1980s into the 1990s. In volume 63, Language as a whole covered only nineteen pages; by volume 84 the chapter had grown to one hundred and twenty nine pages with eleven contributors. When Coates began to review, there was one other contributor, Wim van der Wurff, who wrote in the section on Morphology and Syntax for volume 73. He is still contributing to these sections for the 2006 volume 85. From volume 73, Olga Fischer, from the University of Amsterdam, contributed to Early and Late Syntax and Morphology with Wim van der Wurff, until she focused solely on her Associate Editorship duties for the increasingly voluminous first chapter on English Language.

Three scholars who usually contributed single-authored chapters over the years include Bernard Harris, C.A. Patrides and Ron E. Pritchard. Harris, who was Professor of English and Related Literatures at the University of York, wrote the chapter on Later Elizabethan and Early Stuart Drama from volume 45, published in 1966, until volume 60, by which time the chapter had become English Drama 1550–1660: Excluding Shakespeare. Constantinos A. Patrides, a distinguished early Miltonist, contributed with others to the chapter on the Earlier Seventeenth Century: Excluding Drama, for volumes 50 and 51. With volume 52 (1973), he started writing a section on Milton, which thereafter became a separate chapter,

---

[204] Wilcox lectured at the University of Liverpool from 1979 to 1991 before moving to a Chair at Groningen.

which Patrides continued writing from the University of Michigan when he returned to the USA until volume 63, published in 1985. Another distinguished Miltonist, Gordon Campbell, Professor of Renaissance Literature and Culture at the University of Leicester and a former Chair and President of the EA, then wrote the chapter on Milton for two volumes, 64 and 65.

Another regular *YWES* contributor over many volumes includes Ron E. Pritchard, who taught at the University of Keele from 1965 until 1996. He worked as *YWES* associate editor for volumes 74–78 and wrote the chapter on the Earlier Sixteenth Century from volume 59 (1980) to volume 73 (1995). The latter chapter extended over sixteen pages, the former barely four. Henry Claridge is another regular *YWES* contributor : he contributed with A. Robert Lee, then his colleague at the University of Kent at Canterbury, to the chapter on American Literature to 1900, with volume 68 published in 1990 and is still contributing, sixteen volumes later, with volume 84, covering 2003 published in 2005.

Indeed, the American Literature chapters have maintained considerable consistency of contributors and this is largely due to the associate editors, Janet Beer, who is responsible for the pre-twentieth-century American literature chapter, and Steven Price, responsible for the twentieth-century chapter. Janet Beer, now Dean at Manchester Metropolitan University, first contributed (as Janet Goodwyn) to *YWES* when she wrote with Henry Claridge in volume 71 (1993). She contributed until volume 78 (2000), and became associate editor with volume 79. Steven Price, a specialist in American drama at the University of Wales at Bangor, has written for American Literature: The Twentieth Century from volume 73 published in1995. Then there were only two other contributors to the chapter, which ran for fifty-five pages. By volume 83, covering 2002 (2004), the chapter ran for eighty-seven pages and there were seven other contributors, in addition to Price, who has been associate editor since volume 79. Beer and Price inherited their sections from Lionel Kelly, who taught from 1965 to 2001 at the University of Reading, and who was an associate editor of *YWES* from volumes 70–78 (1992–2000), also contributing on twentieth-century American Literature from volume 68 to 79.

Mention should be made of other *YWES* contributors of long-standing, such as Carole Durix, who contributed the New Zealand and South Pacific sections of the New Literatures chapter between 1987 and 1998; and Trevor R. Griffiths, who wrote the Drama section of the Twentieth Century chapter from volume 65 to volume 75. Owen Knowles, an associate editor from volume 61 (1982) until volume 66 covering 1985 (1988), was a contributor to various areas of Nineteenth-Century Literature from volume 58 (1979) until volume 65 (1988). And finally, an unsung hero of the volume is Ann Dean, who has been responsible for the ever-expanding indexes, which have to be produced accurately under extreme pressure. Her first part index to volume 72 (1993) extended to twenty-four triple-columned pages of Critics, and forty-six double-columned pages of Authors and Subjects Treated. By contrast, her two indexes to volume 83 (2004) encompassed fifty-one and seventy-four double-columned page listings.

The Year's Work in Critical and Cultural Theory [*YWCCT*]

From volume 62 (for works published in 1981) to volume 71, published in 1993, *YWES* included a separate chapter on literary theory. During this period, as Stephen Regan indicates in his Preface to the first volume of *YWCCT* reviewing 1991 publications: 'the field of critical theory has broadened considerably, developing its new perspectives and approaches in close association with the growing appeal and popularity of "cultural studies"'.[205] Regan hoped that the new volume, published in 1994, would be useful for scholars in art history, popular music and media studies, in addition to those working on literature and literary criticism. The first two volumes contained two parts. The first, in the manner of *YWES* consisted of a narrative bibliography; the second part, in a new initiative, contained a selection of guest essays on a particular topic.

The first part of the initial volume, 'The Year's Work in Critical Theory', contained eight essays, five of which were the product of individual contributors, the others written by co-authors. Subjects covered in this first volume, arguably at the height of literary theory's prestige within English Departments, are entirely representative of then-current fields of enquiry and provide a snapshot of dominant approaches: General Critical Theory; Rhetoric and Deconstruction; Psychoanalysis; Feminism; Historicism; Colonial Discourse/Postcolonial Theory; Art History; and Popular Music. These eight chapters expanded into twelve totalling 238 pages in the second volume, which was published in 1996 reviewing works from 1992. In *YWCCT* 3, these chapters increased again to include a chapter on Queer Theories and Cultures, and one on Film Studies. This volume, published in 1997 contained a narrative bibliography, extending to 382 pages in total. It was edited by Kate McGowan, a theoretician and modernist at Manchester Metropolitan University, who was also responsible for the next eight volumes (3–10, covering work published in 1993 until 2000). This stability of editorship permitted the journal to flourish, and the tenth volume—McGowan's last—which covered work published in 2000 in fifteen chapters, appeared in 2002. The eleventh volume, published in 2003 and edited by Martin McQuillan of Leeds University with an Assistant Editor, contained sixteen chapters and 338 pages.

In his Preface to the first volume, Stephen Regan had written that 'Part II of each [volume] will contain a collection of specially commissioned essays on current theoretical issues and debates'. This plan worked for the first two volumes: the first volume contained ten contributions marking 'the occasion of Terry Eagleton's fiftieth birthday in 1991 and his appointment as Warton Professor of English at Oxford University in 1992'.[206] Volume 2 included seven commissioned essays on 'Critical Theory: An International Perspective'. The third volume, the first edited by Kate McGowan, had one part devoted to fourteen chapters of narrative evaluating varying topics in critical theory. Volumes 4 (1996) to 7 (covering 1997) had as their

---
[205] *YWCCT*, 1, 1994, p. ix.
[206] *YWCCT*, 1, 1993, p. ix.

second part 'Culture and Communications'. These parts consisted of six or more chapters (six in volume 4, eleven in volume 5, ten in volume 6, and eleven in volume 7) focusing on the field of cultural theory with particular attention to work developing in the USA and Australia. Australian contributors dominate these volumes. By volume 10, the areas of theory reviewed included Critical Theory: General; Marxism(s) and Postmarxism(s); Feminisms; Multiculturalism; and Marginal Identity, Culture and Art.

In a period of great transformation and constant evolution of theoretical fields, some contributor continuity may be seen in *YWCCT*. One contributor, David Buckley, a Munich-based academic, wrote a chapter on Popular Music for the first eleven volumes. Patrick Williams, at Nottingham Trent University, wrote most of the chapter on Colonial Discourse/Postcolonial Theory for almost all of the first ten volumes. Others who were regular *YWCCT* authors range from Adrian Page of the University of Luton contributing the chapter on Semiotics from volumes 2 to 7. Vicky Lebeau from the University of Sussex wrote the chapter on Psychoanalysis for the first five volumes. Ian Saunders of the University of Western Australia has written on Unheard Cultures from volumes 5 through 11; and Tara Brabazon on Australian Popular Culture and Media Studies from volumes 5 to 10. The title page of *YWCCT* also displays an impressive list of up to twelve Advising Editors for each volume. These include the most distinguished names at the time in the field of critical and cultural discourse, among them Steven Connor at Birkbeck; Terry Eagleton, currently at the University of Manchester; Linda Hutcheon (University of Toronto); Fredric Jameson from Duke University; Christopher Norris at Cardiff; Elaine Showalter (then at Princeton); Stan Smith of Nottingham Trent University; and Patricia Waugh at the University of Durham.

VII
Publications: Journals

From *Bulletin* to *English*

The *Bulletin*

If *YWES* represents the annual scholarly face of the EA during the years between the two great World Wars of the twentieth century, much of the history of the association may be found in its *Bulletin*, distributed at least once annually to its membership. The *Bulletin* was first published in 1914 and ceased with issue 81 in November 1935, when it was replaced by *English*. It 'kept members and branches of the association in touch with each other'.[207] Essentially an information missive, the *Bulletin* contained basic information for the EA membership; for instance, *Bulletin* 35 (September 1918) contains details of the Annual Meeting divided into 'Business Meeting', 'The President's Address', and 'The Conference'; a 'Bibliography'; 'Notes'; 'Proceedings of Committees'; 'Proceedings of Branches'; 'New Members'; and 'Notices'. The report to the Business Meeting, communicated that:

> In moving the adoption of the Report and Financial Statement, the Chairman emphasized the fact that, despite the War, the membership of the Central Body had continued to increase. He also alluded to the satisfactory circulation of the Association's Anthology, now in its 13th edition; to the letter addressed to the Vice-Chancellor of the University of Cambridge by the Association, expressing satisfaction with the institution of an English Tripos and criticizing certain of the recommendations of the Special Board for Mediaeval and Modern Languages; to the memorial addressed to the Board of Education on their regulations for Advanced Courses in Secondary Schools commenting on the place assigned to English…[208]

'The President's Address', when Sir Sidney Lee spoke on 'The Perspective of Biography', follows the report, with subsequent reports containing a review of the annual conference held at Bedford College in May 1918. The subject was 'The Place and Value of English Literature and Language in the Later Years of School Life' and the report occupies almost seven pages of the *Bulletin* conveying a considerable diversity of opinion.[209]

An enumerative 'Bibliography' giving details of some of the work in English Language and Literature appearing in the intervals between Bulletins reminds the reader that it 'does not claim to be complete, nor does its mention of a book necessarily imply recommendation'.[210] The remainder of the *Bulletin* is taken up with

---
[207] Hilda D. Spear, '*English*' in Alvin Sullivan, ed., *British Literary Magazines of the Modern Age, 1914–1984*, 1986, p. 165.
[208] *Bulletin*, 35, September 1918, p. 3.
[209] *Bulletin*, 35, September 1918, pp. 7–14.
[210] *Bulletin*, 35, September 1918, p. 14.

miscellaneous notes, proceedings of committees, proceedings of branches, lists of new members and various notices.

In short, the *Bulletin* contains a plethora of factual information about the specific activities of the EA each year on a national and regional basis. Hilda D. Spear writes in her account of *English* that 'It was not until 1935…a proposal for a regular [EA] membership was mooted. In June 1935 a special subcommittee of the association was set up to look into the problems of falling membership and to suggest ways of revitalizing the association'. A recommendation 'was that a special magazine should be started'.[211] This would replace the *Bulletin*, the final issue of which was number 81 for November 1935, consisting of twelve pages of reports, followed by six pages of EA publications and a final note on the demise of the *Bulletin*.

English

Under 'ENGLISH', English Association readers of the *Bulletin* learn that 'It is proposed to issue the first number of the Magazine entitled *English* in January 1936. The magazine will replace the Bulletin', and will 'record the activities and voice the policy of the Association, and…contain literary, university, and scholastic features'. There will be 'special sections devoted to Drama, Broadcasting, Correspondence, and the Association's work in the Empire and Overseas'.[212]

The initial editor of *English* was George Cookson, who edited the journal until he died in September 1949.[213] The first issue of *English* contains a five-paragraph Editorial in which its aims and objectives were outlined.[214] In addition to stimulating engagement with 'Drama, Broadcasting, Music, and Art as well as general literature', it intended to 'bring Teachers into contact with one another', such that *English* will 'promote a generative interchange of thought' on the subject of English—'one of the chief aims of the' EA.

> It is hoped…that the Magazine will be a bond of union between the numerous branches of the Association by focussing attention on common interests and aims, and through the section devoted to Colonial, Imperial, and Overseas activities will bring into close touch with the Association at home the work of Branches and members abroad, where problems are perhaps new and different.

Finally, Cookson hoped that *English* would bring new members to the EA. It didn't, because although members received it free, it was included in the membership fee. Its price initially was 'half-a-crown net', or 12½ pence for ninety pages.

In her excellent account of *English*, Hilda D. Spear (still, in 2006, a dynamic and engaged member of the EA) cites a review from *The Times*, 28 February 1936, which 'gave six and a half column inches to reviewing it'. The reviewer observes that *English* 'is a well-printed and dignified quarto; and, not content with being a medium

---

[211] Spear, p. 165.
[212] *Bulletin*, 81, November 1935, p. 8.
[213] His associate editor, Guy Boas, took over until 1954 when Margaret Willy, the poet and critic, became editor.
[214] *English*, 1, 1936, p. 1.

of communication for teachers of English and a bond between the many branches of the Association, it makes very good reading for the general'. Spear draws attention to the contrary fact that *English* was not well received by all EA members. In 1937, at an EA London Conference, it was attacked for 'lowering the standards and the prestige of the Association'. The editors of *English* should be 'promoting English scholarship rather than indulging in journalism'.[215]

The first issue contained Cookson's Editorial followed by observations drawing attention to the subsequent contents. These include articles by Sean O'Casey, 'His Father's Dublin Funeral', and Dorothy L. Sayers on 'Aristotle in Detective Fiction'. These are followed by eleven poems, variously by John Drinkwater, Laurence Binyon, Edmund Blunden and others. There are reviews of T. S. Eliot's *Murder in the Cathedral*, Caroline Spurgeon's *Shakespeare's Imagery*, amongst other books and plays. Correspondence is followed by a detailed 'Report of the Annual Dinner' held at the Hotel Metropole, on 11 October 1935: here, is included a report of Hilaire Belloc's address, J. E. Talbot and Guy Boas's replies—both of which draw attention to 'the fall in membership' and offer potential remedies to attract more and younger members through *English*. Among these are an increased interest in drama and the 'opportunity of discussing and considering the practical side of their work' on the part of the teachers of English.[216] Following brief accounts of other speakers at the Dinner, detailed summaries of the 'Proceedings of Branches'– in England, Scotland, Australia, India, South Africa and New Zealand follow.

Subsequent issues followed this pattern. The second issue, also published in 1936, reported in its Editorial that there were just over one hundred new EA members. This growth may be 'partly stimulated by the publication of *English*'. It also announced the creation of a library on its premises: 'It is desired to build up gradually a representative library of literary criticism'. This included work on 'the English language and educational books on the study and teaching of English'.[217] The first issue at the end of the report of the Dinner contains J. E. Talbot's one-paragraph tribute to one of the most important founding EA figures, A. C. Bradley, who died in 1935.

Another personality who played an important part in the EA activities during the years between the Wars was J. E. Talbot, music critic for the *Manchester Guardian*. From 1935, Talbot had served as Chair of the EA's Executive Committee. As EA Chair, 'he was always tactful and friendly in the conduct of … affairs'. The record of his death occupies a special blocked page of *English*.[218] In this manner, *English* continues the tradition of its predecessor, the *Bulletin*, in recording the demise of the Association's prominent members; in its reports of the Annual Dinner and details of the Annual General Meetings; and in its notifications of Proceedings of the Branches, both in the British Isles and overseas.

In addition to recording the deaths of founding figures, *English* is noted not merely for the space given over to its reviewing, but in significant attention paid to

---

[215] *English*, 11, 1956, p. 62; Spear, p. 166, respectively.
[216] *English*, 1, 2, 1936, p. 76.
[217] *English*, 1, 2, 1936, p. 95.
[218] *English*, 1, 5, 1937, p. 382.

correspondence from its members all over the world. The immediate pre-War *English*[219] contains a lengthy letter written by D. C. Moorehouse concerning 'one of the most interesting education ventures in New Zealand—the Government Correspondence School'. As the Editorial expressed it using the words of another founding EA father, the EA would 'carry on its activities' in spite of the outbreak of the War. Demonstrating its nationalist impulse, and its stalwart traditionalist outlook, the Executive Committee felt that 'at the present time there is special need for its work'. The Notes and Observations, in an explicit statement of Empire and Englishness, warned that 'even the romantic ideals in which the war of 1914 started found the strain of Shakespeare's *Henry V* before Agincourt, or even of Nelson's Trafalgar signal too lofty'. The black-outs could not be avoided: duty had to be done.

In her account of *English*, Hilda D. Spear notes that '[*English*] has a ready-made readership, for the price of the magazine is included in the annual subscription'.[220] This was certainly true of the period from the outbreak of the Second World War through to the mid-1960s. There were three editors during these years: George Cookson's long period as editor ceased in 1949, when Guy Boas took over until 1954; he was replaced from 1954 to 1975 by Margaret Willy. Three issues a year, in the Spring, Summer, and Autumn, were the norm from 1936, and the Oxford University Press was the continuous publisher. As has been noted, EA journals went through something of a crisis early in 1951 when financial deficits were brought to light. The increasing costs of paper and printing resulted in economies of size and in price increases.

Guy Boas' address, '*English* and its Contributors', given to the Association at a meeting in the Alliance Hall, Westminster in November 1950, and published in *English*,[221] should be seen, then, in the context of retrenchment, impending budgeting restrictions, and a need to defend its existence. Boas opens his remarks, occasioned by the fifteenth year of *English*, with a lament for the demise of *The London Mercury*, a literary magazine which ran from 1919 to 1939. According to Boas, in spite of its excellent contents and gifted editorship, *The London Mercury* was unable 'to maintain sufficient circulation to meet its costs'. He notes that 'since the *Mercury* disappeared prices of production have risen considerably, and it is very much harder today to make both ends meet where printing and publishing are concerned than it was then'. *English* is 'paid for out of the income of the Association, assisted by receipts from advertisements, and is not…primarily dependent on sales'. For Boas, this advantage 'carries a corresponding responsibility'; it should not compete 'with existing and long-standing literary journals, but at providing opportunity for serious writers, and especially poets, to publish work which otherwise they might find difficulty in placing'. This work should be of the highest quality and in areas difficult to place in other literary vehicles, light verse being just one example.

---

[219] *English*, 2, 12, 1939, pp. 396–97.
[220] Spear, p. 166.
[221] *English*, 8, 46, 1951, pp. 180–83. This issue also contains an unusual tribute, probably by George Cookson, to George Bernard Shaw who died in 1950. The tribute takes issue with the 'frequent assertion that as a dramatist, [Shaw] comes second to Shakespeare', p. 167.

Boas continues, '*English* should give special attention to the subject of English teaching'. It had not done so due to a lack of response from teachers. Boas writes that 'It is hard enough to teach English: to write about such teaching is more difficult still'. He does draw attention to valuable contributions on the subject from, for instance, Robert Hey Charles on 'English Teaching Today'. Charles, an EA member since 1934, who died in September 1951, served on the EA's Schools Committee and was the Chief Inspector of the Ministry of Education.[222] Boas provides other examples of contributions on the subject of the teaching of English by George Sampson, Nowell Smith, Ifor Evans, and others. Boas also indicates a further editorial problem confronting the journal: that of maintaining 'the balance between technical English scholarship and more purely literary work'. The EA 'has always contained two elements: (1) The professional teachers of English and (2) the amateurs of letters'. *English* must maintain a balance between the academic and the 'popular'; a 'unity of these two outlooks is the essence of what *English* should be'. Regarding the future of *English*, Boas asks each reader to secure more members for the EA: one reader, one new member. Also, and rather curiously, Boas states that it had been hoped to increase the sale of *English* to the general public by changing the colour of its cover 'from Oxford to Cambridge blue', the lighter blue, according to marketing experts, allegedly attracting more buyers at a railway bookstall. The aim of *English* and the EA, in the words of its first editor George Cookson, was 'to bring the best attention to the language and literature most widely known'. Boas closes on a nationalistic note, writing that 'England with the fortune of its temperate climate and its long experienced history has an example of stability and moderation still to give'. For him the EA can 'contribute to this influence' and *English* is part of that national influence.

Guy Boas was speaking and writing in a post-World War II era, which experienced traumatic change, and in Britain on the eve of the Festival of Britain, Boas' words represent a restatement of Britain's attempt to remind itself and others that it still had a role to play in world affairs. It is remarkable that, even in the darkest days of the Second World War, *English* maintained its production, interest, and quality. The fourth volume (numbers 19 through 24, Spring 1942 to Autumn 1943) is a fine illustration. The volume consists of 204 pages, with issues running to approximately 35 pages each. In number 19 (1942), the editor, George Cookson, uses the occasion of Faber and Faber's publication on 11 December 1941 of T. S. Eliot's *A Choice of Kipling's Verse …with an essay on Rudyard Kipling* to reflect upon the quality of Kipling's verse and Eliot's criticism. In his reflections, Cookson draws attention to an essay by Amaranatha Jha, Vice-Chancellor of Allahabad University, on 'Kipling the Poet'.[223] Cookson's Eliot on Kipling essays (4–8) is followed by a contribution from Wilfrid Wilson Gibson (1878–1962), better known for his poetry than prose exposition, and Una Ellis-Fermor writing on 'The Plays of G.B. Shaw'. These are followed

---

[222] See *English*, 9, 48, 1951, p. 268.
[223] Jha's exposition appeared in a publication which otherwise would be neglected in this history and represents an important part of the EA's overseas branches activities. Jha's essay appears with K. K. Mehrotra's 'Kipling and "the bubble reputation"' and others in *Essays and Studies by Members of the English Association, United Provinces Branch* (Allahabad, 1938).

by eleven reviews including those written by Nowell Smith, Dorothy Margaret Stuart, Vivian de Sola Pinto, and Margaret Willy, for example. There are also very brief 'Shorter Notices' of short singular paragraphs mostly of volumes of verse.

English 20 (1942) opens with an obituary notice (39–40) written by Nowell Smith for George Gordon, EA President in 1942, President of Magdalen College and Vice Chancellor of Oxford University, and Oxford Professor Poetry from 1933 to 1938.[224] Other contributions to this issue, include Lawrence Binyon writing on 'Berkshire and the Poets', Laura M. Ruggon 'Our Verbal Losses' and Una Ellis-Fermor reflecting on 'University Dramatic Societies'. Following reviews, there is 'Correspondence' consisting of a short letter; 'Association Notes', an account of London meetings held in spite of the war; and 'Proceedings of Branches' with details of English Association membership. The subsequent issues for volume four follow a similar pattern. In number 21 (1942) essays of interest range from Nowell Smith's extensive review of Eide Selincourt's *The Journals of Dorothy Wordsworth* and E. C. Pettit writing on 'A Study of Abraham Cowley', to Una Ellis-Fermor's 'Propaganda and the Drama'.

Number 22 for 1943 opens with a five paragraph unsigned 'Notes and Observations'. The subjects covered in the editorial range from 'The Public Schools Conundrum' to controversy 'On the subject of English usage'. Articles range from Arundell Esdaile's 'Dr. Johnson and the Young' to Harold Goad's 'International English' and the journalist S. R. Littlewood's account of 'Civic Theatres in Prospect'. By 'Civic Theatres', Littlewood refers to those paid 'out of national taxes and local rates' when peace emerges.[225] Reviewers in Number 22 include E. K. Chambers on C. J. Prouty's *George Gascoigne*; E. H. W. Meyerstein on C.S. Lewis' *A Preface to Paradise Lost*; Geoffrey Tillotson on G. Wilson Knight's *Chariot of Wrath*; and Vivian de S. Pinto on S. Sassoon's *The Weald of Youth*. Notice of the death of Professor Caroline Spurgeon, who was an original member of the EA, is included in 'Association Notes'.

The remaining 1943 issues devote much space to the deaths of Laurence Binyon and Lascelles Abercrombie. The former died in 1943, the latter in 1938. Nowell Smith leads number 23 with 'Thoughts on Laurence Binyon's Poetry' in which he makes high claims for Binyon as 'a visionary, a seer, and an orator'.[226] Number 24 is largely devoted to 'Lascelles Abercrombie—the Homage of Friends'. The contributions were intended to form part of a memorial volume consisting of tributes, since 'The war has prevented the publication of the volume as a whole'.[227] The tributes are in prose and also in poetry, including poems by Edmund Blunden, a lengthy one by Wilfrid Gibson, and J. Redwood Anderson.

Poetry is a noticeable feature of the war-time issues of *English*. In volume 4, 19–20 (Spring 1942–Autumn 1943), for example, there are ten poems of varying length. An eleventh poem, 'City Panorama', is by Evelyn Janes, aged 15. Poets included range from E. H. W. Meyerstein (two), to Patric Dickinson (two), and Ian L. Serraillier. Indeed the next issue of *English* finds space for Serraillier's 'The Bishop and the

---

[224] In 1923, Gordon contributed an essay on 'The Trojans in Britain' to *Essays and Studies*, 10, pp. 9–31and ran an EA Branch at Leeds University (*English* 20.4 [1942], p. 37).
[225] *English*, 4, 22, 1943, p. 123.
[226] *English*, 4, 23, 1943, p. 145.
[227] *English*, 4, 24, 1943, p. 174.

Devil', a lengthy eight-paragraph narrative poem based upon the naming of 'the high Alpine Mass joining Zermatt with the plains of Italy' after Theodule who was the first Bishop of Valais in the Rhone Valley, 381–391AD. Serraillier, a frequent contributor to *English*, and the author of *The Silver Sword*, was instrumental in the conception of the influential 'New Windmill Series' published by Heinemann, which was used in schools in the 1950s and 1960s to introduce the work of contemporary poets.

Poetry remains a regular feature of *English*. As Hilda D. Spear indicates, from its inception '*English* received and published a considerable number of poems, though it never became a popular vehicle for the short story'. She notes that 'While the poets who published in *English* subscribed to no "school", many works had a faintly Georgian flavour. This perhaps reflected the interests and age of the editor, George Cookson, who was himself an occasional writer of poems'.[228] Spear also draws attention to 'a noticeable absence of poems from the left-wing political writers of the 1930s such as W. H. Auden, C. Day Lewis, Louis Mac Neice, and Stephen Spender, as well as…W. B. Yeats and T. S. Eliot'. However, many poets, well known at least as anthology poets, contributed to *English* in its earlier years. These included W. W. Gibson, Edmund Blunden, Phoebe Hesketh, Walter de la Mare, and Patric Dickinson amongst others.

During the editorship of Margaret Willy from 1964 to 1974, *English* introduced 'Special Numbers' devoted to special topics. These began appropriately with the 'Shakespeare Quarter Centenary Number' in 1964 (number 86). The Scottish number (96), which appeared in the autumn of 1967, included poetry interspersed throughout the text by George Mackay Brown, Robert Garioch, Norman Mac Gacy, Hugh MacDiurmid, Ian Crichton Smith, and Sydney Goodson Smith. Analysis of this Scottish number reveals that the basic formula for *English* had changed little over the years, although there were far more publishers' advertisements than in earlier years. Content ranged from a two paragraph introduction to the 'Scottish Number of *English*' by the editor, Margaret Willy to an eight-line single stanza by George MacKay Brown. Four general articles concern 'James VI and Renaissance Poetic Theory', 'A Note on *Tam O' Shanter*', and essays on Edwin Muir and Hugh Mac Diarmid. Between them is a survey, 'Scottish Writing Today', subdivided into 'Poetry' and 'The Novel and Drama'. The 'Review of Books' section contains five reviews of books with Scottish content, ranging from *The Oxford Book of Scottish Verse* to an anthology of Scottish Poetry.

Another issue of *English* during the post-war years is the 'Shakespeare Quarter Centenary Number' (86) for the summer of 1964. This included 'A Shakespeare Message' from the playwright and novelist Clemence Dane, President of the EA in 1961. The issue has seven articles, seven poems, the usual reviews of books (not confined to Shakespeare), 'Shorter Notices', 'Recent Reading', a 'Poetry Review', additional reviews and reports, and notes on EA activities. The seven articles on Shakespeare, by contributors such as Guy Boas, William A. Armstrong, and R.A. Foakes, extend from the general to 'Shakespeare and the Medieval Stage', 'The

---

[228] Spear, p. 167.

Sonnets', '*Hamlet*', 'Shakespeare Out of School', 'Shakespeare on Record', and 'Shakespeare in Southwark'.

As noted above, Margaret Willy edited *English* from 1954 until 1975, when Martin Dodsworth succeeded as editor until 1987. In 1984, Michael Baron became a joint editor with Dodsworth. From 1987 until the autumn of 1974, Michael Baron, who taught at Birkbeck, and Peter Barry jointly edited the journal initially in consultation with Martin Dodsworth. In 1995, Ken Newton, Professor of English at Dundee, took over and shared the editorship with Peter Barry, the same team editing *English* to this day. Peter Barry, the author of the best-selling *Beginning Theory* (1995; 2nd ed. 2002) and *Contemporary British Poetry and the City* (2000, selected by the American Library Association's *Choice* as an 'Outstanding Title'), comments:

> My involvement with *English* and the English Association started in the late 1970s, when I began sending academic essays to the then editor Martin Dodsworth. He didn't take the early ones, but his comments were extremely shrewd and helpful, and Martin is another of the 'teachers' to whom I owe a great deal. He published one of my essays in 1980, and asked if I'd like to review for the journal. I did so throughout the early 80s, and also provided a number of reports, up to 1990, on the Higher Education Teachers of English (HETE) conferences, which were a major UK powerhouse for the theory revolution of the period.
>
> In 1986, Martin, and Michael Baron, who was then co-editor of *English*, invited a number of regular reviewers to a meeting at Birkbeck College...what emerged a few months later was that Martin wrote to say that Michael was about to go to the States for a year's exchange, and would I take over the 'front half' of the journal (that is, the essays) for that period. So I edited the 1987 issues, and then took over as permanent 'front half' editor (I thought of *English* then as a kind of pantomime horse) from 1988, when Martin moved on to Chair of the Association.
>
> The 'back half' (or Reviews) editor also wrote what was then called 'The Editorial Miscellany'—a formidable task. Martin wrote erudite paragraphs on books which we wanted to 'notice' but couldn't review at full length: he produced several pages at a time, and told the printers to use as much as they needed (each issue had to be, if I remember, 92 pages precisely), holding over the rest till next time. Michael continued this impressive tradition, until he stood down in 1995 to develop his work in other areas. I took over as 'back half' editor, and Ken Newton (whom I'd first met at HETE in the mid 1980s) became 'front half'. I was better suited to writing on 'issues' affecting the discipline, rather than doing a Miscellany in each issue, as I felt that English as a subject was increasingly being shaped by pressures from outside, pressures which the Association should identify and challenge. So we changed the name the editorial some years ago to 'The Editorial Commentary'.
>
> I should add that the poetry side of the editing role has always been very important to me. At King's, and for several years after, I was part of the group 'Alembic Poets', so named because the Alembic is a three-legged instrument, the other legs being Robert Hampson—now Professor at Royal Holloway—and Ken Edwards, who now runs the 'Reality Street' press. We tended towards minimalism, and the scrutiny of 'unnecessary' words was so intense that many poems disappeared entirely under the Alembic workshop treatment. Hence, as poetry editor I have a compensatory leaning towards 'maximalism' and often publish quite wordy and 'relaxed' poems.[229]

---

[229] Private correspondence between Peter Barry and William Baker, 13 May 2005.

Aimed at readers within universities and colleges and presented in a lively and engaging style, then, *English* contains essays on major works of English literature or on topics of general literary interest. There is a substantial review section, in which reviewers have space to situate a book within the context of recent developments in its field, and present a detailed argument, rather than just a brief evaluative commentary as one often feels. *English* is unusual among academic journals in publishing original poetry; this policy embodies the view that the critical and creative functions, often so widely separated in the teaching of English, can co-exist and cross-fertilise each other.

During the 1960s and early 1970s, Margaret Willy introduced 'Special Numbers' of *English*, with an average of one a year appearing from 1964 to 1974. As noted, they began with the 'Shakespeare Quarter Century' in Summer 1964 (number 86) and concluded with an issue on the 'Twentieth Century Novel' for Autumn 1974 (Number 117). As Hilda D. Spear indicates in her account of *English*: 'When Martin Dodsworth became editor in 1975 he made a number of sweeping changes, which he discussed in the editorial of the issue for Spring 1976 (25, no 121)'. Spear adds

> The change in format was intended to 'put more into each number of *English*', but it was decided that the 'more' should also be different. *English* was becoming, perhaps, too much like other journals, and so certain deliberate changes in policy were brought about. A major proportion of the available space was allotted to more substantial reviews: 79 of 127 pages in the first new issue. The review section also contained an 'Editorial Miscellany', a briefer 'survey of recent editions, reprints, and so on'. The other innovation was to give space to the longer essay on a major work of English Literature, and the first such essay was '*Middlemarch*: Public and Private Worlds' by Barbara Hardy. The shape of today's *English* is much the same.[230]

The 1984 issue, volume 33 (numbers 145–47), edited by Dodsworth and Baron, contained nine literary essays, ten poems, seventeen book reviews, an argument, a report, and three editorial miscellanies. The essay subjects ranged from the poetry of Sir Thomas Wyatt, Henry Vaughan, and John Milton, to the literary criticism of F.R. Leavis, and the fiction of Samuel Richardson and William Golding. In his 'Editorial Miscellany' in number 145, Martin Dodsworth comments that he has 'tried for three kinds of article: reassessments of major works, reassessments of minor authors, and articles on general topics of interest'.[231] He noted that English does 'not set out to develop a common point of view' and that 'the extended review section at least maintains an air of contemporaneity and reflects a choice which if not uncircumscribed is at least individual'. Volume 38, 157 in the Spring of 1988 contains, in Michael Baron's words, 'the first Miscellany in which Martin Dodsworth does not have a hand'. Baron enumerated 'in the form of a check-list the kind of critical work' he and the new editor Peter Barry 'are interested in publishing'. The listing was not meant to be either comprehensive or to indicate an order of preference:

---
[230] Spear, p. 167.
[231] *English*, 33, 145, 1984, p. 87.

1) Articles which evaluate aspects of the work of major writers through close reading and argument.
2) Articles dealing with significant points of literary history (such as Paul Norgate's on Wilfred Owen in the Spring 1987 issue).
3) Articles dealing with issues raised by recent critical theory and debate (such as Garry Watson's in the present issue).
4) Articles which make fruitful (if sceptical) use of specific methodologies in the reading and evaluation of literary works.
5) Discussions of problems concerned with the teaching and examining of literature, and of 'English' in a more general sense, sixth form or higher level.
6) Articles which convincingly argue the merits of neglected writers or genres. (82)

Each issue of *English*, in addition to information for subscribers and advertisers, contained details of the EA and those on its Executive Committee. The Autumn 1989 volume 38, number 162 was the last to be published by the Oxford University Press, and the journal has subsequently been published by the English Association. Michael Baron penned his last 'Miscellany' with the Autumn 1994 volume. The 'Miscellany' became the 'Editorial Commentary' with the next issue, which Peter Barry thought 'seems in keeping with other changes we have introduced in the last few years, such as including contributors' academic affiliation in the signatures and setting up a more formal and systematic referencing system'.[232] Clearly *English* was no longer, as it was in the days of Margaret Willy's editorship, catering to both a University academic audience, teachers in the schools, and a general audience. Now, it aimed primarily at the academic audience as a response to pressure during the 1990s for increased publishing and research activity amongst University Departments as a result, principally, of the invidious Research Assessment Exercise. In the language of the period, *English* should appeal to 'RAE-driven academics', a motivation that still pertains today, of course.[233]

The Spring number 193 for 2000 (volume 49) saw a re-designed front cover containing contents details rather than the previous sparse front cover containing simply the name of the journal, its editors, volume number and date. The subscription for 2001 had risen to £48.00 or $115.00. In 1975, the annual subscription to non-members of the EA was '£3 post free'. By 1983, this had risen to £12.00 in the UK, or $29.00 for subscribers in the United States, and £15.00 for those elsewhere with no distinction for EA members. In 1996 these figures had risen to £33.00 or $75.00. By 2005 these costs had again increased to £65.00 or $150.00. *English* still, however, remains one of the most reasonably priced of all general journals in the field.

The Summer 2004 issue, Volume 53, Number 206, contains three critical articles: on Mansfield Park by Valerie Wainwright; on 'Robert Lowell and Marvell: Poetry and Patriotism'; and an article comparing the poetry of A. E. Houseman and Geoffrey Hill, by Steven Matthews. These articles are followed by four poems by

---

[232] *English*, 44, 178 (1995), p. 92.
[233] *English*, 48, 192 (1999), p. 241.

Michael O'Neill and Peter Barry's 'The Editorial Commentary' providing judicious 'practical advice to Ph.D. students on how to make themselves better conference speakers'. The issue concludes with reviews. Andrew Hadfield covers nine books on various aspects of Shakespeare , followed by four reviews of individual academic monographs. The journal, in its most contemporary manifestation, is ranked among the top general journals in the field, and is set to flourish in the next one hundred years of the English Association.

Occasional Publications of the EA

The Best Seller: *Poems of To-day*

It was during the First World War that the EA produced perhaps its most successful publication in terms of sales. Nowell Smith writing in 1942 observes: 'The most remarkable achievement of the Association during the war, and indeed the greatest success with the general public during the whole course of [its] history, was the publication of that handy and inexpensive volume called *Poems of To-day*, which appeared first in August 1915, was in its 13th edition in 1917, its 35th in 1927, its 52nd in 1938'.[234] He adds: 'It was a garland culled by many hands, but the final selection, the arrangement, and the telling Prefatory Note were almost wholly due to the fine judgement and care of Sir E. K. Chambers'. Chambers, a distinguished civil servant and author of *English Literature at the Close of the Middle Ages* and *The Mediaeval Stage*,[235] was President of the EA in 1940. Chambers's *Poems of To-day* was published for the EA in 1915 by Sidgwick and Jackson, and it continued to sell until 1955. It contained 32 pages of introductory materials and 174 pages of poetry selections. The first series was followed by numerous subsequent series. The second series published in 1922 by Sidgwick and Jackson was edited by Aldous Huxley; and subsequent series, as will be seen, continued to make this a profitable and highly valuable publication of the EA.[236]

The publication of *Poems of To-day* served an EA function not included in *Essays and Studies* and the subsequent *YWES*: it catered to its 'Secondary or Primary Education' constituency. The majority of the poets, Chambers wrote, 'are living' unless victims of the war. Further 'the intention has been to represent mainly those poetic tendencies which have become dominant as the influence of the accepted Victorian masters has grown weaker, and from which the poetry of the future, however it may develop, must in turn take its start'.[237] There is a 'sequence of themes', with three main divisions: 'poems of History'; 'poems of the Earth, of England again

---

[234] Smith, 1942, p. 8.
[235] Chambers's four-volume *The Elizabethan Stage*, published in 1923, is still, of course, considered indispensable.
[236] According to the *Bulletin*, *Poems of To-day* (June 1932) was 'in its forty-third edition… In all 467,600 copies of these works had been sold… *The Anthology of Prose To-day* had sold 15,275 copies. *Anthology of Prose* never ascended to best seller, so that was very gratifying' (*Bulletin*, 75, December 1932, p. 3).
[237] Chambers, *Poems of Today*, p. vii

and the longing of the exile for home';[238] and 'poems of Life itself, of the moods in which it may be faced, of religion, of…virtues, of friendship and childhood, of passion, grief, and comfort'.[239]

Forty-seven poets are represented in the first anthology with 'Biographical Notes' preceding the poems, which begin with Walter de la Mare's 'All That's Past', and conclude with Alice Meynell's 'At Night'. All but one of the poets included in the anthology were alive in 1900—virtually contemporary writers, then, the exception being Robert Louis Stevenson who died in 1894. He and Robert Bridges are the most represented poets with eleven poems each in the anthology. Also well represented are Laurence Binyon (seven poems), Alice Meynell (nine poems), Francis Thompson (six poems) and William Butler Yeats (eight poems).

The second series was published on 31 May 1922. John Bailey reported to the EA in May 1923 that 'the second volume, for which the [EA] were much indebted to Miss Sellon, who took the principal part in preparing it, was already in its fourth edition'.[240] A volume combining the first and second series was issued in November 1924. The popularity of both series is gleaned from the imprint details of *Poems of To-day: First and Second Series*.[241] The data on the verso of the title-page reveals that there were '57 impressions, 1915–1943' of *Poems of To-day: First Series*, and '21 impressions, 1922–1943' of *Poems of To-day: Second Series*. The edition combining both series was reprinted nineteen times following its first issue in January 1954. The consequences of its success were astutely critiqued by Nowell Smith, who observed in his 1942 Chair's Address to the EA that 'there may have been somewhat of a false sense of security [during the inter-war years] induced by the great success of *Poems of To-day*…and a tendency to rely on the profits of such publications to offset the fall of revenue from membership'.[242]

The second series of *Poems of To-day* reflects a change of mood and tone from that of the first series published initially in 1915. The subsequent volume published seven years later reflects the experiences of war in 'the impassioned memories of the poet[s]'. The Prefatory Notes, dated January 1922, conclude with the comment that in this second series 'Romance is blended with realism', and escape from the contemporary is reflected 'sometimes by looking back into the past, more often by way of the sea and far wanderings, sometimes by magic'. Also 'the mystery of death has quickened…perception[s] of the mystery of life and of the immanence of spirit'.[243] The second series expands the number of poets and their work: of poets from the first series, the second series includes three more poems by Robert Bridges, four more by Walter de la Mare, John Drinkwater, James Elroy Flecker, Newbolt and Francis Thompson. Four Hardy poems are included, but only one by A. E.. Housman, 'Epitaph on an Army of Mercenaries'. Of the 'War Poets', Siegfried Sassoon is represented by 'Everyone Sang', and Charles Sorley by 'Marlborough'

---

[238] This is, of course, an overtly nationalistic theme reflecting the period immediately following World War I.
[239] Chambers, *Poems of To-day*, p. viii.
[240] *Bulletin* 49, December 1923, p. 3.
[241] (London: Published for the EA by Sidgwick & Jackson, Ltd.); reprinted in January 1954.
[242] Smith, 1942, p. 10.
[243] *Poems of To-day* 2, p. viii.

and 'The Song of the Ungirt Runners'. There are five James Stephens poems whereas there were none in the earlier volume, and three by Edward Thomas. The useful biographical notes included in the earlier anthology are missing from the combined volume. The later collection is notable for its inclusion of many more women and Irish poets.

Poems of To-day: Third Series was published in 1938. The Prefatory Notes reinforce the EA's traditional bias, stating that the anthology's aim is 'to bring together a selection of contemporary poetry…and at the same time sufficiently in accordance with tradition to avoid excursion into the fields of ultra-modernism'.[244] 73 poets are included in the third series, with their 161 poems arranged in alphabetical order of poet, beginning with Lascelles Abercrombie and concluding with three poems by Andrew Young. Detailed Biographical Notes on each of the poets are reintroduced following their loss from the Second Series. New poets not included in the previous volumes represent the great majority, new poems replace those of established poets presented in the Second Series, and other poets are squeezed to achieve this new look: Laurence Binyon, for example, represented by seven poems in the earlier anthologies, is reduced to one work; Yeats' eleven early works are reduced to six from his middle and later periods. The poems of W. H. Davies, Thomas Hardy and Walter de la Mare are different from those previously published.

4 May 1951 saw the publication of *Poems of To-day: Fourth Series*, priced at 8/6d, and produced by Macmillan for the EA. This edition was the collaborative work of the EA Publications Sub-Committee, chaired by Admiral Sir Arthur Hall. The aim of its compilers was 'to bring together a selection of the best English poetry published in this country between 1938 and 1947', and included 'no less than 110 poets'. As the edition was aimed at schools 'the compilers agreed to abandon five of the poems originally chosen and to substitute others by the same authors'.[245] According to the EA Minutes for the 23 February 1947 Report of the Publications Sub-Committee, these included poems by George Burke, Robert Graves, and J. F. Hendry.

Poems of To-Day: Fourth Series was based on eclecticism: 'the compilers have tried to exercise as catholic a judgment as possible and to avoid prejudice either in favour of or against any one school, movement or generation'.[246] The prime consideration was stated to be quality; and there are extracts from poems by writers such as Sidney Keynes, who was killed in the Second World War. As chronology (1938–1947) was one of the determining principles of inclusion, there is one Yeats poem, the very late 'Under Ben Bulben'. The only lines included from Eliot are from 'The Family Reunion'. Of other poets, a surprise, perhaps, is the inclusion of five poems by Richard Church, who was a poet, novelist, and literary critic. Though he is largely forgotten today, he was President of the Royal Society of Literature and EA President in 1965. An indication of his waning reputation is seen in the inclusion of only one of Church's poems in the fifth edition of *Poems of To-Day*.

---

[244] *Poems of To-day: Third Series*, 1938, p. v.
[245] p. v.
[246] *Ibid*.

Poems of To-Day: Fourth Series includes three Auden poems, including 'In Memory of W. B. Yeats', and four poems by Dylan Thomas, Louis MacNeice and W. W. Gibson. Edmund Blunden, who regularly contributed to *English* and served as EA President in 1967, is represented by two poems. The largest selection goes to Edith Sitwell and Andrew Young with six each, and Walter de la Mare with seven.

The *Fourth Series* of *Poems of To-Day* did so well that in 1963 Margaret Willy's *Fifth Series* was published by the EA. Willy, in her 'Prefatory Note', observes that 'Poetry of much diversity and accomplishment has been produced in post-war England since the publication of *Poems of To-Day: Fourth Series*. It is the aim of the present anthology to afford some idea, within an allotted compass of 140 poems, of the scope of this activity between 1947 and the end of 1961'. Willy's selection includes nearly 80 poets and includes some of the last work of an older generation of writers, ranging from Edwin Muir (three of his poems were in the earlier anthology, four in Willy's selection) to Dylan Thomas (two in Willy, four in the earlier selection). Roy Campbell, a single poem of whose is in the earlier volume, is not included. In the 1963 *Poems of To-Day*, Sitwell is reduced to one poem; de la Mare has four. Young and T. S. Eliot are excluded due to the 'length of their later poetry'. Willy gives attention to 'the continuing development…of such established and important poets as W. H. Auden and Robert Graves'. The earlier selection contained only three poems by the latter: Willy includes four and the same number by Auden. More importantly perhaps she draws attention to 'the most notable features of these years [1947–1961]…the emergence of many younger writers, unknown in 1947'. She includes amongst those 'who have steadily consolidated their reputations during the past decade' Ted Hughes (two poems), Thom Gunn (two poems), D. J. Enright (two poems), John Wain (three poems), Thomas Blackburn (three poems), and Charles Causley (two poems). Four poems represent the largest individual selection for a poet; only Walter de la Mare, Robert Graves, Edwin Muir, and R. S. Thomas achieve this number in Willy's selection.

Twentieth-century poetry, or in other words 'Poems of Today' was not the only production of the EA in the post-war years. In 1953 George Allen & Unwin published for the EA a volume entitled *The English Association Book of Verse: An Anthology of English Poetry of the British Isles from Chaucer to the Present Day* selected and arranged by Peter Leyland in collaboration with M. Alderton Pink. The aim of the anthology was 'to show man's experience through the poetry which has expressed it, and on this basis to make a representative selection of the English poetry of the British Isles, including poetry of the twentieth century' (p. 5). Accordingly the anthology is divided into eight sections along thematic principles: Action, Love, Art, Fantasy and Symbol, Man and Nature, the Span of Life, Man and Society, and Man and God.

Aimed at a school and school textbook market, each section has a prefatory explanatory paragraph. The anthology concludes with brief notes and an 'Index of Authors', alphabetically arranged. Twentieth-century poets living in 1953, when the anthology was published, include Auden, de la Mare, T. S. Eliot, C. Day Lewis, Masefield, Siegfried Sassoon, Stephen Spender, and Andrew Young.

Short Stories, Prose and Miscellaneous Publications

The EA *Bulletin* for July 1928 noted in its regular 'Notes' section that Longmans had published on behalf of the EA its 'Anthology of Contemporary Prose…under the title of *Prose of To-day*'. It was priced at 3s. 6d. or 2s. 6d. (School Edition).[247] Chairs' reports to the EA Annual General Meeting published in the EA *Bulletin* indicate that the publication was an attempt to follow upon the success of *Poems of To-day* and shore the Association against falling membership and hence falling revenues. J. E. Talbot, the Treasurer, pointed out to the twenty-second Annual Business Meeting held in June 1928 'that the royalties received on account of *Poems of To-day* really kept them going, and he felt this to be an unsatisfactory position. They should be self-supporting and their liabilities should be balanced by their subscriptions'.[248] The following year the Business Meeting of the AGM was informed that there had been a 'slight falling off in the membership of some of the Branches', but that sales of *Poems of To-day* and *Prose of To-day* were satisfactory. Talbot 'pointed out the investment of a further sum of £1,000 received by way of royalties on *Prose of To-day* in five per cent War Stock'.[249] However, as Talbot reported to the Business Meeting on 23 May 1930, 'the Royalties on *Prose of To-day*, which last year were entered at £249, this year were only £75'. He realistically confessed 'that the financial prosperity of the Association was largely and rather undesirably due to the success of *Poems of To-day*'. Further 'it was not to be expected…that the sales of a prose anthology should be anything approaching the magnificent success of *Poems of To-day*'.[250]

Prose of To-day was primarily the work of Guy Boas, and, in its first manifestation in 1928, contained extracts from 59 authors. Alphabetically arranged under author, and including Biographical Notes, the first entry is a paragraph from Lascelles Abercrombie's 'Empedokles' and the last is two paragraphs from W. B. Yeats 'Per Amica Silentia Lunae'. The Prefatory Note states the aim that 'The present volume intends to exhibit the range and variety of good prose usage among representative writers of our own time'.[251]

Some idea of the success of *Prose of To-day* is reflected in its reissue in 1932. By this year, *Poems of To-day* had sold 467, 600 copies and *Prose of To-day*, 15,275 copies.[252] It is clear from Guy Boas's 'Editor's Foreword' that an additional section, 'Notes and Questions', is intended for school rather than university use. The 'Notes' explicate, for instance, '*Empedokles*' and replace the specifically 'Biographical Notes' found in the earlier volume.[253] 59 Essay Questions are meant to guide analysis, suggesting, for instance, that in relation to *Empedokles* students might 'Define the difference between what is meant by the words 'classical' and 'romantic', and show why the life of Empedokles is appropriately called romantic'.[254]

---

[247] *Bulletin*, 63, July 1928, p. 4.
[248] *Bulletin*, 64, December 1928, p. 3.
[249] *Bulletin*, 77, November 1929), p. 3.
[250] *Bulletin*, 80 November 1930, p. 4.
[251] *Prose of To-day*, p. vii.
[252] *Bulletin*, 75, December 1932, p. 3.
[253] *Prose of To-day*, pp. 193–218.
[254] *Prose of To-day*, p. 219.

Another EA publication that began with the intention of exploiting the success of *Poems of To-day* and aimed at a school rather than a university audience is *English Short Stories of To-day*. Published for the EA by Oxford University Press in 1939, by 1948 it was in its fifth impression. A second series selected by Dan Davin was published in 1958; a third series selected by T. S. Dorsch in 1965 and a fourth series selected by Roger Sharrock in 1976. The 1938 first publication included 13 short stories and Biographical Notes on authors, such as Stella Benson, John Galsworthy, Richard Hughes, Montague James, Somerset Maugham, Leonard Merrick, Naomi Mitchison, Geoffrey Moss, Frank O'Connor, 'Saki' (H. H. Munro), Dorothy Sayers, Hugh Walpole, and H. G. Wells.

Indeed, the Post-War period was a very active one for EA publications, which included, in alphabetical order:

- *English Essays of Today*. London: Oxford University Press, 1960.
- *English Historians: Selected Passages*. Ed. Bertram Newman. London: Oxford University Press, 1957.
- *English Short Stories of Today: First Series*. London: Oxford University Press, 1939 [fifth impression, 1948]; *Second Series*, 1958; *Third Series*, 1965; *Fourth Series*, 1976.
- *A Guide to English Courses in the Universities*. Ed. Eric Arnold. London: John Murray, 1965.
- *Literature and Life: Addresses to the English Association*. 2 vols. London: Harrap, 1948.
- Maurice Alderton Pink, *An Outline of English Grammar; with suggestions on the method of teaching*. London: Macmillan, 1954.
- *The Teaching of English in Schools*. Ed. Vivian de Sola Pinto. Foreword by Sir Fred Clarke. Foreword. London: Macmillan, 1946, 1947.
- Miscellaneous Pamphlets; for example, Presidential Addresses; Individual Pamphlets.

These publications are a mixture of the pedagogical, the academic, and the general, depending upon the markets at which they are aimed. The 1965 *A Guide to English Courses in the Universities* sold 11,000 copies. Its market was the expanding student population as it listed university English Departments and courses available in the post-Robbins report era. The publication proved to be so successful that by 1980 it had been through five different incarnations and revisions under differing editors.

The Teaching of English in Schools: A Symposium, edited by Vivian de Sola Pinto with a Foreword by Sir Fred Clarke, on the other hand, was aimed at what the EA Executive members felt was an under-represented part of the EA constituency. Directed at schoolteachers, the symposium included contributions from L. A. G. Strong on 'Poetry in the School', D. C. Whimster on 'Drama in the School', M. M. Lewis on 'Spoken English in the School', Pamela Gradon on 'The Teaching of Grammar', A. M. C. Latham on 'The Teaching of Prose', Guy Boas on 'School Examinations in English', W. A. Claydon on 'The School Library', and A. H. Stewart and V. de Sola Pinto on 'The Training of the Teacher of English'. Such subjects reflect the great changes in the education system in the aftermath of World War II and the Butler Education Act. The choice of Sir Fred Clarke, a very eminent and long-established educator, to write the foreword was no accident, since his status lent credence and authority to the volume.

English Essays of Today, published for the EA by Oxford University Press in 1960, on the other hand, drew upon the sales success of its initial incarnation. Published in 1936 with 'Biographical notes' at the end, this contained essays by thirty-eight authors. The writers included ranged from Maurice Baring, Max Beerbohm, Hilaire Belloc, Edmund Blunden, and Neville Cardus to Lytton Strachey, H. M Tomlinson, G. M. Trevelyan, Helen Waddell, Virginia Woolf, and W. B. Yeats. Aimed at the school and general market, this generated income, and even as late as 1957, 17,000 copies were sold in India.

The EA drew upon the marketing appeal of illustrious names to write forewords. Another example of an EA publication aimed at the school market, and yet with a general interest, is the popularist historian, Bertram Newman's *English Historians: Selected Passages*, published for the EA, again by the Oxford University Press. Published in 1957, it contains a foreword by C. V. Wedgwood, who herself served as EA President in 1956.

As indicated earlier, *English Short Stories of Today*, published in 1939, was by 1948 in its fifth impression. Appealing to a wide market, a second series was published in 1958, a third in 1965. A steady money-maker and seller, a fourth series selected by Roger Sharrock was published in 1976. All were published by the Oxford University Press for the EA.

Davin's selection for *English Short Stories of Today, Second Series*, still in print in 1978, includes twelve short stories followed by brief 'Biographical Notes' on the authors. They include Elizabeth Bowen, Joyce Cary, Walter de la Mare, Graham Greene, L. P. Hartley, Somerset Maugham, Frank O'Connor, V. S. Pritchett (two stories), William Samson, Dylan Thomas, Evelyn Waugh, and Angus Wilson. Only Somerset Maugham survives from the *First Series* published in 1939. Dorsch's selection for *English Short Stories of Today Third Series*, published in 1965, contains twenty stories. L. P. Hartley, William Samson, and Angus Wilson are also found in Davin's selection. Dorsch's volume follows the format of the previous selections with brief 'Biographical Notes' at the end. His authors range from Mary Lavin, Dal Stivens, Viola Meynell, Maurice Shadbolt, and Bill Naughton to John Wain, L. E. Jones, Peter Ustinov, May C. Jenkins, Morley Callaghan, Norah Lofts, and Rhys Davis—in other words, a wider selection than previously, including well-established writers from a previous generation (Viola Meynell, for instance, 1885–1956). His selection also includes emerging Commonwealth writers either living in London or writing overseas, such as Nadine Gordimer, Ruth Prawer Jhabvala, George Lemming, David Owoyeles, and Maurice Shadbolt. Such writers were to figure prominently in Roger Sharrock's 1976 selection.

In addition to the publication of miscellaneous pamphlets such as the Presidential addresses, EA publications also included occasional lectures to EA groups such as F. S. Boas' 'Ovid and the Elizabethans'. However, mention should be made of the 1948 publication in two volumes of *Literature and Life: Addresses to the English Association*, published by Harrap in collaboration with the EA and reprinted by the Kennikat Press, Port Washington in 1970. Harrap and the EA 'decided to use this means of making available to a wider circle outstanding lectures delivered to the central body'.[255] The first volume contains ten undated addresses; the second nine. Contributions of addresses to the first volume range from Sir Idris Bell, Guy Boas, Osbert Lancaster, and C. S. Lewis to Vivian de Sola Pinto, G. Rostrevor Hamilton, H. V. Routh, Lawrence G. Tanner, S. C. Roberts, and Reginald W. M. Wright. Lawrence Edward Tanner, author of various histories of Westminster Abbey and its environs, gave his address to the EA on 'Westminster Abbey in English Literature'; another address, by Reginald N. Wright, focuses on 'The City of Bath and its Literary Associations'. The opening address on 'The Problem of Translation' is of interest because its speaker, Sir Idris Bell did not become an EA President. Another interesting address is C. S. Lewis' 'Kipling's World' delivered as a lecture to the EA on 24 November 1948, and reprinted in *The Kipling Journal*.[256]

The second volume of *Literature and Life* contains addresses from Margaret Willy on 'Keats and His Letters' to Joyce Cary speaking on 'What Does Art Create?' Other contributors and subjects include Viscount Herbert Samuel, the politician who served as EA President in 1941, on the subject of 'English Poetry of To-Day', and Hermann Peschmann, whose subject was 'New Directions in English Poetry, 1920–45'.

Other EA publications were aimed, as has been noted, at specific markets. This is especially true of those by Maurice Alderton Pink who wrote various reference books and dictionaries including *English Grammar, Composition, and Correspondence* with Thomas S. Evelyn. First published in 1926, this was its twelfth edition in 1979. Pink's *Procrustes: Or the Future of English Education*, published in 1927, demonstrated in the words of Guy Boas 'a remarkably fresh insight into the relationship of education, philosophy, and politics'. In addition to co-editing the EA's *Books of Verse* published in 1953, he also wrote *An Outline of English Grammar*. Published by Macmillan in September 1954 for teachers, Pink shared the royalties on all copies sold with the EA. Pink was actively involved with EA affairs, having served in the early 1950s as Chairman of its Publications Committee. He was, in the words of Guy Boas (in his obituary tribute published in *English*) 'the always perfectly accomplished editor of many stimulating books for class-room and study groups'.[257]

Other Journals and Publications

During the last decade of the twentieth century and the first years of the next, the EA has expanded its publishing profile. Martin Dodsworth noted in his observations to celebrate the EA's 90th birthday that the EA's 'publishing programme . . . includes the two annual volumes of *The Year's Work*, the series of *Essays and Studies* and the

---

[255] *English* 7, 41, 1949, p. 251.
[256] 25, Nos. 127–28, September, 1958, pp. 8–16; December 1958, pp. 7–11.
[257] *English*, 10, 59, 1955, p. 180.

journal *English*, all primarily aimed at trends in the world of higher education'. For schools, on the other hand, the EA 'produces *The Use of English* and *Primary English*, as well as the series of *Bookmarks* designed to stimulate and guide reading by middle-and upper-school age children'. He adds that 'some of these publications are well established, but others are new: *The Year's Work in Critical and Cultural Theory* and *Primary English* have come into being only in the last five years and *The Use of English* only transferred to [the EA's] wing in the nineties'. It transferred from the Scottish Academic Press in the Autumn of 1991. He adds that 'the range reflects both the diverse academic strength of the Association and its qualifications for participating in public debate'.[258]

The EA *Annual Report* for the year ended December 31, 2004 recorded seven publications during the year: the annuals, *Essays & Studies*, *YWES*, and *YWCCT*; and the journals *English*, *The Use of English*, *English 4–11*, and the EA *Newsletter*.

The Use of English

The Use of English edited by Andrew Stables of the University of Bath and Ian Brinton from Dulwich College, is the oldest journal serving English teachers in schools and colleges in the UK. Following on from a forerunner called *English in Schools* founded in 1939 by the distinguished educator Denys Thompson, a former student of F. R. Leavis, who taught at Gresham's School in Norfolk, *The Use of English* began in 1949 as a forum for practical debate about the teaching of English. Published by Scottish Academic Press for many years, *The Use of English* was taken on by the English Association in 1991 when its long-time editor, Roger Knight, joined the English Association Executive.

The journal's website notes 'Vigorous, independent comment on theory, policy, and practice has always been its forte. Such comment has never been so necessary as it is at the present time: a time of change, uncertainty, and a high level of central intervention in the teaching of English'. In other words, *The Use of English* provides 'a lively, critical forum' in the 'era of compulsory testing, of Shakespeare for all and the new Order for National Curriculum English'. Indeed, Roger Knight became well-known for his trenchantly expressed views on the National Curriculum and other issues pertaining to the teaching of English.

The journal also has an extensive reviewing section focusing on reviews of books on the teaching of English, literary criticism, anthologies, and editions. To take a representative example from *The Use of English* 55, Number 1, Autumn 2003, issue 1, in addition to Andrew Stables' Editorial, it contained an essay by the EA's Patron, Randolph Quirk, on 'From Latin to English'. Other articles range from two on Shakespeare, one on 'Approaches to Data-Based Language Study Examination Questions for AS and A-Level English Language', and a general essay on 'The Importance of Reflecting in Reading'. There are ten book reviews followed by 'Short Notes and Books Received'.

---

[258] Martin Dodsworth, 'The Way Ahead', *English Association Newsletter*, no. 152, Summer 1996, pp. 3–4.

English 4–11

English 4–11 on the other hand is aimed at those who teach a different age group. The EA's journal for primary teachers was first published in Spring 1992 as *Primary English* and was re-named in 1998 to reflect an increasing range of coverage. Writing in the first issue the editors noted

> This may seem the wrong time to be starting a new journal for primary teachers of English. Will it, we hear you ask, be just another unread item littering the staff-room table at a time when you and it are already groaning under the weight of glossy communiqués from SEAC, the NCC, the NFER and the rest.?
>
> Well, we hope that you will read it, and that you will think of writing for it. We want it to be a constant reminder that totting up the code numbers of Attainment Targets will always be peripheral to the real business of teaching.
>
> **Primary English** is the first journal exclusively concerned with the teaching of English in primary schools. It is being launched with the support and encouragement of the English Association, the only body concerned with English across the whole spectrum of primary, secondary and higher education. The consulting editors are all professionally involved in primary education. For this first issue we have collaborated in writing articles with teachers in our various local schools.

This collaboration between teacher and editorial board is an integral part of the journal today which contains material produced by, and for, the classroom teacher, practical resources and reports on successful major projects. This first issue included articles on 'Singing Games for Children', 'Parents and Children Sharing Stories', 'Children Responding to Literature', 'Writing as Emotional Release', 'Organising a Slideshow Presentation' and 'Poetic-Prose: Non-Chronological Writing with Junior Children'. An extensive book review section was added in issue 2 and over time reviews of videos and software have also been added.

Between 1994 and 2004 the journal also held annual conferences for primary teachers. The first conference, 'Talking and Teaching: Children's Literature' held at LSU College in Southampton, featured poet and broadcaster Michael Rosen discussing the role which children's poetry played in the classroom; children's novelist Chris Powling who talked about writing and teaching children's fiction; and editorial board member Rita Ray who focused on ways of encouraging children's own writing and drama using puppets and masks. The final conference, 'Creativity in English: Opening up the Literacy Hour', was held at the West Yorkshire Playhouse in Leeds and included contributions from teacher and writer Huw Thomas who talked about how to make literacy lively and relevant; literacy specialist Sue Palmer on how speaking, listening and drama could be integrated into literacy teaching; drama consultant Colin Jackson talking about drama as a creative process; and storyteller Ansell Brodrick.

In 1995 the journal established an award for the 'Best Children's Illustrated Book' of the year. The first winner was Colin Thompson for his splendid and intricately detailed book *Ruby*. In 1999 the awards were extended with prizes being made in each of four categories: Key Stage 1 Fiction, Key Stage 2 Fiction, Key Stage 1

Non-Fiction and Key Stage 2 Non-Fiction. Winners to date include Shirley Hughes, Mick Manning and Brita Granström (twice), Meredith Hooper (twice), Helen Ward (twice), Neil Gaiman and Dave McKean, and Michael Rosen and Quentin Blake.

From 1992 to 1996 *Primary English* was edited by Anne Hogan (LSU College Southampton) and Patrick Wood (University of Sunderland). In 1996 Henry Pearson (University College, Chester) replaced Anne Hogan and in 1998 long-time editorial board member John Paine, an LEA Advisor from Salford, took over from Patrick Wood. In Autumn 2004 the EA welcomed the United Kingdom Literacy Association as a partner in publishing the magazine.

An idea of the scope of the journal can be gleaned from the contents of the Autumn 2005 issue which contains articles on 'A Pirate in the Literacy Hour', 'What Do I Read to My Class?', 'Custardise your Curriculum!', 'Using Art and Drama to Inspire and Motivate Young Readers', 'Re-making Role-Play in Barnsley' together with 'News, Notices, Research' and reviews of 'Quality Software' and books for children and teachers.

EA *Newsletter*

The thrice-yearly *English Association Newsletter* was first published in 1946 'to supplement the information given in the Annual Report and *English* concerning the activities and personalities of the Association'. The format remained essentially unchanged until December 1985 when changes were made in the content of the *Newsletter* which the Association hoped would make it 'livelier, more informative and easier to read'. As well as altering the size, type face and heading 'We are also extending our regular features by introducing short topics likely to be of general interest to members'.[259]

Several re-designs later, the *Newsletter* is published in the Spring, Summer, and Autumn/Winter. It still aims to keep members informed of all the activities and publications of the Association and contains articles on Higher Education, Secondary Education, and Primary Education matters; reports on English Association Conferences; book reviews; new publication news, plus notice of English Association and other conferences. Edited by Helen Lucas, it contains articles, current events, and news for all areas of English in education. Number 180, for example, printed in Autumn/Winter 2005, contains an article by Professor Peter Kitson, Chair of the EA, on 'The Research Assessment Exercise 2008'; 'The EA's response to English 21' by Ian Brinton, Chair of the Secondary Education Committee; an article on a recent addition to the EA's *Issues in English* series: *Second Reading: a report debating the present state of English at AS and A Level and identifying priorities for revising the English Subject Criteria*, by Adrian Barlow, former Chief of Examines for English, OCR; 'Whose Heroes? 200 Years of Nelson and Trafalgar in British Maritime Fiction' by Yolanda Courtney, Head of the Leicestershire Museums Service; a letter from Emeritus Professor Derek Brewer, University of Cambridge, responding to an

---

[259] Miriam Allott, *English Association Newsletter*, December 1985.

article on the RAE 2008 Panel by Peter Barry in the Summer 2005 Newsletter; an obituary of Michael Gearin-Tosh and four pages of EA Conference and Centenary Year news. There are also Subscription Rates for 2005, a Calendar of Events for the Year, and details concerning other EA publications.

Pamphlets

English Association pamphlets were published almost from the Association's inception. Usually these pamphlets were no longer than a maximum of eighteen pages in length, and just over 10,000 words per pamphlet. Selling for one shilling, some were reprinted, but most could hardly be referred to as best sellers. The pamphlets were produced throughout the years of the First World War, and indeed, the years between 1914 and 1918 saw seventeen of these produced. They ranged from the poet and essayist Lascelles Abercrombie's twelve-page pamphlet, *Poetry and Contemporary Speech* (No. 27) published in 1914 to F. S. Boas' *Wordsworth's Patriotic Poems and Their Significance To-Day* (No. 30) published in 1916. The 1918 Presidential Address was that of the former Prime Minister, H. H. Asquith, entitled *Sir Henry Wotton—With Some General Reflections on Style in English Poetry* (No. 44, published in 1919). Three pamphlets appeared in 1915 alone: these were *The Use of Comic Episodes in Tragedy* by the music specialist and lecturer, Sir William Henry Hadow, published in February; *On Concentration and Suggestion in Poetry* by Sir Sidney Colvin, President of the EA at the outbreak of WWI, published in June; and six months later, the redoubtable J. H. Fowler's pamphlet *School Libraries*.

In 1915 W. P. Ker was President of the Association. His Presidential Address, *The Eighteenth Century*, focusing particularly on Gibbons, was published in 1916 as one of two EA pamphlets for that year. The *EA Bulletin* for July 1916 comments on Ker's address: 'In the course of a delightfully allusive address, which the Association have been allowed to publish and which is unfortunately bound to lose almost all its delightful flavour in any compressed account. Professor Ker took up the cudgels on behalf of a more sympathetic understanding of that much misunderstood period'.[260]

1917 was a productive one for EA pamphlets. September 1917 saw the publication of the Marquis of Crewe's Presidential Address as pamphlet 38. Crewe's *War and English Poetry* surveyed 'English war poetry from the fourteenth to the twentieth century'. Crewe indicates 'that the periods of great wars had not always produced great war poetry, nor heroic deeds roused contemporary poets to commemorate them adequately', and this conclusion is poignant, of course, in the light of the great poetry produced during the 1914–1918 war by Wilfred Owen, Siegfried Sassoon, and Robert Graves, among others. For Crewe 'personal experience did not appear necessary to inspire the finest battle poems, and on the other, from the evidence of the poetry written by soldiers in this present war, it would seem that topics of home and peace were more likely to be chosen by soldier poets. It must be allowed also that little war poetry had reached the highest levels of literature'.[261]

---
[260] *Bulletin*, 29, July 1916, p. 4. Also published in 1916, was John Dover Wilson's 'Poetry and the Child'.
[261] *Bulletin*, 32, September 1917, pp. 4, 6.

Again, these sentiments are dramatically undermined by the extraordinary poetry that emerged from the contemporary conflict, and which seems to herald a new world of literature from that experienced by Crewe.

Three other publications were produced in 1917: Caroline Spurgeon's *Poetry in the Light of War*, published in January; the anonymously compiled *Eight Examination Papers for Pupils of School Age in England and Wales*, which followed in May; and in December, A. C. Bradley's *The Reaction Against Tennyson*.

September 1918 saw the publication of two pamphlets. One was the Presidential Address of Sir Sidney Lee as pamphlet 41, *The Perspective of Biography*. Lee, the chief editor of the *Dictionary of National Biography*, presents his biographical vision, which responds to 'a whole nation's commemorative aspirations'.[262] He examines biographical examples including Boswell and Lockhart, Carlyle, Froude, Moore's *Life of Byron* and Hare's *Life of Sterling*, together with the subject of 'historical bias'. He concludes by referring 'to the need of maintaining a high biographical ideal at a time when the commemorative instinct of men was being strongly aroused as at present [during war]'.[263] The other pamphlet to be published in the last year of the First World War was Ernest de Sélincourt's *The Study of Poetry*, published in March 1918, in which national ideals and male heroism were emphasized, very much reflecting the milieu of production.

The EA's series of separately published pamphlets continued until No 93 in November 1935, which was Guy Boas' lecture to the Association on Lytton Strachey.[264] These numbered EA pamphlets (42–93), produced from 1919 to 1935 followed the pattern of the previous pamphlets with presidential addresses and incidental publications. The former include work by such figures as Viscount Grey of Fallodon (1923), Galsworthy (1924), Stanley Baldwin (1927), Newbolt (1928), and Laurence Binyon in 1934. Missing are addresses by Lord Curzon, President in 1925, who died during his year in office. His address to the EA was given by Sir Rennell Rodd (himself President in 1933), the diplomat and scholar as a 'tribute to the memory of his lifelong friendship with Lord Curzon', about whom he spoke in his pamphlet, *The Essential Characteristics of Poetry*.[265] Also missing from the pamphlets is an address by William Cosmo Lang, Archbishop of Canterbury and EA President in 1931. Given that Lang was too ill to give his lecture on 16 October 1931, the novelist Hugh Walpole spoke in his place on *Novel Building*.[266]

Non-Presidential lectures published in pamphlet form focus largely on individual writers. Dorothy Margaret Stuart, a regular contributor to the *Year's Work in English Studies* and other EA publications, took the opportunity provided by a meeting of the EA on Milton's birthday 'to honour the centenary of Walter Scott's death'. Her *Sir Walter Scott: Some Centenary Reflections*, pamphlet 89, published in 1934, is a tribute to

---

[262] *Mapping Lives: The Uses of Biography*, ed. Peter France, William St. Clair, 2002, p. 79
[263] *Bulletin*, 35, September 1918, p. 7.
[264] The EA subsequently issued occasional unnumbered pamphlets, such as Nowell Smith's 1942 Chair's Address on 'The Origin and History of the Association'.
[265] A summary of his talk is found in the *Bulletin*, 55, November 1925, pp. 5–6.
[266] Lang afterwards commented that Walpole had 'so marvellously weaved together the evolution of his own art and the history of the English novel' (*Bulletin*, 74, April 1932, p. 3).

Scott's fiction and narrative poetry at a time when Scott was decidedly out of fashion. Pamphlet 88, published in 1934, is 'a reply to the essay "Shakespeare and the Drama" written by Tolstoy which appeared in *Tolstoy on Art* published by the Oxford University Press in 1926'.[267] The pamphlet is longer than usual and demonstrates that the EA had no official line on literary works, but was eclectic in its approaches and in its publications. In terms of scholarly debate, it is interesting to observe, as does Michael Taylor in his *Shakespeare Criticism in the Twentieth Century*, that '[i]n the 1930s the Shakespeare critic who most uncompromisingly rejected everything that Bradley stood for...and embraced with religious fervour the doctrine of the play as poem was G. Wilson Knight',[268] the author of pamphlet 88. As discussed, A. C. Bradley, the fifth President of the EA in 1911 played a significant role in its foundation and early development. In an obituary note Bradley was asserted to be 'most properly called the father of the English Association' and 'a mainstay of the Association'.[269] That did not prevent the EA a year before his death from publishing G. Wilson Knight's essay. Despite their differences, in his *Shakespeare and Tolstoy*, Knight does not mention Bradley, but focuses upon defending Shakespeare from attacks by Tolstoy and Robert Bridges. Both, according to Wilson Knight, 'have failed to appreciate Shakespeare primarily through neglect of his imaginative and symbolic effects, due to the excessive emphasis placed on Shakespeare's characterization throughout nineteenth-century commentary'.[270]

Another EA pamphlet of interest from this inter-war period, and now a collector's item, is that by T. S. Eliot, *Charles Whibley: A Memoir*, which was published on 14 January 1932 at one shilling as 'English Association Pamphlet 80'.[271] In his Memoir, Eliot mentions little of his subject's political or social attitudes, though clearly he is in sympathy with Whibley, whose neo-conservatism in his criticism and attitudes are evident. This publication by the EA in December 1931 at a time of social, political and economic disorientation and upheaval in Britain is revealing: it further demonstrates the EA's catholic and eclectic approach, adopting no specific political or ideological stance in the material it produced. Eliot's pamphlet had been distributed to members of the English Association during December 1931. According to Donald Gallup there were 'probably 4000 copies printed, of which 1205 were issued without wrappers as part of *The English Association Pamphlets: Writers, Poets, Playwrights* in June 1964, and "roughly 850", also without wrappers, as part of *The English Association Pamphlets: A Selected Miscellanea* in August 1964'. Gallup notes that Eliot's 'essay was given as a talk to the English Association 20 February

---

[267] *Shakespeare and Tolstoy* by G. Wilson Knight, 1934, p. 3.
[268] Michael Taylor, *Shakespeare Criticism in the Twentieth Century*, 2001, p. 109.
[269] *Bulletin*, 31, November 1935, pp. 7–8.
[270] p. 19.
[271] The journalist and author Charles Whibley (1859–1930) was a patron for *The Criterion*, the first number of which in October 1922 contained Eliot's 'The Waste Land'. Whibley had some connections with the EA. He edited the *Collected Essays* (1925) of his close friend W. P. Ker. Whibley had, according to Eliot 'what is perhaps the first of all critical gifts, without which others are vain: the ability to detect the living style from the dead' (p. 11). Incidentally, Eliot's Whibley essay was not his sole contribution to the English Association. *Essays and Studies* 21, published in 1936 and edited by Herbert Read, contains T.S. Eliot's 'A Note on the Verse of John Milton' (pp. [32]–40). It is included in his *On Poetry and Poets*, 1957.

1931. It was not separately published in the United States, but it is included in [Eliot's] *Selected Essays* [published in 1932]'.[272]

The publishing statistics here provide some guide to how many copies of their pamphlets the EA was actually selling and how many members actually acquired them. The December 1932 *Bulletin* reports a total membership in 1932 of 5,595 and in the previous year 5,962'.[273] Eliot's *Charles Whibley* was distributed to members during December 1931, but as Gallup records above, 'probably 4000 copies were published a month later'. Over three decades later, in June 1964, '1205 were issued without wrappers', and in August of the same year 'roughly 850 also without wrappers' were published.[274] So either just over 2000 of the original 4000 or so copies remained with the EA or the pamphlet was reprinted as part of subsequent reissues.

Sir Henry Newbolt's Presidential Address given at Bedford College in June 1928 was published a month later as pamphlet 70. Newbolt's *The Idea of an English Association* presents the first twenty-one years of the EA's existence from a historical perspective. A rather brief pamphlet of just over ten pages of printed text, it is notable for its generalities. He reflects upon the 'certain points of view' held in common by the founders of the EA 'to promote English scholarship, to raise the standard of education and especially of self-education, to increase our membership to the utmost, and to recruit it from the whole British Commonwealth'. Newbolt also perceives a 'fourth aim' of the EA, the 'desire for fellowship and for a wider and more immediate touch with contemporary English writers and critics'.[275] Newbolt places the need for the EA within a perspective of national transformation, which he attributes not to the 1914–1918 War but to 'the French Revolution and the war of 1793 to 1815'![276]

Newbolt's address, pervaded by a prophetic sense of impending 'social disunion which threatens us',[277] advocates 'the humane education sought by Wordsworth', which 'would ally itself with all those men and women in every neighborhood who have grasped the fact of today…that the present frame of society is wholly inadequate'.[278] Newbolt is in the tradition of so many other prominent members of the EA, who were 'avowed disciples of Wordsworth'.[279]

---

[272] Donald C. Gallup, *T. S. Eliot: A Bibliography*, 1947; rev. ed. 1969, Appendix 20a, p. 45.
[273] *Bulletin*, 75, 1932, p. 3.
[274] Gallup, *op. cit.*
[275] *The Idea of an English Association*, pamphlet 70, 1928, pp. 3–4.
[276] He writes at p. 4, 'I believe that we shall not be far wrong if we attribute the chaotic social conditions of To-Day to a wrong turn taken in the early years of the nineteenth century'.
[277] *The Idea of an English Association*, p. 8.
[278] *The Idea of an English Association*, pp. 12–13.
[279] Indeed, according to Ian Reid, *Wordsworth and the Formation of English Studies*, 2003, p. 91, Newbolt's pamphlet is 'infused with idioms and notions that have an explicitly Wordsworthian colouring'.

VIII
Provincial Branches

The Early Years

The 1907–1908 Membership List of the EA reveals a membership of 332 'Central' members. Within three years of its foundation, the EA had seven branches in England: at Birmingham, Bristol, Croydon, Liverpool, Newcastle and Yorkshire. Of affiliated provincial branches, J. H. Fowler established the first in March 1907 in Bristol with 66 names, of whom 32 were Associate Members and 42 women. Fowler was the President, and Professor R. P. Cowl of University College, Bristol, was Vice President. The Treasurer, also from the University College, was F. E. N. Campbell; the Secretary, W. A. Freeman, taught at the Bristol Grammar School. A four-person Executive Committee consisted of three women: a Miss George; Miss Burns from Clifton High School for Girls; and Miss Pease of the Day Training College, Berkeley Square, Clifton; and one man, F. Pickles, who taught at the Higher Grade School, St. George, Bristol. Of the full and associate members, the overwhelming majority taught in the various schools in the Bristol area concentrated in the Clifton area, representing a fair cross-section of higher and school education establishments across the private and public educational spectrum.

G. E. S. Coxhead was the dominant force behind the establishment of the Birmingham branch. Its President, John Churton Collins, became Professor of English at Birmingham University in 1904. In common with so many prominent EA personalities, Churton Collins was both a product of Balliol College, Oxford, and a prolific writer and editor, whose publications show that he was fully in sympathy with the underlying aims of the EA: that the teaching of English should be conducted in a serious professional rather than an amateur fashion. Coxhead and Professor A. Hughes of Birmingham University were Vice-Presidents and C. P. Stevens from Wellesbourne House School, Acock's Green, Birmingham, served as Secretary and Treasurer. The Birmingham branch had an Executive Committee of seven, including three women: Miss Cox from Hall Green and Miss Jones, from Sutton Coldfield, and Miss. M. A. Hollins, who taught at the Church of England School for Girls in Edgbaston. Of the four men, A. H. Angus was from George Dixon Secondary School, Rotton Park, A. Grant from King Edward's Grammar School, Five Ways, A. Cohen from the Council School, Rea Street and E. C. Keeg from the Council School, Bristol Street. With the exception of R. Cary Gilson from the King Edward's School, nineteen others were Associate Members (thirteen being women), most of whom were teachers.

The Liverpool branch was much larger with an Executive Committee of seventeen and a membership of seventy-one, of whom sixty were Associate Members, mostly engaged in education in Liverpool and its surrounding area as far afield as Chester. The President was the redoubtable Professor Oliver Elton, who, of course, served as President of the EA in 1932.

The Scottish Branch

The strength of the EA in its early years lay in its membership north of the border, which exceeded the numbers of the association in England and Wales in 1907. Its constitution was slightly different from that in England. The Officers as of 31 December 1907 consisted of a Chair (Professor George Saintsbury), four Vice-Chairs, an Honorary Treasurer and a Secretary, and a Council of Management of forty of whom only seven were women. The large Council represented the various regions of Scotland; indeed, there were seven Secretaries of local centres in Glasgow, Edinburgh, Dundee, Aberdeen, St. Andrews, Kelso and Stirling. The membership consisted of 418 of which 143 were women; 205 were Associate members. Members represented head teachers and teachers from private and public schools, the universities, teacher training colleges, clergy, and prominent dignitaries such as the Lord Provost of Glasgow. There were civil servants, educational inspectors, bank officials, librarians, and well-known writers, such as Andrew Lang.

In his 21 October 1910 article in *The Educational News*, J. C. Smith notes that the Scottish branch of the EA had its own special activities. In Scotland 'we have interests and problems of our own which are national rather than merely local', which included 'the work of the Dialect Committee, which has undertaken the pious task of collecting and classifying on scientific principles all the fast-vanishing phenomenon of spoken Scots'. In addition, English had gained in importance in Scottish universities at the end of the nineteenth century, and a Royal Commission on the Scottish Universities (1889–92) effectively reconstituted the curriculum, among other things, making English Language and Literature a full degree subject.[280]

Part of the remarkable strength and growth of the EA in Scotland must be attributed not only to educational theory and practice, but also to individual leadership. E. S. Valentine and J. Inch Low played important formative roles in the creation of the EA in 1906. There were other notable figures including George Saintsbury, at that time, Regius Professor of Rhetoric and English Literature at the University of Edinburgh.[281] Saintsbury served as the first Chair of the Scottish branch and became the third President of the EA in 1909, giving his Presidential Address on *Shakespeare*. Other notable figures active in the early years of the Scottish branch include Mrs. Rachel Annand Taylor, a noted London-based poet and writer who sat on the Council of Management, and three notable Vice-Chairs: Andrew Lang, the writer; Professor Rev. Alexander Lawson, the first Berry Professor of English Literature at St. Andrews University; and Sir Henry Craik, the Head of Scottish Education.

In terms of its constitution, the Scottish branch also differed slightly from the English EA. The 1907 papers contain a letter dated 1 January 1907 to prospective membership, which was signed by the Chair, George Saintsbury, J. C. Smith, Convenor of the Finance Committee and J. Inch Low, the 'Hon. Secretary', and

---

[280] D. Daiches, 'Sir Herbert Grierson', *Proceedings of the British Academy*, xlvi, 1960, p. 322
[281] Among his publications are *A History of Criticism and Literary Taste in Europe from the Earliest Times to the Present Day* (1900–1904), *A History of English Prosody from the Twelfth Century to the Present Day* (1908–1910), plus his *A History of English Prose Rhythm* (1912).

which illustrates clearly that subscriptions were on a sliding scale with a definite commitment to publish 'Transactions' at certain times during the year. Other extant documents from this period contain only minor differences from those drawn up by the EA in England, but do show that the branch retained its own sense of identity throughout its history. It was active at least until 1959, the year in which its records, now in the Special Collection Division of Edinburgh University and in the EA Archive at the University of Leicester, cease.

The Growth of the Branches

The EA *Bulletin* and its successor *English* during the years between the two World Wars gave considerable space to recording the activities of branches in the United Kingdom and overseas. Implicitly these activities, or lack of them, reveal the extent of the EA's influence, prestige and actual situation in terms of membership. In 1922, EA membership was around the 5,000 mark and in its twenty-first year in 1927 membership was over 7,000. At the annual 1927 dinner held at the First Avenue Hotel, High Holborn, on Friday 28 October, with Stanley Baldwin the Prime Minister in the Chair, the Presidents and Secretaries of nineteen branches attended as guests. J. C. Squire, Chairman of the Executive Committee, proposed a toast in their honour: 'We who work in the London Office know that as far as the English Association is concerned, the Branches are the most important part of the tree'. In common with other organizations of a similar nature 'From the earliest years the relationship between the parent body and the local branches was fraught with problems'.[282] Such problems included different categories of membership and attempts by the Central Body in London to impose regularity. As Nowell Smith indicates 'in May 1914, there was a conference between some of the Executive (John Bailey in the Chair) and five representatives of the Branches, because, whereas membership of the Central Body had increased by 100 in the previous two years, that of the Branches had decreased by about 150'.[283]

At the 1927 Annual Dinner present as guests of the Association, in addition to the French Ambassador, were the Presidents of the Bristol, Cambridge, Cheltenham and Gloucester, Darlington, Eastbourne, Leeds and District, Liverpool, Middlesborough, Nottingham, Sheffield, Southampton and Edinburgh Branches. In addition there were the Secretaries of the Brighton and Hove, Bristol, Cambridge, Chelmsford, Darlington, Durham, Liverpool, Nottingham, Southampton, Stafford, Stockton, Edinburgh, Glasgow, and the Scottish Branches.[284]

'Proceedings of Branches' were recorded in the *Bulletin* in some detail. These reports contain both the dates of meetings and the subjects and, in some instances, also contain citations from and summaries of lectures and addresses, many of which

---
[282] Barbara Finney, 'The Ups and Downs of Branches', in Christopher Stray ed., *The Classical Association: the First century 1903–2003*, 2003, p. 160.
[283] Nowell Smith, p. 8.
[284] *Bulletin*, 61, November 1927, which also reported on p. 5 that 'a new Branch of the Association was instituted in Sunderland on October 18'.

were given by leading literary lights. For instance, the November 1927 *Bulletin* reported that E. M. Forster lectured to the Darlington branch on 13 October on 'People in Life and People in Books'. John Galsworthy gave a lecture to the Manchester branch on 14 October, and Michael Sadler addressed the Oxford branch on 13 October. The full length report from this issue of the Bulletin is worth citing in its entirety as a convincing demonstration of the vibrancy of the EA Branches during this period, and as a clear illustration of the genuine, extracurricular interest in language and literature:

DARLINGTON

On September 22, 1927, Mr. E. A. Greening Lamborn lectured on 'English Lyrical Poetry as illustrated in Palgrave's *Golden Treasury*, Mr. J. Strachan in the Chair. Mr. Lamborn gave a detailed criticism of a large number of poems, including Milton's 'L'Allegro', 'Il Penseroso', and 'Lycidas'; Dryden's 'Alexander's Feast'; Collins's 'Ode to Evening'; Gray's 'The Bard' and 'Elegy'; Wordsworth's 'Ode on the Intimations of Immortality'; and Shelley's and Wordsworth's poems on 'The Skylark'.

On October 13, Mr. E. M. Forster lectured on People in Life and People in Books'. He emphasized his point of view that fictitious characters and real characters were essentially different. The men and women created by novelists were fully revealed and understood by him, but the novelist could never understand any living man.

Mutual secrecy was one of the conditions on which life in the world was based. If a novelist could create a man true to life that character would act true to life and in so doing would either kick the book to pieces or kill it by dying himself.

Mr. Forster proceeded to differentiate between what he called the round and the flat characters of fiction, explaining that the flat type was that which could be summed up in a single sentence, while the round type was the reverse. The test of a good round character was whether it could surprise the reader in a convincing way. A large number of characters in modern fiction surprised, but did not convince. They were merely flat characters pretending to be round. Flat characters were regarded in literature as the disreputable characters, but on the other hand they were sometimes very useful for a novelist's purpose.

On November 3 Miss Marjorie Gullan lectured on 'Speech as an Art'. She described her experience in Glasgow, where she founded the Marjorie Gullan School.

Her aim, she said, was to make poetry speaking a real art. The movement had been greatly helped by the British Federation of Musical Festivals and by the democratic character of the Scottish festivals. Her work was essentially democratic.

The Glasgow movement had been the forerunner of the Oxford recitals, and had received the heartiest support from Mr. John Masefield and other well-known poets.

It was necessary to differentiate between the teaching of speech as an art and the old form of teaching elocution.

Miss Gullan held the audience spellbound by her wonderful powers of speaking verse. She recited passages from the literature of the Elizabethans and the Stuarts, and also ballads and Biblical passages.

The Programme for the remainder of the Session is as follows:

On November 24, Mr. B. Colgrave on 'St. Wilfrid of York' (joint meeting with the Historical Association).

On January 20, 1928, Professor Allen Mawer, on 'The How and Why of Place-Name Study'.

On February 2, Professor A. Hamilton Thompson, D.Litt., on 'Medieval Ghost Stories'.

On March 1, Professor W. L. Renwick on 'Shelley and Music'.

On March 8, Mr. G. H. Cowling on 'Yorkshire Dialect Poetry'.

DURHAM

On October 22, 1927, Dr. R. W. Chambers lectured on 'The Legend of King Offa', Mrs. Ellershaw, the President, in the Chair.
    On November 10, Mr. R. S. Elmes lectured on 'The Eddas and Norse Mythology'.
The Programme for the remainder of the Session is as follows:
On December 1, Miss N. M. Lunan on 'C. E. Montague' (1867–).
On January 28, 1928, Miss R. E. D. Donaldson on 'The Novel of Suspense'.
On February 16, Mr. A. Ecclestone on 'Thomas Lovell Beddoes' (1803–49).
On March 1, Mr. R. Rich on 'Thomas Love Peacock' (1785–1866).

EASTBOURNE AND DISTRICT

On October 17, 1927, Mr. G. S. How opened a discussion on 'The Teaching of English'", Mr. G. J. Pass in the Chair.
    Teachers in different types of schools gave the results of their experiences.

MANCHESTER

On October 14, 1927, at the inaugural lecture of the Session Mr. John Galsworthy addressed the members of the Association on 'English'. So great was the number of those who attended that Mr. Galsworthy most kindly agreed to address an overflow meeting in the Whitworth Hall. In the course of a magnificent panegyric on the English tongue, Mr. Galsworthy said:

'There is no end to the extension of the forms or moulds into which we may run this language of ours—the greatest medium of expression in the world to-day. Including its American variety, the English language is the word coin of 170 millions of white people spread over nearly half of the land surface of the earth. It is the language of practically every sea, the official tongue of some 350 millions, brown, black, and yellow people, the accredited business medium of the world, and more and more taught in South America and Japan.

'It would appear indeed to have a certain start of the artificial languages, Esperanto, Volapük, Ido, in the race for the honour of being the second language used in every country. In fact, any impartial scrutiny made at this moment of time must place English at the head of all languages as the most likely to become, in a natural, unforced way, the single inter-communicating tongue.

'There is a tide in the affairs of languages as in the affairs of men. The Napoleonic wars left French the predominant medium of mental exchange. French is still, perhaps, the leading speech in Europe, but French will never now spread effectually by natural means beyond Europe and North Africa. The decline of Europe, the expansion of the British Empire, the magnetic and ever-increasing power of America, are making English the real world-language.

'Its tide was never before so high, and on us private English-speaking people, directly or indirectly concerned with the welfare of that language, there seems to rest the duty of never losing sight of its world-destiny. Surely we are not entitled to be slipped, unbraced stay-at-homes. We need an attire of language, braced and brushed and fit to meet all glances, for English is on view as never language was.

'I often wonder if only I did not know English what I should think of the sound of it, well taught. I believe I should esteem it a soft speech, pleasant to the ear, varied but unemphatic, free from guttural or metallic sounds, restful, dignified, and friendly.

'How prejudiced one is! I should choose it—well spoken—before any language in the world as the medium of expression of which one would tire last. A blend though it be, a hybrid from two main stocks, tinctured by many visiting words, it has acquired rich harmonies of its own and a vigorous individuality. It is worthy of any destiny, however wide.

'A man taking a bird's-eye view of English from Chaucer to this day, and noting the gradual but amazing changes it has undergone, will find on considering Chaucer, Shakespeare, the makers of the Authorized Version, Defoe, Swift, Addison, Johnson, Burke, or Bright, that you cannot crown the English of any one of these and say: "Here a definite pinnacle was reached". They were masters of expression, they used supremely well the English language of their day, tuning the instrument for their contemporaries, enlarging it for those who came afterwards.

'But the possibilities of this great organ of expression transcend even Shakespeare or the Bible. Dare we say that English is past its prime? We cannot judge as yet the English of our day. We see the trees, tall or rank, leafy or dead, but the wood itself we cannot see. Every generation is tempted to depreciate itself. This habit, however amiable and wholesome, is insincere, for there is in nearly all of us that which secretly stands by the age we live in.

'I like to regard English as still in the making, capable of new twists and bold captures. Yet I think our attitude towards it should have more reverence, that we should love our mother-tongue as we love our country, and try to express ourselves in it with vigour, dignity, and grace.

'And here I end this wandering discourse, with an affirmation of belief in the vitality, the variety, the supple strength, the subtle tones of this our rich and ancient language, and of hope that we may come to use it, man for man, woman for woman, speaking and writing, throughout our island as it has ever yet been used, with a full sense of its music and its expressive power.'

In the course of the winter Session Mr. James Stephens, Mr. Philip Guedalla, Mr. Walter de la Mare, Mr. Ivor Brown, and Miss Storm Jameson will lecture.

OXFORD

On October 21, 1927, Mr. Michael Sadleir lectured on 'An Apology for Tales of Terror', Dr. J. Wells, the President, in the Chair. Starting from his title, the name of a pamphlet issued by Walter Scott and others in the 1770s, he led up with art to his main subject, which was to have the history of the stories of sentiment and terror, of which we get glimpses in Miss Austen's novels, and which most of us associate with the name of Mrs. Radcliffe. It would be idle to try to summarize a lecture in which Mr. Sadleir, who has already discoursed on the *Northanger Novels*, distinguished the true 'Gothistic' from the 'imitation Gothic', and explained their relation to the general romantic movement, and to such novels by Charles Dickens and Wilkie Collins. His knowledge of the subject is unmatched, and he was able to give us some extracts from his own collection, concluding with a passage from a story by Mr. Ros, published in 1897, which is in style in the direct line of succession from the tales of a hundred and fifty years ago, so long and so persistent is the tradition. The quiet humour of Mr. Sadleir's delivery and the artistic arrangement of his matter were as remarkable as the subtle analysis of the different species of this *genre*.[285]

Five years later at the AGM of 10 June 1932, the Chairman of the Executive Committee, the novelist Hugh Walpole, reported that the EA 'membership was 5,595 this year, as compared with 5,962 in the previous year. The membership of the Central Body decreased by 169, of the Branches in England by 134, and of the Branches abroad by 77'. The trend reversed North of the border: 'The Branches in Scotland … showed an increase of 13 members'.[286] In spite of the reduction in

---
[285] *Bulletin*, 61, November 1927, pp. 18–22.
[286] *Bulletin*, 75, December 1932, p. 3.

branch membership, eleven pages of this *Bulletin* record 'Proceeding of Branches'. These include meetings, lectures and other activities including, for instance, discussions 'on Virginia Woolf's 'Orlando' (Chelmsford, 7 June), 'Reviews of Books' and so on. Branches included those in Birmingham (nine meetings), Bristol (six meetings), Chelmsford (ten meetings), Darlington (three meetings), Hull (four meetings), Leeds and District (six meetings), Leicester (seven meetings), Liverpool and District (four meetings), London, East (two meetings), Manchester (six meetings), Middlesborough (ten meetings), Nottingham (three meetings), Oxford (four meetings), Plymouth (three meetings), Sheffield (six meetings), and Southampton (six meetings). Staffordshire had three branches: Leek and District (six meetings), Northwest Staffordshire (seven meetings), and Stafford (eight meetings). There were also meetings in Sunderland (two) and York (three). The Scottish branch was active in Aberdeen (two meetings), Dundee (one meeting), Edinburgh (eight meetings), Glasgow (six meetings), St. Andrews (six meetings) and West Fife (eight meetings).

Some of the reports from the branches, as we have seen, contain detailed summaries of lectures. The Leicester branch, for instance, reports in detail on papers by A. S. Collins on 'Hugh Walpole', Roger Manvell on 'The Literature of the Stage', and Professor A. A. Cook on 'Alice Meynell'. The report from Sheffield contains a summary of the Ifor Evans Centenary lecture given on 17 October 1932 on 'Sir Walter Scott'. Of special interest is the report from the Stafford branch, which is frank in its assessment of the real state of affairs in the branch, in addition to outlining activities. The report reads:

STAFFORD

The Branch suffered like other institutions from the economic and political difficulties of the time. A considerable number of Members and Associates resigned, and its activities suffered from the occurrence of the General Election in October, at the beginning of the Winter Session, which diverted to Politics much of the attention that might have been given to Literature and the formation of Reading Circles.

The drawing up of the Winter Programme of Lectures was particularly difficult, and one lecturer had to withdraw his promise owing to ill health.

A very successful reading circle was held by Mrs. B. Wilson during the spring and summer, the subjects of the papers and discussions being first Biography and later some novelists. A successful variation was the writing of a short story by each member of the circle, the stories having the same title and an evening being given to their reading.

The visit to the Birmingham Repertory Theatre and the Summer Excursion for 1923 were abandoned for this year.

The attendance at some of the lectures was disappointing, the only one really well attended being Colonel Wedgwood's lecture on 'The Personnel of Parliament before 1832'.

The Summer Excursion in June 1931 to Ludlow was most enjoyable.

The following is the programme arranged for the session 1932–3: On October 13, 1932, Miss Doreen Wallace on 'Contemporary Novelists'.

On November 10 Mr. Hugh Ross Williamson on 'The New Movement in Poetry'.

On December 8, Lord Charnwood on 'Some English Historians and Historical Novelists'.

On January 24, 1933, Miss M. Maitland Davidson on 'Heroines of Modern Fiction'.

On February 24 Professor Mary Williams on 'King Arthur and the Knights of the Round Table' (illustrated with lantern slides).

On March 16, Mr. W. S. Peach on 'Matthew Arnold as a Poet'.[287]

The decline of the membership and impact of the EA is reflected in the reports of the period preceding the World War II and in the 'Proceedings of Branches' accounts of each year of the War. These reports move from a record of dynamic activity to less optimistic reading. *English* for 1938 contained two numbers. The earlier number 7 records branch activities in Bath (eight meetings); Birmingham (seven meetings, of which one was a Joint Meeting with the Classical Association on 1 March 1938, when Professor George Thomson spoke on 'The Myth of Prometheus in Literature'); Durham (four meetings); and Hull (four meetings of which one of was a joint meeting—in this instance, with the Historical Association at which Dr. Philip Corder spoke on 'The Roman Remains at Brough'). Leicester was a more active branch with six meetings; London East also had the same number and a business meeting. Also active was the Norfolk and Norwich branch with eight meetings, two of these being a Members' Night with Readings and Discussions. There is no account of the 24 February 1938 meeting at which Alec Waugh spoke on 'Whither the Novel?' Plymouth had four meetings; Reading held one; Sheffield and Southampton were more active with seven and five meetings respectively. Of the seven Sheffield meetings, one was a discussion on 'Training in Taste' and the other on 'Visit to the Graves Art Gallery'. A note prefacing the Durham report observes that 'in arranging the programme for the session the Committee of the Branch have aimed at broadening the scope of its series of lectures, so as to include subjects of a general artistic and historical importance as well as those specifically confined to literary history and criticism'. The four sessions began with Gordon Bottomley on 'The Meaning of Poetry' (20 October 1937). On 24 November, Robert Lyon, described as 'Master of Painting in King's College, Newcastle' spoke on 'Expression in Painting' with 'lantern illustrations'. On 2 February 1938, Irvine Mason, who was Professor of Chemistry at the University of Durham, spoke on 'The Beginnings of Painting'. A fortnight later Professor Bonamy Dobrée lectured on 'Trends in the Modern Novel'.

Noticeably the section in *English* 'Proceedings of Branches' reduced as the political situation got worse. Only two branches, Darlington (six meetings) and Southampton (three meetings) sent reports for the second issue of *English* in 1938. Unfortunately the Darlington branch doesn't record the contents of lectures by John Dover Wilson on 'Shakespeare's Universe'; Clifford Leech on 'Document and Ritual: an Essay on Critical Theory'; Edwin Muir on 'The Contemporary Novel'; or L. A. G. Strong on 'Tradition and Experiment in the Modern Novel'. It does record that the 6 December 1937 meeting consisted of a 'Lecture Recital by the Martin Harvey Miniature Ballet on "Dancing Through the Ages"'.[288]

The third issue of *English* for 1938, number 9, was fuller. It gave accounts of programmes at Bath (seven meetings), Plymouth (four meetings), Reading (two meetings) and Southampton (four meetings). The final issue of *English* (no. 12, in 1939) notes

---
[287] *Bulletin*, 75, December 1932, pp. 41–2.
[288] *English*, 11, 8, 1938, p. 129.

that only two reports reached it for inclusion. The Nottingham branch noted that four meetings had been arranged for the Autumn of 1939, and Plymouth, nine for Autumn 1939 and Spring 1940. The EA in order to encourage a younger membership instituted 'Junior Branches' and an 'award of a prize for the best essay, but the outbreak of War … made it impossible for the competition to be held in the present circumstances'.[289] *English* lists in alphabetical order over two pages 'of Schools enrolled under the Junior Branch Scheme'.[290] The numbers, 13, 14 and 15 of *English* published in 1940, note unsurprisingly, that although the 'Junior Branch' competition for the best essay was held, it 'proved disappointing…in no case did an essay reach prize standard', only twenty-four essays being submitted from 11 schools compared with fifty-five from two schools previously. Branches reporting their activities to *English* are reduced to Edinburgh, which was very active with six meetings; Nottingham with five; Durham with four; and Plymouth with three in 1940. As Nowell Smith comments in his 1942 Chairman's Address 'some 130 Junior Branches [were established] in secondary schools', which was partly the result of a 1935 Executive Committee's decision to construct a 'Schools Sub-Committee' and individual initiative by EA members. 'The latter experiment was cruelly cut down by the frost of War'.

Overseas Branches

Reports from the overseas branches regularly occur in the *Bulletin* and *English*. The dates of the actual foundations of individual overseas branches are somewhat obscure. Some of the earliest were probably formed in the Indian sub-continent, for a 'Mr. F. E. Corley (South India)' is amongst the names nominated by the branches and elected at the AGM, 10–11 January 1913, at University College, London.[291] Corley's name, with that of G. M. Parkin from the Toronto Canadian branch, occurs amongst the branch nominations for 1916–1919 when a Mr. S. V. Blake, also from Toronto, was added to the nominations.[292] The Report of the Executive Committee for the Year Ended December 31st 1919 records that 'the Branch in Toronto [has] 119 full members'[293] The Accounts for 1919 show that the Toronto branch contributed £18 for subscriptions, the third highest amount (the Scottish branches contributing £69 2s. and Manchester £24. 8 6d.). The names of Corley, Blake and Parkin are the only representatives nominated by branches until another name also appears, a Leigh Smith from Ceylon in 1921.[294] Blake's name remains for Toronto in the 1922 listings of nominations.

There was also interest in the EA from elsewhere. At the May 1920 Annual Dinner held at the Royal Adelaide Rooms in the Strand, one of the guests was the Hon. A. Sanderson from Australia who spoke on behalf of the guests. Sanderson 'assured the members of the Association that the figures indicating the consumption

---

[289] *English*, 12, 1939, p. 401.
[290] *English*, 12, 1939, p. 402–4.
[291] *Bulletin*, 19, September, 1913, p. 4.
[292] *Bulletin*, 38, September, 1919, p. 5.
[293] *Bulletin*, 40, May, 1920, p. 1.
[294] *Bulletin*, 44, November, 1921, p. 4.

of English literature in Australia were really amazing'. For Sanderson 'The Dominions of the British Empire looked to England for the standard of written English; but, speaking as one who had travelled widely, he deplored the absence of any standard of spoken English'. Sanderson 'wished the Association could find and fix some standard of English speech, for the sake of those from other lands who desired to know what true English was'. Notably no comment was made publicly on the EA's position on this at the dinner.[295]

In his Presidential Address at the annual EA dinner held at the Café Monico on 27 May 1921, Lord Ernle, President in 1920 and 1921, was 'glad to notice that we [the EA] have recently opened branches in South Africa and in Ceylon'. Ernle added, with imperialistic hyperbole: 'we send out the great models of English literature as the missionary pioneers which interpret to the world, as well as to ourselves, the best side of our national characteristics, and represent our finest thoughts and ideals expressed in their purest forms'. He then asserted that 'It is for that missionary work and enterprise, ladies and gentlemen, that the English Association exists'.[296] There is no more explicit statement of the EA's early 'missionary' activities and colonial endeavours, long since abandoned!

John Bailey reported to the AGM in May 1923 that the EA had branches in 'Canada, South Africa, Ceylon, and other parts of the British Empire'. He believed that 'a Branch was about to be opened in Australia'. Nominees by the branches for election to the EA General Committee for 1923 include 'Mr. Leigh Smith (Ceylon); Professor H. Clement Notcutt (South Africa); Mr. F. E Corley (South India); Mr. Alan Sullivan; Mr. M. D. C. Tait (Toronto)'. Amongst the guests at the 1923 Annual Dinner held at the Trocadero Restaurant was the Spanish Ambassador who spoke of the influence of Shakespeare upon Spanish Literature. Also present was Dr. George McLean from the USA who mentioned the possibilities of forming close links between the USA and the EA.[297] This, of course, was a possibility frequently mentioned, but one which never actually materialized.

Committee nominations from branches as reported in the *Bulletin* for December 1924, reveal a decided growth in overseas branch activity. Nominations are noted for Ceylon, South Africa, Sydney Australia and Toronto. Interestingly at the AGM for May 1926, 'Major Kenneth Colvile raised the question of the South India Branch, whose activities had been suspended for some time'. The *Bulletin* notes that Colville 'was of the opinion that the name of this Branch should be deleted from the List, as its presence there discourages any one from attempting to form other Branches, and in India there was a great field for Branches'.[298]

Some extent of the actual nature of Overseas branch activities may be gleaned from the reports from branches. These are recorded following the activities of the 'Scottish Branch' in the *Bulletin*. For instance, no. 59, April 1927, records details of activities in Ceylon, Fort Hare, Cape Town, South Africa, Sydney, New South Wales

---

[295] *Bulletin*, 41, September, 1920, p. 14.
[296] *Bulletin*, 44, November, 1921, p. 8.
[297] *Bulletin*, 49, December, 1923, pp. 3, 6, 13.
[298] *Bulletin*, 58, November, 1926, p. 5.

(Australian English Association). Ceylon recorded that 'During 1926 there has been a considerable increase of members. In 1925 there were 91 members, of whom 85 were Full Members, and 6 Associate Members. In 1926 there were 120 members, of whom 114 were Full Members, and 6 Associate Members'. *Bulletin* no. 60, August 1927, reported activity from two branches in Australia. The Queensland programme for 1927 included short papers on 'Education in France'; a 'Presidential Address'; 'Report on "English in Schools"'; the topic of 'Scholarship Examinations'; a lecture by Professor H. Alcock on 'The Great English Historians as Writers'; an evening on 'The Dalton System'; and finally, a 'social evening'. The Sydney, NSW branch gave even fuller details of three events which had taken place and four to follow. The Cape Town, South Africa, branch attracted distinguished authors. John Galsworthy, EA President in 1924 and in 1932, gave his address on 'Expression' on 4 March 1927, which was published as pamphlet 59. It covered, in part, the same ground as his presidential address of 1924. The report adds that 'So much interest was aroused in Mr. Galsworthy's only appearance in public that the hall proved quite inadequate to hold the number that wished to hear him, and some hundreds of people had to go away'.

The visit on 18 March of a writer much more neglected today than Galsworthy, Leonard Merrick, was also popular. Merrick 'read one of his short stories—"The Doll in the Pink Silk Dress' from *A Chair on the Boulevard*…and held a large audience spellbound'. When Merrick's father lost money, at the age of eighteen the young Leonard was sent to South Africa from London to the Kimberley goldfield area. Kimberley and its surroundings form the backdrop for his short stories and the novel *The Worldlings* (1900), which starts in Kimberley and then moves to London. The report of Merrick's response to the EA Capetown branch audience's reception is revealing:

> When I was a very young man I lived in your city. It was in Capetown that I first aspired seriously to become a novelist. It was in Capetown that I made my first acquaintance with a public library. It is around Capetown that some of my most pleasant memories linger. When my first novel was published I used to wonder whether it would be read in Capetown. I can hardly say how touched I am at the honour which has done me of having been able to read one of my stories to a Capetown audience.[299]

The Report from the Cape Town branch noted that 'An increased interest has been taken in the work of the Association since the visits of…John Galsworthy and … Leonard Merrick, and the membership now stands at 78'. The Toronto branch of the Association reported in the same issue, no. 60 for August 1927, that 'the number of members in now 95', and it reported seven meetings for October 1926 through April 1927. This membership was not as extensive as that of the Ceylon branch, which reported in *Bulletin* no. 62, March 1928, that 'During 1927 there has been a further increase of members, the number being 140 as compared with 120 in 1926 and 91 in 1925'. The same number of the *Bulletin* records branches in Australia (Queensland, Sydney, NSW), Canada (New Brunswick, Toronto), Ceylon (Colombo), India (Allahabad), New Zealand (Christ Church), South Africa (Cape Town, Fort Hare,

---

[299] *Bulletin*, 60, August, 1927, p. 33.

Witwatersrand, Johannesburg) and a branch at the University of Chicago.[300] The next year another branch had formed in Rangoon.[301] The March 1930 *Bulletin* recorded branches formed in Melbourne, Hong Kong, Wellington, and South Africa; however, Chicago seems to have lapsed with no contact address given. The situation of overseas branches five years later was not unhealthy. There were four Australian branches (Adelaide, Melbourne, Queensland, and Sydney); one only in Canada (Toronto), Ceylon (Colombo), New Zealand (Christ Church) and Hong Kong; three in India (Allahabad, Madras, Rangoon); and five in South Africa (Cape Town, Fort Hare, Pretoria, Wellington and Witwatersrand/Johannesburg).[302]

Some optimism in the early days of the Second World War must have been kindled by the reports from 'Overseas Branches' recorded in the third volume, number 13, of *English* published in 1940. Two meetings were held at the Melbourne branch in Australia. In South Africa Fort Hare, Witwatersrand, and the Wellington branches were active. Indeed in the Autumn of 1939, five meetings took place in Witwatersrand with subjects ranging from Jane Austen, to acting at the time of Garrick and Kean, and 'American Books for South Africans'.[303] But the outbreak of World War II saw the 1940 closure of the Wellington South Africa branch started in 1932; the Cape Town branch, formed in 1932, closed five years later; Rangoon, started in 1932, lapsed after two years; and Hong Kong, also a product of 1932, closed in 1941.

The EA Executive Committee meeting minutes, materials in the EA archives, and personal evidence presented by those involved, and 'Proceedings of Branches' for the period after 1941 convey a mixed message. During the Second World War, as has been noted, activities of the Branches, together with various Branches themselves, were curtailed. Representative of wartime Branch 'activities' is the report of 'Proceedings of Branches' recorded for the Plymouth Branch. Plymouth, a naval centre, suffered particularly intense German bombing raids during the war, and this is commented upon in these proceedings:

> At the Annual General Meeting, which was held at Swarthmore Settlement, a blitz having rendered our former meeting-place—the Arts Club—uninhabitable in the early summer, the election of the Committee by ballot paper was announced: the Vice-President, Sir William Munday, became President, and Mr. R. R. Brown was elected Vice-President for 1942; while the Hon. Treasurer and Hon. Secretary were asked to continue their respective duties. The Hon. Secretary reported the loss of four members—Mr. Whitfield (President for 1941) and Mr. Dundas were 'called up', and the evacuation of schools had withdrawn Miss Saville and Miss Herbertson from the city. These were all staunch members who had served or were serving on the Committee, and who had, on many occasions, entertained the Branch. No dates for lectures were missed during 1941, lectures being provided by the members themselves, except on 5 November when very generously L. A. G. Strong gave us 'A talk on Broadcasting and the Writer' which created enthusiasm and much laughter in an audience of about seventy persons. Membership on 7 January was 37 (including 3 Associate Members).[304]

---

[300] *Bulletin*, 62, March, 1928, pp. 33, 36.
[301] *Bulletin*, 64, December 1928, p. 40.
[302] *Bulletin*, 81, November, 1935, p. 12.
[303] *English*, 3, 13, 1940, p. 47.
[304] *English*, 4, 19, 1942, p. 35.

The next issue of *English*, volume 4, number 21, 1942 recorded from Plymouth, a programme of lectures each day, lectures on 'The Nature of Art', 'Alexander Pope and his Friends', 'Shakespeare's Sonnets', 'Benet's John Brown's Body', and 'Mark Rutherford'. In spite of wartime difficulties, Plymouth was the only branch whose reports are published in *English* for 1942–1943.[305] Other Branches to send in reports during the War, apart from Plymouth, include Durham in 1944 and 1945. At the AGM held on Tuesday 10 July 1945, the EA Chairman, Arundell Esdaile, specially commended the Plymouth Branch 'for having carried on so successfully during the war years' and reported that the year witnessed the start of a new EA Branch at Chichester, Sussex.[306]

Reports for 1946 record four meetings at the new Chichester Branch in the Autumn of 1945 with talks on the poet William Collins, Shakespeare's *Henry V*, 'Twentieth Century English Poetry' and 'What is Prose?'[307] Branch activities, especially in the southwest of England and the London surroundings, picked up considerably in the immediate post-war period. Proceedings in Bath, Bristol, Kent, Plymouth, and Southampton are noted in 1947, although there may well have been activities in other parts of the country.

A few years later, for 1951 and 1952 lecture programmes are recorded in *English* in Bristol, Manchester, Kent, Edinburgh, Nottingham, Reading, Southampton, and York. The Nottingham Branch seems to be more directly related to the English Department at its University than the other branches. These, from the programme of events, seem to be a combination of the University and the general public, as in the instances of Manchester and Southampton with academic affiliated speakers, in particular. The York Branch's honorary secretary was from St. John's College, with a local clergyman as the President of the Branch. In addition to lectures on subjects as varied as 'Tennyson as a Humorist', 'A Natural Dialect Survey', and 'Macbeth' in the Autumn of 1951, the late Spring of 1952 programme includes on 7 June a 'visit to the newly reconstructed Georgian Theatre at Richmond, Yorkshire'.[308]

A decade later, in the early 1960s, *English* still records 'Proceedings of Branches'. For instance, volume 14 in 1962 records active branches with meetings in locations as diverse as Edinburgh, Kent, Nottingham, and Southampton. Volume 16 in 1966–67, however, records no Branch activity whatsoever. In fact, lists found in the EA archives reveal lists of Branches closed in the 1950s, with a few revivals the exception rather than the rule. These reveal, in alphabetical order: Bath closed at the end of 1950; Birmingham closed in 1952; Bristol closed in 1954; Cardiff 1953; Chichester 1954; Coventry 1952; Darlington 1947; Durham 1950; Edinburgh 1950; Exeter 1951; Hull 1950; Leeds 1951; Manchester 1964; Plymouth 1951; Reading 1949; Rhondda 1949; Rugby 1947; South-West Wales 1951; Worthing 1949; and York, which closed in 1954. For these very numerous closures, only three Branches were revived: Dundee was revived in 1966; Glasgow was revived in 1965; and Middlesborough in 1966.

---

[305] *English*, 4, 22, 1942, p. 139; 23, 1943, p. 203.
[306] *English*, 5, 30, 1945, p. 221.
[307] *English*, 6, 31, 1946, p. 46.
[308] *English*, 9, 51, 1952, pp. 118–19.

In each instance, there were local circumstances resulting in closure, extending from disinterest in the EA's activities or the demise of the active organizing member. The lack of people coming forward to put in the work to keep the branches active and growing was clearly a major factor. Such closures reflect the history of the EA, which increasingly in the post-War situation became an organization that was metropolitan based and focused, and perceived to be specifically London-orientated and relatively 'closed'. James Alison, a retired HM inspector of Schools and an active Scottish member, offers an explanation for the demise and revival of the Scottish branches during the period. He writes: 'historically there was a Scottish Branch of the EA, which at one time had three constituent centres, in Edinburgh, Glasgow, and Dundee; but this structure had collapsed before I came on the scene in 1963, when I helped to re-form the Glasgow Centre'. A 'small Edinburgh group' was also kept going but both of these, Glasgow and Edinburgh 'petered out around 1969–1970 as people moved on or retired and could not be replaced'.[309] He adds:

> There is now no EA presence in Scotland; there may still be individual Scottish subscribers but I don't know of any...None of the Scottish Branches went in for publications or journals but did supply brief reports to the national journal *English*. They were mainly societies which offered members monthly lectures and an annual conference . . . For a time both centres [Glasgow and Edinburgh] benefited, indeed survived, through the willing cooperation of their local universities, colleges of education and HM Inspectors. In the 1960s they were regarded as offering useful professional development for teachers of English. But then educational priorities changed! Moreover by 1970 the tide of cultural nationalism was moving against a London body titled 'The English Association'. It was significant that in that year a new scholarly society called 'the Association for Scottish Literary Studies' was founded, which competed for the same mix of university, school and lay membership.

Overseas Branches 1940–67

During the Second World War, *English* carried reports from overseas branches active in Australia (Melbourne and Sydney), India (Allahabad, Madras and Calcutta) and South Africa (Fort Hare, Witwatersrand, which reported on 30 June, 1942 a membership of 42, Pretoria, and Wellington in the Cape Province). Allahabad even, apparently, had time for what appears to be internal disputes. The war had not impacted upon it directly, and emerging independence movements apparently did not impact upon the EA's activities. At the EA Executive Committee meeting of 26 January 1944, an extract was read 'from a letter received from the Hon. Secretary of the Allahabad Branch of the Association'. This 'stated that, as the result of a resolution adopted by the Branch in 1931 whereby the head of the English Department of the University of Allahabad became *ex officio* President of the United Provinces Branch, the Hon. Secretary of the Branch since its inception in 1925, would be relinquishing his position'. The resigning secretary, Professor S. C. Deb, 'added that he would continue to work in the interests of the Association as President of the Branch and would communicate the name of his successor in due course'.

---

[309] Personal correspondence, May 2004.

The 'Proceedings of Overseas Branches' for Allahabad, India, published in 1945, record that 'Professor S.C. Deb, who had been Secretary of the Branch for almost twenty years, has been elected President'. Eight meetings from 28 August 1944 through 21 April 1945 are reported, which included papers on 'The Plays of Eugene O'Neill', 'The Technique of the One-Act Plays', 'Nehru as a Writer', 'The Short Stories of Somerset Maugham', and a discussion on 'The Position of English in the post-War Educational Schemes of the Province'.[310]

The Fort Hare Branch in South Africa report for 1942 included membership data. It had twenty-five full members and sixty-two associate members. The branch held six meetings during 1942, all apparently well attended. The head of the Bible School at a Missionary Institution was President of the Branch and spoke on 'Inspiration and Craftsmanship'. The Principal of the Missionary Institution lectured on J. M. Barrie. Other lectures included one from a lecturer in Social and Economic Anthropology at Rhodes University College on '"The Ways of the Wizard": an account of the magical beliefs of the Majaji tribe of the Northern Transvaal'. The Professor of English at the South African Native College, Fort Hare spoke on 'Tradition and Design in Russian Civilization'; and the Rabbi of the East London Hebrew congregation spoke on 'The Jews and English Literature'.[311]

An interesting example of activity is seen in reports in *English* of the foundation in January 1945 of an EA Branch in Alexandria, Egypt. Five monthly meetings are recorded from February through June 1945 on subjects ranging from James Joyce to readings on the part of members from 'English Literature on Egypt'. A full report relates that there are 'some thirty local members. The nucleus of our membership is drawn from the Professors, Staff, and Graduates of Farouk el Awal University of [Alexandria], and, to a lesser degree, from the teaching staff of English and Egyptian Schools...members are of various nationalities, less than half being British'.[312] The report adds that 'the Chairman for this year [1946–1947] and many members are Egyptian, and we have Irish, American, Syrian, Greek, Armenian, Italian, and Russian members'. The reporter, the Honorary Secretary, is Chilean; the Chairman is a colonel from the Egyptian Police; and the Committee consists of three Professors and two University lecturers, the Director of the Alexandria British Institute, a representative from the English Girl's College and an Egyptian journalist plus the Secretary. Monthly lectures included papers on Anthony Trollope, the development of Arabic literature, *Don Quixote*, the Welsh Literary tradition, George Meredith and Ernest Hemingway. On 29 May 1946 D. J. Enright, then a lecturer in English Literature at the Farouk el Awal University in Alexandria, spoke on Contemporary Poetry. Enright's *Memoirs of a Medical Professor* (1964) recall his experiences as a wandering English professor in Japan, Egypt, Singapore and elsewhere as the sun set on the British Empire and the influence abroad of Britain.

Overseas Branch activity is recorded in *English* until Spring 1964 and then ceases in subsequent issues. This is somewhat curious as the Autumn 1965 issue of *English*,

---
[310] *English*, 5, 36, 1945, p. 224.
[311] *English*, 4, 22, 1943, p. 139.
[312] *English*, 6, 36, 1947, p.328.

is a special 'The Commonwealth: Past and Present' one with contributions on Canadian writing, 'The Indian Background of Eliot's Poetry', the Contemporary scene in New Zealand, 'Nigerian poetry in English', and 'Teaching Speech in Tasmania', and 'Recent Trends in South African Writing'.[313] The West Indies and other areas are excluded. Between 1947 and the Spring of 1966, regular reports of Branch activities are recorded from Australia, South Africa and India. Sydney, and Brisbane, Queensland, which resumed meetings in March 1947 following a wartime break, held nine meetings in 1947. Both were particularly active Australian branches. In Sydney, H. M. Butterley retired in 1961 after thirty years of working for the EA as Honorary Secretary of the Sydney Branch.[314] By 1962, the Sydney EA, established in 1932, created its own journal, *Southerly*, edited by G. A. Wilkes, 'Sydney University's Professor of Australian Literature (the first to be appointed to such a chair in any Australian University, and a long-standing member of the Committee of the Sydney Branch)'.[315]

The last published report in *English* from Alexandria in Egypt appears in 1950, with the programme for 1949 to 1950 and three meetings: 'What Makes a Great Poem'; to 'Charles Reade'; 'Six Weeks in the U.S.A'. Reports from Allahabad in India are included until volume 13 published in the Autumn of 1961, with the illustrious R. N. Deb, who seems rarely to be absent from its activities, lecturing on 'Some Aspects of Shakespeare'. Over ten years earlier, the Allahabad report reflected well the situation of chaos following the British withdrawal from the Indian sub-continent. The report reads: 'Owing to the stress and strife in the country following the great political changes, and also owing to other diversions in the University, the Association could not function as actively in past years. Only one meeting could be held on 19 November 1947 at which...P. C. Gupta read a paper on 'The Aesthetics of Galsworthy'; ...I. Greenberg gave also a Shakespearean recital'.[316]

Regular reports were received throughout the period from Fort Hare and, to a lesser extent, Cape Town, South Africa. The Fort Hare Branch 'met without a break since 1923 and in 1956 the usual six meetings were held during the winter months'.[317] It was still reporting activity in 1964. Another active branch was Salisbury, in what was then Southern Rhodesia. In the Autumn of 1961 and through to August of 1962 eleven meetings are recorded plus the note that 'Membership of the Branch has increased this year [1962] from 30 in 1961 to just over 50'.[318] Three years later, from February to October, ten meetings were announced.[319] Curiously, no reports are recorded from New Zealand, Canada or from non-Commonwealth countries. The West Indies and South America are represented by a sole report from British Honduras, which records a number of events organised in Belize on a

---

[313] *English*, 15, 90, 1965.
[314] *English*, 14, 80, 1962, p. 127.
[315] *English*, 14, 84, 1963, p. 258.
[316] *English*, 7, 39, 1948, p. 102.
[317] *English*, 11, 66, 1957, p. 249.
[318] *English*, 14, 81, 1962, p. 126.
[319] *English*, 15, 87, 1964, pp. 124–25.

monthly basis from February to September 1956. These included a lecture on 'The Images of Caribbean Poetry'.[320]

Papers in the EA archives contain a record of when payments from the overseas branches began and ceased. As such, they constitute something of a record of the establishment, existence and demise of the overseas branches. In Australia, the Adelaide Branch, founded in 1932, closed eight years later, but was revived in 1960. The last payment recorded is in 1976. Melbourne and Queensland have the same 1932 foundation dates. They last contributed funds to the London EA in 1974. In India, Allahabad made its last recorded payment in 1964, Delhi in 1970, Madras in 1968. In South Africa, Cape Town first paid in 1932, closed in 1937, was revived in 1956 and still survives today. Pretoria ceased payment in 1950, as did Witwatersrand in 1952. Interestingly, a branch was still active in Salisbury up to 1975. The sole country in which the English language did not play a prominent role, Spain, had a branch of the EA active in 1968 but the last note of its existence in the EA archives is in 1969!

The 1960s to the present day

In spite of the diminution of branch activity in the 1960s and 1970s, a few prospered and flourished in the last years of the twentieth century and beginnings of the next. As indicated by Miriam Allott, the English Association North (EAN) was active and focused on Liverpool University in the 1980s. Members of the English Department, especially Helen Wilcox and the specialist on Romantic Literature, Bernard Beatty, 'organised conferences and events for schools, brought together academics from northern English departments (especially Liverpool, Manchester and North Wales) and even had a journal—the 'Proceedings of the English Association North'.[321] According to Bernard Beatty, the Chair, the English Association North is more than simply a branch of the EA, and from it emerged a subsequent journal, *The Reader*:

> EAN is not officially different but practically it is. We used to have a little Magazine PEAN (Proceedings of EAN) and *The Reader* is in a way a continuation of that. When it first started up it flagged this association; I am not sure whether it still does so. EAN basically did two things, it organised conferences for teachers (which was the original idea). The latter worked well for a time but it became increasingly difficult for teachers to get time off to attend unless the conferences were geared to school or teacher profiling of a utilitarian and even philistine character, so bit-by-bit enthusiasm (a lot of it about in the beginning) dwindled. It was very much subject-based first of all rather than geared to 'education', as such, though of course, the two can't be wholly sundered, but there seemed less and less allowed space for this sort of thing.[322]

The Reader is currently, in 2005, active as a journal 'supported by the School of English at the University of Liverpool and by the Arts Council' and, according to its

---
[320] *English*, 11, 63, 1956, pp. 124–25.
[321] Private correspondence, May 2005, between Helen Lucas and William Baker.
[322] Email correspondence, May 2005.

website[323] has an office at the University of Liverpool. It features poems and literary criticism. Issue 3 for 1998, for instance, contains poems by Elizabeth Jennings, Richard Hall, and Alison Chisholm, and an article by Bernard Beatty, 'Talking About Byron'. *The Reader* claims on its website association with the EA, and provides information that:

> The English Association North is an independent part of the English Association promoting the collaborative study and enjoyment of English literature throughout the North, and building partnerships between Universities, Colleges of Further Education, schools and the general reading public. It is currently centered in the English Department of the University of Liverpool, whose members regularly give sixth-form lectures in schools, raising funds which are used to sponsor further talks, theatrical events, prizes, scholarships, and this magazine, in the interest of continuing education in English Literature throughout the region.

In terms of other literary publications, as noted earlier, G. A. Wilkes, Challis Professor of English Literature at the University of Sydney, edited *Southerly*, the journal of the Sydney Branch of the English Association since 1963. Initially on its foundation in 1939 called *Southerly: A Literary Magazine*, it became from 1957 to 1993 *Southerly: A Review of Australian Literature*. Subsequently it was known as *Southerly*. Professor Elizabeth Webby took over the editorship in 1994 and edited it with Ivor Indyk until 1999. In 2000, Noel Rowe and David Brooks, also from the English Department at the University of Sydney, jointly took over the editorship. Its pages contain articles, interviews, poems, short stories and reviews on Australian literature. S. E. Lee's 'The First Fifty Years, II: *Southerly*, 1939–1974', and 'The Golden Years: A History of *Southerly* from 1974 to 1989',[324] gave an account of its genesis and history. Robert Jackson, from the English Department at the University of Sydney, notes:

> The Association has been going through a rather lean period here, being unable to recruit new blood, having been a bit superseded among English teachers in the schools by a rival professional body, The English Teachers' Association.[325]

He adds that it also suffers 'from ennui and general exhaustion among the increasingly older people who run it. But we did, after a hiatus of a couple of years, run in March a very successful conference, attended by some 150 teachers, on the HSC [Higher School Certificate] units of study'. Jackson also notes that, 'the conference was dedicated to Helen Willis, a dedicated and inspirational teacher who for many years organized, just about single-handedly, the annual conferences for teachers and HSC students'.[326]

---

[323] www.thereader.co.uk
[324] *Southerly*, 34, 1974, pp. 121–41 and *Southerly*, 49, 1989, pp. 335–52, respectively.
[325] Email correspondence, May 2005.
[326] Willis taught at Chatswood High School in Sydney and the conference papers were published in her honour under the title *Creativity and Transformation: Papers from the English Association Teachers' Conference 2005 Published in Honour of Helen Willis*. They were edited by Richard Madelaine, the current President of the Sydney Branch of the EA, and published by the EA, Sydney in 2005. The last two sentences of the tribute read that for Helen Willis, 'the goals and joys of the enriched world of life and teaching English' are inextricably linked with a 'sense of transformation'. Also, while the Sydney Branch of the EA manifests its gratitude to her in the publication of the volume, she expresses '[her] gratitude to the English Association for its contribution to [her] life and the lives of others' p. 2.

The website of the 'English Association Sydney Branch' is linked to *Southerly* and provides as its URL the English Department of the University of New South Wales 'EAS'.[327] The information provided forms a suitable coda to the history of the EA:

> The English Association [London] was founded in 1906 by a group of English teachers and scholars concerned that English, then struggling for recognition as a subject in its own right, should be given due recognition in secondary and tertiary curricula. Its broad aim was to create opportunities of co-operation between teachers of English at all levels and to promote in the community, the knowledge and appreciation of English language and literature by holding conferences and lectures, and publishing journals, books and leaflets.

The Sydney Branch was founded in 1923 with the same aims in view.

> The Association runs at least two conferences each year for teachers of senior school English; a public lecture by an eminent local scholar for HSC English students; publishes pamphlets and books for English students and their teachers; and publishes a quarterly review of Australian literature called Southerly in which, among other things, appear scholarly and critical articles on HSC set texts and authors.

Among its objectives, it comments on its desire to

- Encourage and promote creative writing and criticism of Australia through the publication of a periodical literary journal titled Southerly.
- Establish or to assist in and contribute towards the establishment in Australia of other branches of the Central Association.
- Correspond with and co-operate in such ways as the Association shall think proper with the Central Association with branches in Australia and elsewhere and with any corporations, companies, clubs, associations, institutions or organisations whose objects are altogether or in part similar to the association.

Forever protean, the aims of the original EA founders in 1906 are still valid and have relevance one hundred years later. In a world transformed beyond all recognition by the electronic revolution, and unimaginable conflicts, the founders' ideals transcend time and place and continents. There is still a pressing need 'to promote the due recognition of English as an essential element in the national education and to help in maintaining the effectiveness of the language in both its spoken and its written use' in the twenty-first century. The vision and pioneering labours of E. S. Valentine, G. E. S. Coxhead, A. C. Bradley, F. S. Boas, and others planted seeds, which have not withered over the century. Thanks to their combined efforts and those of their successors, the EA flourishes and prospers in its founding island in the northern hemisphere and on a continental vast island thousands of miles away—Australia.

---

[327] http://hsc.csu.edu.au/pta/members/ea.html

Bibliography

Abrams, M.H., *A Glossary of Literary Terms*, 8th ed., Boston, MA: Thompson Wadsworth, 2005.

Anon, *The Teaching of Shakespeare in Schools*, English Association Pamphlet 7, 1908.

Anon, *Essays and Studies by Members of the English Association, United Provinces Branch*, Allahabad, 1938.

Attridge, Derek, *The Rhythms of English Poetry*, London: Longman, 1982.

Balchin, W.G.V., *The Geographical Association: the First Hundred Years 1893–1993*, Sheffield: Geographical Association, 1993.

Bald, Marjorie Amelia, *Women Writers of the Nineteenth Century*, Cambridge: Cambridge University Press, 1923.

Barry, Peter, *Beginning Theory: an Introduction to Literary and Cultural Theory*, 2nd. ed., Manchester: Manchester University Press, 2002.

Barry, Peter, *Contemporary British Poetry and the City*, Manchester: Manchester University Press, 2000.

Bellamy, G., 'The Genesis of the Newbolt Report on the Teaching of English in England: a Study of the Early Years of the English Association', unpublished master's thesis, University of Leicester, 1977.

Clement, G. *The Teaching of English in Girls' Secondary Schools*, English Association Pamphlet 6, 1908.

Colls, Robert, *Identity of England*, Oxford: Oxford University Press, 2002.

Doyle, Brian, 'The Invention of English' in Robert Colls and Philip Dodd, eds., *Englishness: Politics and Culture, 1880–1920*, London: Croom Helm, 1986.

Doyle, Brian, *English and Englishness*. New Accents Series. London: Routledge, 1989.

Eliot, T.S., *On Poetry and Poets*, London: Faber & Faber, 1957.

Esdaile, Arundell, 'A Half-Century of the English Association', *Essays and Studies*, Vol. 9, 1956, p. 1–6.

Fowler, J.H., *English Literature in Secondary Schools*, English Association Pamphlet 5, 1908

France, Peter and William St Clair, eds., *Mapping Lives: The Uses of Biography*, eds., Oxford: Oxford University Press, 2002.

Gallup, Donald C., *T. S. Eliot: A Bibliography*, London: Faber & Faber, 1947; rev. ed. 1969.

Harding, Jason, *The Criterion: Cultural Politics and Periodical Networks in Inter-War Britain*, Oxford: Oxford University Press, 2002.

Hudson, Derek, 'Thomas, Sir William Beach (1868–1957)', rev. Marc Brodie, *Oxford Dictionary of National Biography*, Oxford: Oxford University Press, 2004.

Kumar, Krishan, *The Making of English National Identity*, Cambridge University Press, 2003.

Leavis, F.R., *The Great Tradition. George Eliot, Henry James, Joseph Conrad*, London: Chatto & Windus, 1948.

Mackail, J.W., 'A.C. Bradley', *Proceedings of the British Academy*, 1935, p. 390.

Madelaine, Richard, *Creativity and Transformation: Papers from the English Association Teachers' Conference 2005 Published in Honour of Helen Willis*, Sydney: English Association Sydney, 2005.

Mathieson, Margaret. *The Preachers of Culture: A Study of English and Its Teachers*. London: Allen and Unwin, 1975.
Maude, Aylmer, *Tolstoy on Art and its Critics*, London: Humphrey Milford, 1926.
McKerrow, Ronald B.,*An Introduction to Bibliography for Literary Students*, Winchester: St Paul's Bibliographies, 1994 reissue.
Newbolt, Sir Henry, *Teaching of English in England being the report of the Departmental Committee appointed by the President of the Board of Education to inquire into the position of English in the educational system of England*, London, 1921.
Newbolt, Sir Henry, *The Idea of An English Association*, English Association Presidential Address, 1928.
Palmer, D.J., *The Rise of English Studies*: *An Account of the Study of English Language and Literature from Its Origins to the Making of the Oxford English School*, Oxford: Oxford University Press, 1965.
Perkin, Howard, *Key Profession: The History of the Association of University Teachers*, London: Routledge, 1969.
Putt, S. Gorley, *Wings of a Man's Life*, London: Claridge Press, 1990.
Reid, Ian, *Wordsworth and the Formation of English Studies*, Aldershot: Ashgate, 2004.
Robbins, Lord, *Higher education: appendix one to the report of the Committee appointed by the Prime Minister under the Chairmanship of Lord Robbins, 1961–63: demand for places in higher education*, London: HMSO, 1963.
Saintsbury, George, *A History of Criticism and Literary Taste in Europe from the Earliest Times to the Present* Day, Edinburgh: William Blackwood and Sons, 1900.
A History of English Prosody from the Twelfth Century to the Present Day, London: Macmillan, 1908.
A History of English Prose Rhythm, London: Macmillan, 1912.
Sampson, George, *English for the English*: *A Chapter on National Education*. Cambridge: Cambridge University Press, 1952.
Schonfeld, Roger C., *JSTOR: A History*, Princeton: Princeton University Press, 2003.
Smith, J.C., 'English Association', *The Educational News*, 21 October 1910, p. 1097.
Smith, Nowell, *The Origin and History of the Association*, Chairman's Address, London: English Association, 1942.
Stray, Christopher, ed., *The Classical Association: the First century1903–2003*, Oxford: Oxford University Press, 2003.
Sullivan, Alvin, ed., *British Literary Magazines of the Modern Age, 1914–1984*, London: Greenwood Press, 1986.
Taylor, Michael, *Shakespeare Criticism in the Twentieth Century*, Oxford: Oxford University Press, 2001.
Tillyard, E.M.W., *Milton*, London: Chatto and Windus, 1930.
Trickett Rachel, *The Honest Muse: A Study in Augustan Verse*, Oxford: Claredon Press, 1967.
Waddell, Helen, *The Wandering Scholars*, London: Constable and Co. Ltd., 1927.
Wilson, John Dover, *Milestones on the Dover Road*, London: Faber & Faber, 1969.
Wylde, Henry Cecil, *The Universal Dictionary of the English Language*, London: Amalgamated Press, 1932.

Index

Abercrombie, Lascelles, 92, 99, 101, 108
Acland, Sir Arthur Herbert Dyke, 12, 16
Allott, Miriam, 43, 128
Amery, Leopold Stennet, 38
annual conference, 16, 22, 36, 87, 106, 125, 129
annual dinner, 22, 23, 89, 114, 120, 121
annual general meeting, 15, 17, 22, 23, 34–36, 39, 45, 69, 89, 101, 117, 120–124
annual luncheon, 23, 26, 27, 32, 34, 48
Armstrong, William, 33, 93
Asquith, Herbert, 23, 24, 108

Bailey, John, 16, 19, 20, 22, 23, 24, 52, 69, 98, 114, 121
Baker, William, 82,
Baldwin, Stanley, 23, 24, 109, 114
Balfour, Arthur James, 17
Balliol College, Oxford, 11, 24, 38, 112
Baron, Michael, 48, 94, 95, 96
Barry, Peter, 94, 95, 96, 97, 108
Beatty, Bernard, 128, 129
Beeching, Canon H. C., 3, 4, 9, 52, 53
Bell, C. F., 61
Binyon, Laurence, 23, 24, 58, 89, 92, 98, 99, 109
Birkett, Sir William Norman, 38, 39
Blackwell, Basil, 49, 66, 81
Blocksidge, Martin, 49, 51
Blunden, Edmund, 38, 48, 65, 89, 92, 93, 100, 103
Boas, Frederick Samuel, 7, 10, 12, 13, 19, 20, 23, 25, 30, 32–35, 39, 52, 68, 69, 70–78, 80, 83, 103, 108, 130
Boas, Guy, 25, 28, 29, 32, 33, 63, 89–91, 93, 101, 102, 104, 109
Bowra, Sir Maurice, 37
Bradley, A. C., 3–7, 9–11, 14, 16, 43, 52, 54, 55, 89, 109, 110, 130,
Bradley, Henry, 11, 14, 52, 54
Brake, Laurel, 43, 80, 81
branches
    England
        Birmingham, 112, 118, 119, 124
        Bristol, 112, 114, 118, 124

        Chichester, 124
        Darlington, 114, 115, 118, 119, 124
        Durham, 114, 116, 119, 120, 124
        Eastbourne and District, 114, 116
        Hull, 118, 119, 124
        Leicester, 118, 119
        Liverpool, 112, 114, 118
        Manchester, 30, 115, 116, 118, 120, 124
        Norfolk and Norwich, 119
        Nottingham, 16, 114, 118, 120, 124
        Oxford, 115, 117, 118
        Plymouth, 118, 119, 120, 123, 124
        Sheffield, 114, 118, 119
        Stafford, 114, 118
        York, 118, 124
    overseas branches
        Adelaide, 123, 128
        Alexandria, 126, 127
        Allahabad, 28, 122, 123, 125, 126
        British Honduras, 127
        Cape Town, 121, 122, 123, 127, 128
        Ceylon, 120, 121, 122, 123
        Fort Hare, 121, 122, 123, 125, 126, 127
        Queensland, 122, 123, 127, 128
        Salisbury, 127, 128
        Spain, 128
        Sydney, 122, 123, 125, 127, 129, 130
        Toronto, 16, 120, 121, 122, 123
        Witwatersrand, 123, 125, 128
    Scotland, 10, 89, 113, 117, 125
Brewer, Derek, 49, 50, 66, 107
Brinton, Ian, 105, 107
Brooke, Stopford A., 3, 4, 9, 70
Bryant, Sir Arthur, 35, 38
Bulletin, 22, 23, 87–89, 97, 101, 108, 111, 114, 115, 118, 120–123
Bullough, Geoffrey, 31, 32, 63, 76, 77
Burchfield, Robert W., 49, 50, 67
Bushrui, Suheil, 67
Butler Education Act, 30, 35, 103
Butler, Henry Montagu, 11, 24
Byrne, Muriel St. Clare, 65

133

Campbell, Gordon, 44, 45, 49, 79, 80, 81, 84
Chambers, Sir Edmund, 10, 23, 24, 34, 72, 73, 92, 97
Chapman, R. W., 56, 59, 60
Chapman, Raymond, 43
Charles, Robert Hey, 58, 91
children's book awards, 106
Church, Richard, 36, 38, 99
Clark, Sir Kenneth, 39
Classical Association, 2, 3, 4, 6, 15, 24, 119
Claxton, Roger, 47
Clutton-Brock, Arthur, 52, 53
Coghill, Nevill, 49, 62
Collins, John Churton, 112
Colvin, Sir Sidney, 108
Cookson, George, 88, 89, 90, 91, 93
Cox, Charles Brian, 64, 65
Coxhead, G. E. S., 5, 10, 112, 130
Craigie, William A., 55, 61
Crewe, Marquis of, 17, 108, 109
Critical Quarterly, 64
Cunliffe, Marcus, 77
Curzon, Lord, 22, 24, 109

Dane, Clemence [Winifred Ashton], 37, 38, 93
Daniell, David, 44
Darbishire, Helen, 59, 64
Davenport, Arnold, 74
de Sélincourt, Ernest, 16, 23, 24, 56, 109
Deb, S.C.,28, 125, 126
Denning, Lord, 38
Dewar, Robert, 70
Dickinson, Patric, 92, 93
Dieth, Eugene, 61
Dobrée, Bonamy, 62, 64, 119
Dodsworth, Martin, 42, 44, 45, 47, 49, 67, 94, 95, 104,
Dorsch, T. S., 33, 40, 77, 78, 80, 102, 103
Dunsany, Lord, 56
Dyson, Edward, 64

Edinburgh, HRH The Duke of, 39, 48
Eliot, T. S., 62, 89, 91, 93, 99, 100, 110, 111, 127
Ellis-Fermor, Una, 59, 74, 91, 92
Elton, Oliver, 5, 23, 24, 53, 112
English, 88–96, 100, 120, 123–127
English 4–11, 105, 106
English Association North, 128, 129

English Association Studies, 48
English Essays of Today, 102, 103
English Historians: Selected Passages, 102, 103
English Short Stories of Today, 33, 43, 102, 103
Ernle, Rowland Edmund Prothero, 1st Baron, 23, 24, 121
Esdaile, Arundell, 2, 25, 26, 28, 33, 34, 35, 52, 59, 62, 64, 71, 92, 124
Esdaile, Katharine A., 60, 62
Essays and Studies, 5, 14–16, 26, 29, 32, 33, 41–44, 46, 50–64, 66–68, 76, 78, 97, 104, 110
Everett, Dorothy, 71, 75

Fallodon, Edward Grey, 1st Viscount, 23, 24, 109
Fiftieth Anniversary, 33
First World War, 12, 16, 22, 23, 39, 97, 108, 109
Foakes, R. A., 63, 93
Forster, E. M., 22, 115
Foster, Professor Sir Gregory, 11
Fowler, J. H., 11, 14, 19, 108, 112
Fuller-Maitland, J. A., 56
Furnivall, Frederick James, 6, 7, 8, 9, 11, 62

Galsworthy, John, 23, 24, 102, 109, 115, 116, 122, 127
Garbett, Cyril Forster, 35, 37
Gardner, Dame Helen, 59, 62, 64
Garmonsway, G. N., 71
Geographical Association, 2, 3, 43, 45
Gibson, Wilfrid, 91–93, 100
Gollancz, Israel, 6, 7, 9, 11, 19
Gordon, E. V., 70
Gordon, George, 34, 37, 92
Gosse, Edmund, 16, 23, 70
Gould, Warwick, 44
Gowers, Sir Ernest, 39, 64
Granville-Barker, Harley, 23, 73
Green, Michael, 66
Grierson, Sir Herbert, 37, 57, 58
Grimmond, Jo, 50
Guide to English Courses in the Universities, 33, 102

Hackett, General Sir John, 50
Hadow, W. H., 56, 108

Hales, John W., 3, 4, 9, 11
Hall, Sir Arthur Edward, 25, 26, 31, 99
Hamilton, Rostrevor, 31, 33, 59, 62, 64, 104
Harlow, Geoffrey, 42, 44, 73, 78, 79, 80
Hartog, Philip, 5–7, 11,12
Heath, H. F., 6, 7, 9, 10
Heath-Stubbs, John, 41, 42
Herbert, Sir Alan, 36, 38
Herford, C. H., 23, 24, 56, 69, 72, 77
Hickie, Eric Wynne, 36
Historical Association, 2, 45, 115, 119
Huxley, Aldous, 97

Issues in English, 48, 107

Jha, Amaranatha, 91
Johnson, Pamela Hansford, 62, 66
Jones, Gwyn, 63
Joseph, Bertram, 63

Ker, W. P., 15, 19, 20, 30, 52, 54, 70, 108
Kingman Committee, 44
Kitson, Peter J., 47, 81, 107
Knight, G. Wilson, 73, 92, 110
Knight, Roger, 49, 51, 105

Lang, William Cosmo, 109
Lawlor, John, 64
Leavis, F. R., 21, 41, 62, 65, 95, 105
Lee, Elizabeth, 11, 12
Lee, Sidney, 6, 10, 11, 13, 68, 69, 71, 72, 80, 87, 109, 129
Levin, Bernard, 50
Lewis, C. S., 35, 50, 57, 60, 92, 104
Lincoln, Andrew, 44
Literature and Life, 102, 104
Low, David, 32, 63
Low, J. Inch, 6, 10, 113
Lucas, Helen, 45, 47, 107
Lyttleton, Oliver, 38

MacColl, Douglas Sutherland, 53
Mackail, J. W., 23, 24, 53
Maclean, Catherine Macdonald, 60
Magnus, Sir Philip Montefiore, 30, 31, 62
Martin, Leonard Cyril, 74
Matthews, Walter Robert, 37, 39
Maurice, F., 60
McGowan, Kate, 85
McKerrow, Ronald Brunlees, 55, 56

Merrick, Leonard, 102, 122
Meyerstein, E. H. W., 92
Modern Language Association, 3, 5, 7, 13, 16, 82
Modern Language Review, 12, 13
Modern Languages Association, 2, 6, 7
Moorman, F. W., 17, 52, 53
Morgan, Charles, 38, 39
Morley, Edith Julia, 75, 83
Muir, Kenneth, 49, 51, 65
Murray, John, 49, 59, 61, 66, 81, 102

Nasta, Susheila, 68
Newbolt Report, 1, 18–22, 55
Newbolt, Sir Henry, 2, 19, 20, 21, 22, 23, 24, 98, 109, 111
Newsletter, 44, 45, 105, 107–108
Newton, Ken, 94
Nicoll, (John Ramsey) Allardyce, 73, 76
Nicolson, Sir Harold, 34, 38, 39

O'Brien, Conor Cruise, 50
office premises, 29, 41, 42, 45

Paine, John, 107
pamphlets, 5, 13–14, 32, 48, 102–103, 108–111, 130
patron, 47, 105
Pink, Maurice Alderton, 100, 102, 104
Pinto, Vivian de Sola, 28, 31, 60–61, 63, 75, 92, 102, 104
Poems of Today, 33, 97–102
Praz, Mario, 56
presidential addresses, 38, 109, 48, 102, 103
presidents, 4, 9–11, 16, 22–24, 37–39, 48–50, 112, 114
Pritchett, V. S., 50, 103
Prose of Today, 101
Putt, Samuel Gorley, 40–41, 48

Quiller-Couch, Sir Arthur, 18, 72
Quirk, Lord, 47, 51

Ramsey, Arthur Michael, 37
Redmond, James, 42, 73, 79, 80
Reed, Arthur William, 71–72
Rees-Mogg, Sir William, 50
Regan, Stephen, 81, 85
Renwick, W. L., 58, 61, 115
Review of English Studies, 56

Richards, I. A., 49, 61
Richmond, Admiral Sir Herbert William, 60
Robbins Report, 40–41, 102
Roberts, Sir Sydney, 37
Rodd, James Rennell, 1st Baron Rennell, 22–23, 109
Routh, H. V., 28, 31, 76, 104
Rowse, A. L., 37, 65
Rücker, Sir Arthur, 6–7

Saintsbury, George, 11, 15–16, 19–20, 52–54, 113
Sampson, George, 12, 19, 21, 54, 91
Samuel, Herbert Louis, 1st Viscount Samuel, 34, 38–39, 104
Schiff, Hilda, 65
Second World War, 11, 23, 25, 34, 37, 69–70, 73, 74, 79–80, 90–91, 99, 123, 125
Serjeantson, M. S., 55, 69, 71, 77
Serraillier, Ian L., 92–93
Shakespeare Survey, 73, 76
Sharrock, Roger, 42, 65, 102–103
Shippey, Tom, 67
Sichel, Edith, 15, 52–53
Simpson, Evelyn Mary, 60
Simpson, Percy, 9, 13–14, 56, 61
Sisson, C. J., 58
Skeat, Walter William, 4, 11
Smith, J. C., 9, 11, 53, 57, 113
Smith, Nowell Charles, 25, 27–28, 35, 59–60, 91–92, 97–98, 114, 120
Southerly, 127, 129–130
Sparrow, John, 49
Spear, Hilda D., 88–90, 93, 95
Spurgeon, Caroline, 16, 18, 20, 59, 73, 89, 92, 109
Stables, Andrew, 105
Stawell, Florence Melian, 53–54
Steiner, George, 49–50
Stuart, Dorothy Margaret, 26, 29, 60, 75, 92, 109

Talbot, J. E., 89, 101
Taylor, A. E., 53
Thackeray, Anna Isabelle, Lady Ritchie, 12

The English Association Book of Verse, 100
The Reader, 128–129
The Teaching of English in Schools: A Symposium, 102
Thomas, Sir William Beach, 61
Thomas, W. Jenkyn, 11, 28–29, 31, 33
Thomson, Clara Linklater, 6–7, 10–12
Tillotson, Geoffrey, 31, 61–62, 92
Tillotson, Kathleen, 62, 65
Tillyard, E. M. W., 37, 57, 64
Tolkien, J. R. R., 50, 55, 63, 70
Treharne, Elaine, 47, 49, 81
Trevelyan, G. M., 16, 37, 103
Trickett, Rachel, 49, 63

Use of English, 46, 51, 105

Valentine, Easton Smith, 2–6, 9–10, 113, 130

Wales, Katie, 68
Walpole, Hugh, 102, 109, 117–118
Webster, A. Blyth, 54
Wedgwood, Dame Veronica, 37, 103
West, Dame Rebecca, 49
Whibley, Charles, 110
White, Beatrice, 33, 41–44, 61–62, 65, 67, 73–75, 77–78, 80
Whitelock, Dorothy, 70, 74–75
Wilkinson, Cyril Hackett, 59–60
Willey, Basil, 60–61, 64–65
Willy, Margaret, 90, 92–96, 100, 104
Wilson, Frank Percy, 61–62
Wilson, John Dover, 18, 20, 56, 72, 119
Womack, Kenneth, 82
Wrenn, C. L., 70–71, 74
Wright, Herbert Gladstone, 63
Wyld, Henry Cecil, 54–55, 60

Yarker, P. M., 41, 77
Year's Work in Critical and Cultural Theory, 46, 79, 81, 85, 105
Year's Work in English Studies, 7, 28–29, 68, 109